STUDIES IN IMPERIALISM

general editor John M. MacKenzie

Established in the belief that imperialism as a cultural
phenomenon had as significant an effect on the dominant
as on the subordinate societies, Studies in Imperialism
seeks to develop the new socio-cultural approach which
has emerged through cross-disciplinary work on popular
culture, media studies, art history, the study of education
and religion, sports history and children's literature.
The cultural emphasis embraces studies of migration and
race, while the older political and constitutional,
economic and military concerns are never far away.
It incorporates comparative work on European and
American empire-building, with the chronological focus
primarily, though not exclusively, on the nineteenth
and twentieth centuries, when these cultural exchanges
were most powerfully at work.

The imperial game

MANCHESTER
UNIVERSITY PRESS

STUDIES IN
IMPERIALISM

The imperial game

CRICKET, CULTURE AND SOCIETY

edited by
Brian Stoddart
and Keith A. P. Sandiford

MANCHESTER
UNIVERSITY PRESS
Manchester and New York

Distributed exclusively in the USA by
ST. MARTIN'S PRESS

Published by **MANCHESTER UNIVERSITY PRESS**
OXFORD ROAD, MANCHESTER M13 9NR, UK
and ROOM 400, 175 FIFTH AVENUE, NEW YORK, NY 10010, USA

Distributed exclusively in the USA by
ST. MARTIN'S PRESS, INC.,
175 FIFTH AVENUE, NEW YORK, NY 10010, USA

Distributed exclusively in Canada by
UBC PRESS, UNIVERSITY OF BRITISH COLUMBIA,
6344 MEMORIAL ROAD, VANCOUVER, BC, CANADA V6T 1Z2

British Library Cataloguing-in-Publication Data
A catalogue record for this book is available from the British Library

Library of Congress Cataloging-in-Publication Data applied for

ISBN 0 7190 4978 4 *hardback*

First published 1998

05 04 03 02 01 00 99 98   10 9 8 7 6 5 4 3 2 1

Typeset in Trump Medieval
by Best-set Typesetter Ltd., Hong Kong
Printed in Great Britain
by Bookcraft (Bath) Ltd, Midsomer Norton

CONTENTS

[v]

GENERAL EDITOR'S INTRODUCTION

Sports history offers many profound insights into the character and complexities of modern imperial rule. However oppressive the political and economic power of the West may have been, imperialism was also a source of cultural exchanges at many different levels. Among such mutual borrowings, sports remain the most prominent and popular in the post-colonial world. But although the transfer of various sporting forms from the dominant to the subordinate people (they also frequently moved the other way) sometimes carries the air of an attempt at social control, the sports themselves soon develop an independent life of their own. Players and spectators swiftly ensure that the sports are modified and adapted to their own ends within the particular cultural, social and political contexts into which they have been planted.

This has certainly been the case with the quintessentially English game of cricket. In the course of the nineteenth century, it was transferred to all the continents in which the British exercised power. But soon it developed social and cultural – and eventually political – mutations. In new climates and environments, in the hands of different peoples and classes, it was converted from an apparent instrument of subjection into a perceived tool of cultural and political freedoms. Its history hence becomes closely bound up with the march of nationalism, decolonisation and post-colonial response. It also becomes a field for the creation and celebration of imperial, colonial and nationalist heroes.

This book examines all these characteristics of the diffusion and conversion of cricket and much else besides. Although cricketing history has become a well-worked field, no other book matches this one in its geographical range and chronological depth. It covers all five continents and spans the years from the early nineteenth century to the 1970s. In thus bringing their analysis up to date, the contributors are able to examine the survival and development of cricket in the face of the emergence of the relatively new sports imperialism of the United States. All historians of imperialism, nationalism, sports, as well as many cricketing enthusiasts, will find much of interest here.

John M. MacKenzie

NOTES ON CONTRIBUTORS

RICHARD CASHMAN is Associate Professor in History at the University of New South Wales, Sydney, Australia, where he is also Director of the Olympic Studies Centre. He has written widely on cricket in Australia and the Indian subcontinent with books on Spofforth, women's cricket in Australia, crowds and other historical aspects. He was General Editor of the *Oxford Companion to Australian Cricket* and *The A–Z of Australian Cricketers*. Professor Cashman has also published widely on other aspects of sport.

CHRISTOPHER MERRETT is the Chief Librarian of the University of Natal at Pietermaritzburg in South Africa. He has written widely on the history and politics of sport in South Africa, and was active in the non-racial sports movement, particularly in cricket where he served as an umpire.

JOHN NAURIGHT is Senior Lecturer in Human Movement Studies at the University of Queensland, Brisbane, Australia, where he teaches sports history. His interests have concentrated on sport in South Africa, New Zealand and Australia, and he now directs the Football Studies Centre. He has published on sport and politics, race and culture, and has taken a particular interest in rugby cultures.

GREG RYAN is a Lecturer in History at the University of Canterbury, Christchurch, New Zealand, where he completed both his MA and PhD. His doctoral thesis was entitled 'Where the Game Was Played By Decent Chaps: A Social History of New Zealand Cricket, 1832–1914'. He teaches New Zealand and Australian history, and is currently researching issues relating to sport in both countries. The author of several articles, he has also published *Forerunners of the All Blacks: The 1888–89 New Zealand Native Football Team in Britain, Australia and New Zealand*.

KEITH A. P. SANDIFORD is Professor of History at the University of Manitoba in Winnipeg, Canada. His early education was undertaken in Barbados and Jamaica, and his doctoral work at the University of Toronto. The author of several articles on sport, he is a regular contributor to cricket magazines such as *Cricket Lore* and *Journal of the Cricket Society*. Among his books are *Cricket and the Victorians* and *The Cricket Nurseries of Colonial Barbados: The Elite Schools, 1865–1966*.

BRIAN STODDART is Pro Vice-Chancellor (Asia) and Professor of Cultural Studies in RMIT University, Melbourne, Australia. From 1995 to 1997 he was the founding Academic Director of that institution's offshore campus in Penang, Malaysia. From 1981 until 1995 he was at the University of Canberra, Australia, where he was a founding member of the Centre for Sports Studies until his appointment as Dean of the Faculty of Communication in 1991. He has published widely in sports history and sociology, and is a regular keynote speaker at international conferences. Professor Stoddart is also a well-known media commentator on sports issues.

Introduction

Keith A. P. Sandiford

The imperial game analyses the forms and fortunes of cricket as it spread to various segments of the old British empire and beyond. A fascinating story, it illustrates in several surprising ways the complexity of cultural imperialism. Fashions and models are seldom replicated exactly as intended. They are invariably adapted to suit parochial needs and traditions. Thus Barbadian cricket, as Brian Stoddart suggests, bears little resemblance to the Trobriand variety. Sometimes, imperial models carry the defects of the metropolis and these warts also assume peculiarly local characteristics when transplanted. Thus the snobberies which afflicted the game in Victorian England, dividing aristocratic amateur from plebeian professional, reappeared in the racial and ethnic divides bedevilling the sport almost wherever it was taken. These are the basic themes of continuity and disjunction with which this anthology is mainly concerned.

The story of imperial cricket is really about the colonial quest for identity in the face of the colonisers' search for authority. Just as the Victorians felt that participation in the noble sport gave them strength of character and a positive image sadly lacking in foreigners, some colonial communities came to associate cricket with gentility and 'civilisation'. Indians and Pakistanis, for instance, refused to accept the Christian and other gospels preached by the Anglo-Saxons, but adopted cricket as a peculiar kind of national symbol and dedicated themselves to playing it at least as well as did the imperialists themselves. Blacks (and browns) in the Caribbean, too, attached surrealistic importance to the game and established a cricket cult there that almost defies analysis or logic. Just as excellence in soccer became synonymous with the essence of being Brazilian, cricketing excellence has come to define the modern West Indian.

For a long time, too, Australians tried to define themselves in this way and offered astonishingly fierce opposition to the English – not-

[1]

withstanding a considerable demographic disadvantage. With a white population about one-tenth the size of England's, stretched over a land mass several times as extensive, they yet gave as well as they got almost as soon as test matches were introduced. This determination to succeed at cricket came at least in part from a colonial psychology which created an endeavour to keep pace with their arrogant and imperialising metropolitan cousins. Cricket was a vital element in Anglo-Saxon culture. Indeed, some observers in the nineteenth century would have termed it the most significant and the most visible, apart from dress and language. As there was no substantial contending European influence in Australia, Anglo-Saxon models prospered without restraint and all of the country's early cricket captains looked upon test match results as an adequate gauge of the community's readiness for independent nationhood.

In New Zealand, similarly, the absence of European competitors allowed British norms and structures to take deep root. But so complete was the New Zealanders' devotion to the 'mother country' that they were prepared to remain subordinated to Britain almost indefinitely, as Greg Ryan observes. They regarded cricket as a very special discipline, even though they played it with much less skill than they did rugby, and waited for an eternity before achieving their first test victory over England. Perhaps their experience might have been different had they established more secondary schools patterned after nineteenth-century Eton and Harrow. Whereas in the Caribbean, during the nineteenth century, a large number of miniature Etons and Harrows appeared, only a few such institutions emerged in Auckland, Christchurch, Dunedin and Wellington. Perhaps, too, it was the weather (more Scottish than English) which served as a deterrent to cricket's growth. (New Zealand's weather, however, had not changed appreciably when, during the 1970s and 1980s, their leading cricketers were performing much more satisfactorily at the international level. This matter of climate and regional success/style, begs for more thorough analysis.)

The fervent devotion to cricket seen in Australia was strangely absent in Canada, even though there was considerable anglicisation of that huge country long before the twentieth century. It is difficult to account for this curiosity, except to surmise that Canadians sought a different kind of identity during their early years of independence. They celebrated the British North America Act of 1867 by devising ludic strategies of their own and gradually abandoned cricket which had seemed so important to their Anglo-Saxon members earlier. Perhaps Canadians needed to do so given the proximity of the emergent United States which rapidly transformed from a republic into an empire during the generation or so following the conclusion of the Civil War. Interestingly, while cricket remained popular among Canada's Anglo-Saxon elite in the emerging urban centres for a number of years, it never captured the imagination of the Canadian masses.[1]

It may be argued, too, that, by the end of the nineteenth century, the European element in Canada contained too many diverse strands after a host of Germans, Poles, Scandinavians, Ukrainians and others came close to swamping the British and the French, the so-called 'founding fathers'. And, yet again, it might have been the weather which contributed to the growing popularity of curling and ice hockey at the expense of cricket, rowing and soccer. Demography, in particular, played a key role during cricket's two peak periods. During 1840–65, before the great European influx, in English Canada clubs were playing a sophisticated brand of organised cricket in the leading centres in Ontario. Hence the inception of the annual classic between the United States and Canada in 1844 – the very first international contest of its kind. Much later, during the 1970s, when emigration from Commonwealth countries had restored some of cricket's popularity, Canada advanced to the finals of the World Cup Competition in 1979 using mainly West Indian expatriates. The Canadian XI, for instance, which faced England at Old Trafford in June that year included no fewer than four Barbadian migrants, and only one indigenous Canadian.[2] Unfortunately, however, the initial influx has dried up and second-generation Canadians, seeking to attach themselves more securely to the mainstream, have resorted to traditional forms of Canadian recreation.

Such phenomena are never easy to explain. Why, for example, did cricket fare so much better in South Africa than in Canada in the face of huge African majorities and the presence of a competing (Afrikaner) European culture? The game survived there, despite extraordinary difficulties. But to do so, it assumed peculiar features of its own. The white minority, feeling forever threatened by black natives who encircled them in all directions, emerged with a strategy for survival which included racial and ethnic segregation and discrimination in brutal and emphatic forms. Cricket, that is to say, survived as a leading sport in South Africa by adhering to the same tenets of *apartheid* that had carefully preserved the European economic and political hegemony. Whether this strategy was necessary is a moot point, since cricket might well have offered the parties a common ground so sadly lacking elsewhere. South Africans might have avoided much anguish by trying to profit from the West Indian experience. But, as André Odendaal and others have shown, the blacks were left to fend for themselves and to develop their own cricket in defiance of European arrogance and opposition.[3] That they did so at all speaks volumes for the awesome power of cultural imperialism which, historically, has proved as capable of inspiring mimicry as enforcing obedience.

Elsewhere in Africa, where European communities remained only minute fractions of the overall population and where the Victorian public school ethos never really took root, cricket made but a pilgrim's progress. Only recently has it shown some vital signs in such countries as Kenya, Nigeria and Uganda. Between the South African and other African extremes, of course, there stood Zimbabwe, very similar in history and attitude to the Union of South Africa. Cricket's roots there went deep enough to survive all the tribulations of the post-war period and, ultimately, to earn that country test match status and a position on the International Cricket Council during the 1980s.

It is by examining these African experiences that we can recognise just how remarkable is the whole West Indian saga. In the Caribbean territories, Europeans seldom accounted for more than a small percentage of the population. But so complete was white mastery over black populations by the nineteenth century that the minority never felt the numbing sense of insecurity which hypnotised whites in Algeria, Angola, Mozambique, South Africa and Zimbabwe. Segregation, already an integral feature of Caribbean life, never had to be legalised.[4] Blacks were routinely excluded from such cricket clubs as Kingston, Queen's Park, Pickwick and Wanderers by accepted convention rather than law. Blacks were not encouraged to enter the elite schools, but could not be excluded totally. They seldom reached the highest positions in the schools, the services, courts and the Church, but (having been trained in Anglo-Saxon colleges) they were appointed to less prestigious positions in the academic, civil, judicial and religious institutions. There were simply too few Europeans to man the citadel, hence the use of native auxiliaries from necessity.

This peculiar accommodation provided West Indian society with a certain stability throughout the long and difficult post-emancipation period. Apart from a few exceptional radicals, educated blacks and browns accepted the system, along with their subordinate roles, and tried not to rock the boat. Trained in Anglo-Saxon morals, ethics, language, literature, politics and history the emergent black bourgeoisie became firm supporters of Anglo-Saxon imperialism, and played cricket with a zeal and a panache that sometimes alarmed even the Anglo-Saxons themselves. Whereas in Africa, the boundaries were basically racial and ethnic, in the West Indies (as in England) the dividing lines were largely social and economic. If England appointed only amateurs to captain county and test teams for an unconscionably long time, West Indies thought it improper to elevate blacks to regional or national captaincy.

Interestingly, as in England, gender provided another of cricket's peculiar boundaries in the Caribbean. Throughout most of the Victorian period, ladies were discouraged from serious participation in cricket in England and the Women's Cricket Association there was not firmly established until 1926.[5] This patriarchal convention took firm root in the Caribbean, as Hilary Beckles has recently demonstrated. It was not until after the Second World War that women's cricket began to flourish in the West Indies.[6] The fact that few authors subscribing to this collection have been able to pay much attention to the issue of gender is itself a commentary on the precarious state of female cricket in other parts of the old British empire. Australia did not establish a Women's Cricket Council until 1931; nor was there a similar organisation in New Zealand before 1934. Although women's cricket was played in several provinces before the Second World War, it was 1952 before the South Africa and Rhodesia Women's Cricket Association was officially founded. And the Women's Cricket Association of India did not come into existence until 1973.[7]

Whereas in Australia, New Zealand and Africa aboriginal populations were generally discouraged from playing cricket, the attitude of the West Indian elite was more ambiguous. Barbados was universally acknowledged as the most racist and snobbish of all Caribbean territories. Its cultural leaders, therefore, excluded manual labourers and working-class blacks from its major cricket (and other) competitions. This was done by classifying all such people as 'professionals' and limiting sports participation to amateurs. But such classification could never be extended to junior clerks in the civil service or teachers and priests at any level. Hence the appearance of blacks in such clubs as Empire and Spartan (who also found it necessary to mimic the cultural elite and establish certain social barriers of their own).[8]

But after so carefully weeding out the 'professionals', Barbadian cricket administrators encouraged manual labourers to play among themselves by allowing them to use the fields and equipment of the clubs for 'friendly' matches, by inviting them to bowl at the nets of the amateurs, and by asking them to play in trial matches so as to 'sharpen up' the regional team.[9] Nor were labourers debarred as spectators. They came in droves to cheer for the local clubs, even though it was obvious they could never gain regular membership. The very snobbish Wanderers, ironically, had one of the strongest and most vocal followings in Barbados from 1877 to 1951 while its headquarters remained in the densely populated black district then known as the Bay Land. Pickwick, another white club, also boasted its loyal army of black enthusiasts residing in the New Orleans area of St Michael.[10]

   While some English amateurs refused to play against South African blacks at the turn of the century, there was no such discussion when the Slade Lucas and other English amateur teams travelled to the Caribbean in the 1890s. Nor was there any objection raised to the selection of four or five blacks to accompany the West Indian teams which toured England in 1900 and 1906. In fact, the young Pelham Warner, himself born in Trinidad and trained in Barbados, strongly urged the West Indians to take a few 'professional' bowlers if they hoped to have any success at all in the 'mother country'.[11]

   The English generally discouraged full social participation in cricket in the Far East, especially since (as Brian Stoddart has shown for the Pacific) it sometimes assumed unusual forms when transported out there, but it is highly improbable that they could have prevented the Chinese from participating had they chosen to do so in substantial numbers. It is more likely that the English would have repeated their Indian and Pakistani programme. They would have promoted some form of segregation while encouraging the natives to play, so long as they did so in an English manner without posing any obvious threat to law and order (as interpreted by the English).[12] When local communities showed determination to adopt the English models at whatever cost, the imperialists generally took the line of least resistance and consoled themselves with the comforting thought that they were succeeding in 'civilising' the natives.

   Sometimes, however, the natives became more civilised than their civilisers and this often provoked unkind remarks from the metropolis. When it was not the Australians playing too hard (almost like an unfriendly team from Yorkshire) and bending the spirit if not the letter of the gentleman's game, West Indians were playing too flamboyantly as one would expect from excitable natives from the tropics. When the West Indians became the most clinically professional team in world cricket, several English analysts concluded that it was the abject poverty in their homes which gave their fast bowlers such unusual verve and ferocity. A well-known English journalist produced *Calypso Cricket*, a famous documentary, in which the terrors of short-pitched fast bowling were stressed even though the film itself was an excellent demonstration of controlled pace supported by brilliant catching behind the stumps and in the slips. Nowhere was it even contemplated that the superb fast bowling produced by Joel Garner, Malcolm Marshall, Andy Roberts and others required practice, hard physical labour, unusual dedication and considerable cricket acumen.[13]

   Metropolitan commentators have sometimes stumbled upon a fundamental truth: the differing forms and styles of imperial cricket reflect such local variables as geography, history and psychology. A once-dominant England, struggling desperately to remain afloat since the Second World War, may well seek refuge in defensive strategies designed to stave off defeat. Her pitches and climate have encouraged the endless production of medium-pace seam bowlers aiming at accuracy as much as penetration; and her batsmen have all too quickly learned the Fabian tactics of attrition. In these circumstances, English selectors have consistently smiled upon the play-safe Geoffrey Boycotts of county cricket and looked suspiciously at the creative genius of the David Gowers. On pitches that favour naked speed and in a tropical environment that discourages patience, Caribbean bowlers aim at conquest rather than containment. Performing before an audience that has traditionally preferred style to substance, Caribbean batsmen play attractive shots which are not necessarily orthodox. Given similar tropical heat but with much slower wickets, subcontinental bowlers have not concentrated so much on sheer pace. India and Pakistan have produced only a handful of great fast bowlers with Wasim Akram, Kapil Dev and Waqar Younis the outstanding exceptions to the Indo-Pakistani rule.

The scholar who made the most persistent effort to analyse the social evolution of cricket was the prolific Trinidadian writer and political activist, C. L. R. James. He explained the fluctuations in England's twentieth-century cricket fortunes by examining the shifting context in which the game was played. If the reign of Edward VII witnessed the Golden Age of English cricket, it was because England felt the need to respond aggressively to the challenges in industry, finance and commerce then being offered by upstart industrialising nations like Germany and the United States. This assertiveness manifested itself in the flamboyance of Edwardian batsmanship. In like manner, the predominating stolidity of England's batsmen since the First World War has reflected the old empire's quest for security and defence.[14] Professor Hilary Beckles, another outstanding West Indian scholar, also sees cricket as the window into the soul of his native community. The brilliance of Gary Sobers, in his view, was a reflection of Barbadian dynamism in one age, while the dearth of creative batsmanship in the following period was an equally clear indication of a 'crisis of social culture'.[15]

There are obvious pitfalls in such analysis. If the flowering of Gary Sobers's genius was indicative of a black renaissance which saw the rise of such remarkable leaders as Sir Grantley Adams, Norman Manley and Eric Williams in the Age of Independence, how can we now explain the dominance of West Indian teams during the Age of Lloyd that followed? At the very time when the West Indies were forging their incredible record of twenty-nine unbeaten test series over a period of fifteen years (1980–95), the entire Caribbean basin was bedevilled by economic and social problems almost defiant of solution.

These considerations combine to make the imperial game a truly fascinating study. While the essays that follow shed some light on the innumerable linkages between cricket and culture, they will no doubt raise as many intriguing new questions as those they seek to answer.

Notes

1 Alan Metcalfe, *Canada Learns to Play: The Emergence of Organized Sport, 1807–1914*, Toronto, 1987, pp. 80–5.

2 *Wisden Cricketers' Almanack* (hereafter *Wisden*) *1980*, London, 117th edn, p. 303.

3 André Odendaal, *Cricket in Isolation: The Politics of Race and Cricket in South Africa*, Cape Town, 1977; Robert Archer and Antoine Bouillon, *The South Africa Game: Sport and Racism*, London, 1982.

4 See, for example, David Lowenthal, *West Indian Societies*, London, 1972.

5 Keith A. P. Sandiford, *Cricket and the Victorians*, Aldershot, 1994, pp. 43–8. See also Nancy Joy, *Maiden Over*, London, 1950, pp. 23–35; and Kathleen E. McCrone, *Playing the Game: Sport and the Physical Emancipation of English Women, 1870–1914*, Lexington, 1988, pp. 42, 72–7.

6 Hilary McD. Beckles, 'A Purely Natural Extension: Women's Cricket in West Indies Cricket Culture', in Hilary McD. Beckles and Brian Stoddart, eds, *Liberation Cricket: West Indies Cricket Culture*, Manchester, 1995, pp. 222–36.

7 Netta Rheinberg, 'Women's Cricket Overseas', in E. W. Swanton, ed., *Barclays World of Cricket*, London, 1986, pp. 379–82.

8 Trevor Marshall, 'Race, Class and Cricket in Barbadian Society, 1800–1970', *Manjak*, 11 November 1973; Martin Ramsay, 'A Critical Examination of Factors Affecting the Formation of Major Cricket Clubs in Barbados', University of the West Indies undergraduate paper, Cave Hill, 1979; and, especially, Brian Stoddart, 'Cricket and Colonialism in the English-speaking Caribbean to 1914: Towards a Cultural Analysis', in J. A. Mangan, ed., *Pleasure, Profit, Proselytism: British Culture at Home and Abroad 1700–1914*, London, 1988, pp. 241–9.

9 See, for example, *Barbados Globe*, 27 March 1899 and 27 December 1899.

10 On the phenomenon of Barbadian cricket, see Keith A. P. Sandiford, 'Cricket and the Barbadian Society', *Canadian Journal of History*, 21, December 1986, pp. 353–70; and Brian Stoddart, 'Cricket, Social Formation and Cultural Continuity in Barbados: A Preliminary Ethnohistory', *Journal of Sport History*, 14, Winter 1987, pp. 317–40.

11 *Barbados Advocate*, 1 February 1898, pp. 6–7.

12 Richard Cashman, *Patrons, Players and the Crowd: The Phenomenon of Indian Cricket*, New Delhi, 1980.

13 Ian Wooldridge, *Calypso Cricket*, London, 1985.

14 Anna Grimshaw, ed., *Cricket*, London, 1988: a collection of essays written over the years by C. L. R. James.

15 Hilary McD. Beckles, 'Barbados Cricket and the Crisis of Social Culture', in Sir Carlisle Burton, Ronald Hughes and Keith A. P. Sandiford, eds, *100 Years of Organised Cricket in Barbados 1892–1992*, Bridgetown, 1992, pp. 50–1.

CHAPTER ONE

England

Keith A. P. Sandiford

The cricket phenomenon which has captured the imagination of succeeding generations of Australians, Indians, New Zealanders, Pakistanis, South Africans and West Indians, among others, was established in nineteenth-century England when the Victorians began glorifying the game as a perfect system of manners, ethics and morals. Far from being a simple physical activity, cricket became a powerful symbolic and representational force for the Victorians who believed that it embodied all that was noble in the Anglo-Saxon character. In a fiercely nationalistic era Englishmen regarded cricket, an exclusively English creation unsullied by outside influence, as proof of their cultural supremacy.

It is difficult to underestimate the importance of cricket in Victorian life. It was a ritual as well as recreation, a spiritual as well as a sporting experience. Its values were used freely by politicians, philosophers, preachers and poets. Its influence on the imagery of Rudyard Kipling and Sir Henry Newbolt was most pronounced and Lord Palmerston, that 'most English minister', used cricketing vocabulary in some of his most telling epigrams.[1] The game itself produced a healthy volume of Victorian verse and fiction, and inspired nineteenth-century art, photography and popular music.[2] Cricket produced its own literature whose social impact went far beyond the details of the game, with cricket language becoming a moral code. The game produced public heroes to rival politicians, actors, writers, philosophers and scientists. Cricket and its social nuances were all-pervasive.

In cricket the Victorians consolidated a Georgian legacy because the game had developed during the Hanoverian age into the general form which its playing aspects display today.[3] Consequently, the Victorians treated cricket with the same awe and reverence applied to other established and durable institutions. The Victorians occupied a world of constant social, political and technological flux so, despite their superficial optimism and confidence, were anxious about the potential state of their present and future. The massive technological changes which they witnessed, for example, instilled conflicting senses of pride and insecurity.[4] This social duality formed the basis of instinctive Victorian conservatism which encouraged a devotion to crown and cricket, two quite different and familiar institutions which, in their judgement, constituted the most powerful and appropriate agencies for promoting organic social harmony. The Victorians played cricket with a greater intensity than the Georgians largely because, in their view, they had cleansed it of its Georgian impurities. They removed gambling and corruption from the game in a deliberate and successful effort to purify it, which was in keeping with their approach to life in general. The majority of them – particularly those belonging to the emergent middle classes – were earnest, prim and evangelical. Such puritanism contrasted starkly with the licentiousness of their immediate predecessors. In many ways, it was a violent reaction against what the Victorians condemned as Georgian laxity. The Georgians had played cricket, as they had done everything else, with spectacular exuberance and panache. This was not in keeping with the Victorian spirit and temper. Whereas the Georgians had played cricket for fun, the Victorians did so for their spiritual and mental regeneration. Georgian enthusiasm gave way to Victorian earnestness, even though the basic form of cricket remained largely unaltered.

Victorian devotion to the game is evident in the rapid spread of its playing patterns, the dimensions of its spectator appeal and in the sheer time devoted to matches. The easiest and most obvious gauge for these is the county championship which was institutionalised by 1873 with its informal genesis considerably earlier. Whereas 9 counties played 31 first-class matches among themselves in 1873, no fewer than 15 county clubs contested 149 games for the championship in 1899.[5] By the later nineteenth century, too, championship matches were played over three days and attracted thousands of spectators to grounds all over England, establishing social patterns which endured for almost a century.

Watching such games was solid social practice. In the very first pages of his monumental *Strangers and Brothers* sequence, C. P. Snow places his central character at a cricket ground watching his beloved Leicestershire and his particular hero, C. J. B. Wood. When Wood failed to play well, the nine-year-old boy 'wanted to cry'. Like countless others, Lewis Eliot became immersed in the game, consumed with excitement as a truly 'passionate partisan' for his team.[6] This fictional account is set on the eve of the First World War and, by then, innumerable Lewis

Eliots had been swept up in the county cricket ritual for thirty years and more.

Yet even that does not capture the full social importance of the game. Its real hold lay in English villages where, by the turn of the twentieth century, the cricket ground and its lovingly tended pitch ranked in symbolic importance with the pub and the church. Indeed, the three were socially intertwined in composition and leadership. These clubs were community enterprises supplying a proletarian need and in many villages they became the focus of intense loyalty and parochialism. Legends grew up around fast bowlers and big hitters in the district, and many a local blacksmith became more famous for his cricket than his craft. Such clubs contributed to local feelings of solidarity and, sometimes, even stimulated the local economy. The Henfield Cricket Club, for instance, became a village institution in Sussex as did the Lascelles Hall club in Yorkshire.[7] Cricket provided entertainment for local folk and gave exercise to hundreds of participants for whom the game also served as a release from the tedium of agricultural and/or industrial labour.

Club cricket had a series of functions, and this was recognised everywhere. As early as 1845 the English parliament legalised cricket which popular usage had for centuries kept alive in defiance of the law.[8] It is significant that, during a public speech at Reading in 1891, George Palmer, the celebrated industrialist, argued that education was perhaps as important as cricket in the lives of the proletariat.[9] Another equally famous industrialist, Sir Titus Salt, did most in 1869 to establish the Saltaire Cricket Club which thereafter revolved directly around the Saltaire Mills.[10] As no one questioned the value of cricket, many teams were kept in operation by local capitalists on the ground that they were as important in a socio-cultural sense as literature, music and the arts.

This social centrality of Victorian cricket was fostered, nurtured and maintained by key institutions and agencies which regarded the game as a major cultural virtue and, therefore, worth promoting. In analysing these supports, it is important to remember that cricket flourished because of an interconnected physical attraction and moral code which tied players, spectators and administrators in a joint enthusiasm and endeavour. A significant support came from the monarchy, with Queen Victoria and Albert, the Prince Consort, encouraging their sons to play cricket and hiring them a professional coach, Frederick William Bell of Cambridgeshire.[11] This was in keeping with the attitudes and policies of George IV and William IV who had taken a genuinely keen interest in the sport. Just before his death in 1837, William IV, who had long served as patron of the Royal Clarence Cricket Club, contributed £20 towards the founding of the Sussex County Cricket Club, in the hope of encouraging 'the manly exercise of cricket, as a game which so peculiarly belongs to this country'.[12] Queen Victoria was instrumental in the foundation of the Home Park Cricket Club in 1850 when a field at the foot of Windsor Castle was placed at the disposal of local residents. Since then, a member of the royal family has always been that club's patron.[13] The Prince Consort was an important cricket figure, serving as patron of the prestigious Marylebone Cricket Club (MCC) from 1846 until his death in 1861. The Prince of Wales (the future Edward VII) followed his father's lead and became patron not only of the MCC but also the Surrey County Cricket Club.[14] Prince Christian Victor played the game with much skill, and his Royal Highness the Duke of Albany was only seven years old when enrolled as a member of the Esher Cricket Club.[15] Royal family members were constantly reported present at the great Victorian cricket festivals, and contributed generously to the Dr W. G. Grace Testimonial Fund in 1895.[16] The Queen did not take an active part in cricket but gave it her stamp of approval. This was of major importance in an age when aristocrats as well as commoners still followed the guidance of the monarchy in matters cultural.

While this royal support was symbolically significant in the widening and deepening hold cricket took during the later nineteenth century, it was the support of the ruling cultural elite which proved critical in the game's social triumph. The aristocracy and the landed gentry became firmly convinced of the inherent social value of cricket, and were joined in that view by the upper middle classes which had largely emerged from the Industrial Revolution. This comparatively tiny group constituted what the Italian political theorist, Antonio Gramsci, would later identify as a hegemonic power bloc whose ruling cultural precepts became accepted as the norm by all social strata.[17] In being adopted by this section of English society cricket's social status and influence were inevitable, and it was eagerly adopted throughout the country.

By the early 1880s, when the MCC membership had grown to more than 2,000, approximately 15 per cent of them were titled.[18] Many Members of Parliament were also members of the MCC, as its president, W. E. Denison, observed in 1892.[19] Six years previously, *Cricket*, one of the best sports journals of the period, marvelled at the high percentage of MPs who had played or were still connected with the game. In the Conservative Cabinet of 1886, cricket was well represented by Lord George Hamilton (MCC) and the Rt. Hon. Edward Stanhope (Kent). W. St John Broderick, A. Akers-Douglas, Lord Harris,

Walter Long, Col. Walrond and the Earl of Latham, all of whom were famous cricketers, were also promoted to important posts outside the Cabinet.[20]

By definition, of course, the titled members of the MCC sat in the House of Lords and many held minor Cabinet posts in the governments of the day, thereby playing influential roles in British political life. Similarly, many others from this power elite dominated senior positions in the civil service where their influence on daily life was enormous. Added to this, MCC government itself was stocked by this group, and being *the* cricket decision-making body these people wielded great influence throughout the cricketing empire as well as the political one. These empires, in fact, were one and the same.

There was a direct link between Victorian politics and Victorian cricket. Even the puritanical Richard Cobden, best remembered now for his role in the repeal of the Corn Laws, became patron of the North of England Cricket Club in 1846.[21] Sometimes, parliamentary members arranged matches between themselves and the civil service.[22] Cricket interests in the Victorian parliament were so strong that, in 1888, they killed a section of the Great Central Railway Bill which threatened the famous Lord's cricket ground with possible extinction. They were strong enough, too, to permit the easy passage of Sir John Lubbock's Bank Holiday Act in 1871 and thus allow the immortal Dr W. G. Grace to thrill massive holiday crowds for the next thirty years.[23] An idea of the intersecting cricket/political culture influence in Victorian life is best seen in individual cases, with the reminder that these are just two of several.

Martin Bladen, seventh Lord Hawke, who was born into a landed family in 1860, was educated at Eton and Oxford, and took his seat in the House of Lords in 1888. He then served as captain of the 3rd Battalion of the Princess of Wales's Own Yorkshire Regiment. Lord Hawke played for Yorkshire from 1881 to 1910, being captain for all but two of those years. In 1898 he became president of the Yorkshire County Cricket Club and held that position until his death in 1938. He led English teams to Argentina, Australia, India, North America, South Africa and the West Indies, and was an English selector from 1899 to 1909. A long-time member of the MCC and its committee, he was president from 1914 to 1919 and a trustee from 1916 until his death. Deeply conservative, Lord Hawke remained a strong disciplinarian in his approach to cricket and its social code. But he did more than any other individual to modernise first-class cricket, to improve the lot (and the image) of the professional cricketer in Yorkshire and to popularise the sport throughout the empire.[24]

Born in 1866, just two years before his father's premature death,

Freeman Thomas was educated at Eton before proceeding to Cambridge where he gained his 'blue' during all of his four years there (1886–89). A steady middle-order batsman, he also played eighteen matches during 1886–90 for Sussex, the same county which his father had represented during the 1860s. He was elected Liberal MP for Hastings from 1900–06 and for Bodmin from 1906 to 1910. After serving for a few years in the army, he was created 1st Lord Willingdon in 1910 before becoming a famous colonial administrator. He served as Governor of Bombay from 1913 to 1919, Governor of Madras from 1919 to 1924, Governor-General of Canada during 1924–31 and Viceroy of India from 1931 to 1936. Everywhere he went, Willingdon encouraged cricket for both its physical and spiritual qualities.[25]

Two major institutions in British life brought about this reverence for and faith in cricket among the ruling elite. The first was education and the second religion, with a good deal of mutual reinforcement occurring between them. Educators encouraged cricket participation among their students in the profound conviction that it produced better citizens as well as scholars. This idea was well expressed by Dr George Ridding, one of the most famous headmasters of that age, who once declared: 'Give me a boy who is a cricketer and I can make something of him'.[26] It was a sentiment shared by public school teachers during the second half of the nineteenth century when cricket became a formal and compulsory feature of the public school curriculum.[27] Such influential educators as H. H. Almond, G. E. L. Cotton, C. J. Vaughan and H. Walford argued that organised sports could bring order and discipline to aggressive groups of rich, spoilt and rebellious brats. They regarded play as a natural tool for the building of adolescent character. Samuel Butler, the great headmaster of Shrewsbury from 1798 to 1836, first tried to monitor play in an effort to develop manliness and discipline. His example was followed almost everywhere, most notably by Benjamin Kennedy at Shrewsbury, John Perceval at Clifton and Edward Thring at Uppingham.[28]

The public schools established the cricketing cult from about 1830 onwards. By 1860 it was an essential feature of their curriculum. So powerful was the cricketing craze that some headmasters could do nothing to resist it. At Uppingham, for instance, the great Thring wrote in his diary, on 28 May 1872: 'I do not want the cricket to get too powerful in the school here, and to be worshipped and made the end of life for a considerable section of the school'. It was, nevertheless, Thring himself who consented to the appointment of a cricket professional at Uppingham in the 1870s, long after most of the other schools had begun to hire coaches for their students.[29]

At first, the public schools depended mainly on amateur coaching as enthusiastic masters as well as faithful alumni taught the boys to play. Old Harrovians like Robert Grimston, Frederick Ponsonby and I. D. Walker devoted many years to this kind of service. Among the most famous of the amateur coaches at Eton were G. R. Dupuis, R. A. H. Mitchell and C. M. Wells. The Revd William James Earle, meanwhile, promoted cricket at Uppingham from 1850 to 1881, showing the longevity of the enthusiastic amateur tradition. He often played for the school XI and was joined regularly by Thring.[30] Masters also took cricket very seriously at Winchester where M. C. Kemp took charge of the game, and even at a small private school like Farnborough cricket was played earnestly around the turn of the century.[31]

The professional influence was even more well established. As early as 1823, a professional bowler was engaged by Harrow whose example was soon followed by Eton.[32] Rugby hired Deacon of Nottinghamshire in the late 1830s as its first regular professional.[33] In the 1850s, it profited from the services of John Lillywhite who was succeeded by Alfred Diver and Walter Price. Tom Emmett, too, spent many years coaching at Rugby after a brilliant career with Yorkshire. By 1849, Westminster had a coach for several weeks annually. Later, Tom Mantle served the school as its senior professional from 1862 to 1883. James Lillywhite went to Marlborough in 1853 before proceeding to Cheltenham in 1855, where he died in harness thirty years later. Brampton was also an excellent coach at Marlborough where he spent twenty years (1859–79), turning out such fine cricketers as F. M. Lucas, C. O. H. Sewell, A. G. Steel and C. P. Wilson.[34]

Alan Gibson Steel typified the amateur product of this coaching tradition, the great player whose cricket prepared him for a busy public and career life. Born in Liverpool in 1858, A. G. Steel was described by *Wisden* as 'the greatest of all Marlborough cricketers'. He was a member of the college XI from 1874 to 1877 and was captain for two years. He was in the great Cambridge XIs of 1878, 1879, 1880 and 1881 and was captain in 1880. He toured Australia in 1882–83 and represented England at home on many occasions. Although his work as a barrister curtailed his appearances, he was one of the great all-rounders, scoring two centuries against Australia and taking most wickets for England on the 1882–83 tour. He led England to victory in all three tests against Australia in 1886. He became president of the MCC in 1903 and all England regarded his premature death in 1914 as a monumental national loss.[35]

By the 1860s public school cricket was systematised with much competition for the services of the better professionals during the spring before the start of the regular county schedule. Many schools, therefore, began their season in late March or early April. This meant that, in addition to the permanent professional, other cricketers were engaged for short periods each year. Thus, by the 1890s, for example, while J. Wootton was the regular professional at Winchester, Tom Richardson and Victor Barton also appeared there for a few weeks. William Caffyn, an excellent all-rounder who toured Australia with the England team of 1863–64, observed in 1894 that many schools like Cheltenham, Eton and Wellington often boasted more than one full-time professional. He himself over a long career coached at Brighton, Cheltenham, Clifton, Eton, Haileybury, Wellington and Winchester. Jack Painter of Gloucestershire also coached at several public schools before his death in 1900.[36]

In 1872, H. H. Stephenson was finally engaged as the senior resident professional at Uppingham. There he remained for several years, establishing an enviable reputation as a gentleman and a tyrannical cricket coach. By the time of his death in 1896 he was a legend in the district. His teams were highly successful and included such renowned players as the Steels (D. Q. and H. B.), G. Bardswell, S. Christopherson, A. P. Lucas, S. S. Schultz and C. E. M. Wilson.

Cricket was highly significant in the development of Victorian public school ideology. At Eton, for example, Oscar Browning was dismissed by Dr Hornsby for his alleged opposition to games.[37] Edward Bowen, a housemaster at Harrow from 1859 to 1901, was given 'three days special leave' in 1888 to compose a poem in celebration of F. Stanley Jackson's mighty deeds against Eton at Lord's that year.[38] Roxburgh ended his days at Charterhouse as a Trinity Exhibitioner but never became a monitor because of his indifference to sports.[39] E. C. Wickham, who 'believed in cricket even more genuinely than did most of the great headmasters of that time', transformed Wellington College into a cricket nursery under the tutelage of John Relf, a professional from Nottinghamshire.[40] At Radley, the playing fields became as important as the chapel,[41] and at Marlborough G. E. L. Cotton established cricket as firmly as he did the classics.[42] Indeed, all the Victorian alumni who left memoirs or histories of their public schools confirm the importance of cricket by devoting larger chapters to that game than to the more academic aspects of the curriculum.[43]

The alumni then took their cricketing skills to the universities, most notably Oxford and Cambridge, where the perceived connection between such skills and the production of appropriate social behaviours was perhaps even more apparent. Cambridge hired over a dozen cricket coaches in 1880 and by 1895 the figure was upwards of eighteen.[44] The universities spawned scores of excellent cricketers and produced such notable administrators of the game as Sir Dudley Leveson Gower, Lords Harris and Hawke, Sir Francis Lacey and Sir

Pelham Warner. As an example of just how important this scholar-athlete nexus was, it is worth considering the composition of some of the great university teams of the late nineteenth century.

When Cambridge beat Oxford by seven wickets in the 1890 match at Lord's, the sides contained several personalities destined for greater things beyond the cricket boundary. Oxford was captained by the Hon. Frederic John Napier Thesiger, an alumnus of Winchester, who was to become a barrister, Governor of Queensland and then of New South Wales before serving as the Viceroy of India. He succeeded to the title of 3rd Lord Chelmsford in 1905 and was created Viscount in 1921. He was appointed First Lord of the Admiralty in the Labour Government of 1924.[45] His Cambridge counterpart was Samuel Moses James Woods, a product of the Sydney Grammar School who played cricket for Australia and Somerset (where he served for many years as secretary to the county club) and rugby for England.[46]

Among the Oxford University blues of 1890 were Hubert Bassett, George Fitz-Hardinge Berkeley, Henry C. Bradby, Maurice J. Dauglish, M. R. Jardine, W. D. Llewelyn, L. C. H. Palairet, Henry Schwann, Ernest Smith and G. L. Wilson. That great stylist, Lionel Palairet, who was also an accomplished archer, hunter, footballer and long-distance runner, became in 1907 captain of the Somerset CCC, over which he also presided after 1930. He was a land agent for the Earl of Devon's sizeable estate. While Schwann went down to the city as a stockholder, Bassett, Dauglish and Smith became teachers, with Dauglish rising to the post of headmaster and Smith, who captained Yorkshire occasionally in the 1890s in Lord Hawke's absence, eventually opening his own preparatory school in Eastbourne. Berkeley and Wilson became barristers, the one in England and the other in Australia. Berkeley also served in the Worcestershire Regiment and saw service in the First World War as a Brigade musketry officer. An accomplished author, he published the popular *My Recollections of Wellington College* (1946) when he was more than seventy-five years old. Malcolm Jardine became a professor of law at Bombay University before being appointed Advocate-General of Bombay. Returning to England, he served for several years as vice-president of the Surrey County Cricket Club, of which his son (the more famous Douglas) was long a distinguished captain.

The Cambridge blues of 1890 included R. N. Douglas, C. P. Foley, P. G. J. Ford, R. C. Gosling, Harold Hale, A. J. L. Hill, F. S. Jackson, D. L. A. Jephson, Gregor McGregor and E. C. Streatfield. The eventual star of this side was the Rt. Hon. Sir Frank Stanley Jackson, one of England's finest all-rounders, who made a name for himself in politics. He was MP for the Howdenshire Division of Yorkshire from 1915 to 1926, financial secretary to the War Office in 1922 and chairman of the Unionist Party in 1923. He then served as Governor of Bengal at the height of the nationalist agitation there during 1927–32, barely escaping assassination on more than one occasion. While Jephson and McGregor joined Schwann at the Stock Exchange in London, Ford became a teacher and Streatfield an inspector of schools. A noted all-round sportsman, Robert Cunliffe Gosling was a brilliant inside forward who represented England five times in soccer and was the donor of the Arthur Dunn Cup. He served for some years as the sheriff of Essex. Hill was another versatile sportsman of some renown. He captained Hampshire at both rugby and field-hockey and was a superb racquets player as well as a boxer. He became a successful shipowner. Hale, an Australian, went into business in South America, while Foley joined the army and participated in the Jameson Raid in 1895. His exploits in this episode earned him the nickname of 'The Raider'. He served with distinction in the Boer War and, as Lieutenant-Colonel, commanded the 9th East Lancashire Regiment during the First World War.

Robert Noel Douglas, who opened the batting for Cambridge, typified the cricket-education-religion triad. The second son of Sir Robert Douglas who was connected with both King's College, London, and the British Museum, Douglas attended Dulwich before going on to Cambridge. Graduating with an MA, he taught at Uppingham from 1892 to 1910. He then served as headmaster of Giggleswick until 1931 when he took holy orders, becoming a priest in 1932 and running a parish until 1947 when he was seventy-nine. At the age of eighty-eight, Douglas died on 27 February 1957 when the president of Oxford University Cricket Club was D. R. Jardine, the son of his old rival and the man who led England on the troubled 1932–33 MCC tour of Australia. Such were the networks created by this cricketing ideology.

The composition, recreation and preservation of the ruling elite is very clear here, and it is easy to see why the cricket ideology persisted so strongly. With shared backgrounds, educations, careers and beliefs, the ruling ideology was self-perpetuating. The number of schoolmasters is especially important because of their impact upon subsequent generations, while the offspring of all these cricketers were destined for similar life paths.

The academic institutions, then, indelibly marked English cricket and English society. Their graduates founded countless cricket clubs in the second half of the nineteenth century, over 100 of which are listed in Arthur Haygarth's monumental *Scores and Biographies*.[47] They encouraged and popularised the game, giving it a social cachet. And their products, the cultural elite, took cricket not only into MCC and county cricket government but also into politics and the civil service. It is not surprising that the Clarendon Commission of 1864 should have supported cricket as a positive force capable of fostering loyalty, courage and team spirit.[48]

The educational institutions were aided and abetted by the established Church of England, particularly as that body itself was a major force in education with many of its officers being schoolmasters and academics as part of their holy mission. Most of the Victorian educators, in fact, became ardent apostles of 'muscular Christianity' which dominated the late Victorian mindset. This doctrine revolved around the notion that there was something good and godly about brute strength and power so long as it is not exercised cruelly against the aged, feeble and helpless. Physical frailty was considered unnatural because it was a manifestation of moral and spiritual inadequacy which could be overcome by prayer, upright living, discipline and exercise. Bullying, of course, was immoral but brawn a virtue.

The leading preachers of this gospel were Bishop Fraser, Thomas Hughes, Charles Kingsley and Charles Wordsworth. Through their teachings godliness became more and more associated with manliness, and by the 1870s the transition was complete.[49] The work of Thomas Hughes was of major importance. His *Tom Brown's Schooldays*, published in 1857, sold 11,000 copies in its very first year. His glorification of the cult of athleticism was immensely popular. He equated manliness with robust power and raw courage, and articulated a philosophy which the majority of Victorians were anxious to uphold. Hughes himself recognised some of the dangers inherent in such an ideology and tried to correct the damage with the more moderate *The Manliness of Christ* which, however, made little impact. The later Victorians preferred the classical Greek ideal of the perfect man being at once handsome, wise and mighty.[50]

Charles Kingsley felt that a healthy mind was impossible without a robust body since so much depended upon the absolute harmony between body, mind and soul. In a sense, he fused Thomas Carlyle's concept of the hero with Cardinal Newman's ideal of the perfect gentleman to emerge with his model of the muscular Christian, even though he did not like the term. Like Herbert Spencer, who considered athletic training more important than the narrowly intellectual, Kingsley allowed his philosophy to be governed too much by physiological concepts.[51]

The pervasive influence of muscular Christianity can be detected in all branches of nineteenth-century English literature. The medieval concept of the chivalrous knight was revived and transformed into the Christian cricketer. Godliness and manliness, spiritual perfection and physical excellence became inextricably interwoven. It was no longer thought possible that a feeble body could support a powerful brain. Hence, for instance, even Leslie Stephen, despite his physical frailty, could ironically pose as a staunch champion of muscular Christianity. His response to chronic illness was to become a fanatical athlete. Like most of his contemporaries, he sincerely believed that he could over-come all weakness by strengthening his physique.[52]

In this climate, it was difficult for clerical and other leaders to resist the trend towards athleticism. As it was, Victorian churches gradually accepted play as an 'adjunct to work'.[53] Even the Nonconformists, who had earlier tried to check the expansion of sport, revised their strategy and attempted to control it. They established cycling clubs, sports teams and Pleasant Sunday Afternoon Societies wherever they could. In fact, the Evangelicals adopted cricket as their special propaganda weapon after 1880. By the turn of the century, Revd Thomas Waugh could write *The Cricket Field of a Christian Life*. Cricket, morality and religion became so intermixed in the Victorian ethos that in Waugh's book the Christian team batted against Satan's devious and immoral bowlers who blatantly disregarded the rules of the game. The godly batsman had to cope with the quality of the bowling itself as well as the attitudes of the ungodly bowlers.[54]

The Victorian clergy gave cricket their unqualified blessings. Churchmen of all persuasions played the game and encouraged others to do likewise. Revd James Pycroft, a curate of Dorset from 1856 to 1895, gave his long life to reading and writing about cricket after having played for Oxford against Cambridge at Lord's in 1836. He remained for about thirty years an important member of the Sussex County Cricket Club committee.[55] Revd Archdale Palmer Wickham kept wicket very well and regularly for Somerset between 1891 and 1907.[56] Revd A. R. Ward contributed more than any other single indi-vidual to the development of first-class cricket at Cambridge Univer-sity.[57] Cardinal Manning, before his ordination, represented Harrow against Eton and Winchester.[58] Revd George Leopold Langdon, who briefly represented Sussex in 1839 and the Gentlemen against the Players in 1841, was the first honorary secretary of the Sussex County Cricket Club.[59] Revd Charlton George Lane, who played cricket for Westminster when only thirteen years old, represented Oxford at both cricket and rowing and went on to play more cricket for Buckingham-shire, Hertfordshire and Surrey in his adulthood. At the age of 51, he made his last public appearance on the cricket field, representing the Veterans against the MCC in the MCC Centenary Week at Lord's in 1887.[60] Dr John Peel, the Dean of Worcester and brother of the great Sir Robert, permitted the Worcestershire County Cricket XXII to play against an All England XI on his estate at Waresley in 1848, and Revd R. Peel (presumably a relative) was one of the founders of the Worcester City and County Cricket Club in 1855.[61]

The relationship between Victorian cricket and religion was direct, and the church influence was doubly profound since several clergymen served as headmasters in the emerging public schools where they implemented their ideas of muscular Christianity and tried to train outstanding civic leaders by exposing them to organised sports. In their view, the requisite civic virtues could best be inculcated in a physical education programme that made cricket, soccer, rugby and rowing essential features of the public school curriculum. So important had the physical aspects of Victorian secondary education become that Thomas Hughes, for example, was assigned to teach boxing, cricket and rowing, in addition to law and public health at the Working Men's College.[62]

This dedication to cricket as a social instrument should be seen in the context of a wider concern which sprang from the gradual improvement in the standards of living even among the labourers, the steady reduction of working hours, and the development of a more positive attitude towards 'manly' exercises. The steady increase in workers' free time was accompanied by fear on the part of the elite that the lower orders might not use it constructively. Hence the frantic search for 'improving' and 'rational' recreations which led to the formation of Friendly Societies and an extraordinary assortment of clubs. Most of these institutions became directly involved in the organisation of manly sports. Industrialisation and urbanisation had significantly interfered with many traditional popular recreations and given rise to modern music halls, seaside resorts and sports clubs.[63] So the late Victorians became even more sportsminded than their predecessors and gave a considerable fillip to such activities as archery, badminton, bowls, boxing, canoeing, dog-racing, golf, hockey, horse-racing, polo, rowing, soccer, swimming, tennis and yachting.

While they enjoyed their new forms of entertainment and recreation, the Victorians argued about the meaning of sport in their lives. They worried that playing games was socially unproductive, perhaps even destructive, and that it threatened established social patterns because it might blur class boundaries. The aim of the discourse was clear: the sport phenomenon had to be given proper social direction so as to be of productive use.[64] The muscular Christians adopted cricket as their special game and moulded it into an important national symbol. The Victorians viewed it as the game least tainted by human foibles. It became so closely identified in their minds with religion, morality and public health that it could loom large in every discussion from

[21]

education to imperialism. Cricket had to be encouraged in the academic institutions because it was an indispensable aid to intellectual pursuits.

Given the pervasive nature of cricket, then, with its deep roots in education and religion, it was naturally expected to play a role in social relations in Victorian England, serving as a healing bond between the classes. Indeed, as muscular Christianity spread its influence, this philosophy of social reconciliation became dominant. Dr W. G. Grace, the greatest of all Victorian cricketers, had no doubt that cricket could advance the cause of civilisation and hold together, as by a common bond, peoples of vastly differing backgrounds.[65] Charles Burgess Fry, another famous batsman, thought that 'there is something in the game that smothers pretence and affectation, and gives air to character'. To him, cricket's special virtue was that it could bring out the best features of human character. It was a 'form of recreation free from all tendency to degrade either those who play or those who pay'.[66] And Albert E. Knight, of Leicestershire and England, viewed the game as a panacea for a multitude of ailments.[67]

Several of their counterparts felt exactly the same way. Revd G. J. Chester, in a sermon delivered at Sheffield in 1859, saw cricket as promoting purity of life as well as bodily health. It could also serve, in his judgement, 'to break down barriers which unchristian pride has built up between class and class, and to cement bonds of goodwill and brotherly feeling'.[68] Richard Cobden concluded that cricket was 'the most innocent of all outdoor amusements'.[69] Lord William Lennox, as early as 1840, referred to cricket as the 'national game' which 'preserves the manly character of the Briton, and has been truly characterized as a healthful, manly recreation giving strength to the body and cheerfulness to the mind'.[70] To Edward Thring, the educator, cricket was the greatest bond of English-speaking people.[71] The Bishop of Hereford, in a typical eulogy of W. G. Grace in 1915, remarked that the good Doctor 'was the best known of all Englishmen and the King of that English game least spoilt by any form of vice'.[72]

Supplementing this rhetoric was the entry to cricket of several social movements aimed at improving the social climate: Sunday schools, church societies, alumni associations, rational recreation movements, the Young Men's Christian Association, reformist town councils and a wonderful hotchpotch of progressive movements.[73] The objectives were simple: through cricket a better populace and, therefore, a better nation and national life. For many civic leaders, cricket was an instrumental form of socialisation.

Yet it must be understood that this cricketing egalitarianism was an illusion because cricket did nothing to remove class barriers. Despite all their rhetoric about 'unchristian' segregation, the Victorian elite remained conscious of their class and determined to protect their status, that all-important badge of 'respectability'. Consequently, the separation of the classes was deliberately preserved at all levels of the game. At the street level, working-class boys played with rudimentary implements, and were constantly at the mercy of the local police. There was no mingling of the classes there. At the village level, lower middle-income players were encouraged by local teachers, priests and businessmen and there was considerable co-operation with working-class participants. The Harrogate club, for instance, was ultimately sustained by the support of the northern proletariat, although it was for a long time administered by its bourgeois founders. In the 1880s, too, the Penrith club deliberately tried to encourage working-class partici-pation by admitting 'workingmen, apprentices and youths' for 5s a year while gentlemen continued to pay 10s 6d. As Gerald Howat and others have shown, village cricket in the Victorian age was characterised by effective socialisation and a noticeable degree of benevolent paternal-ism, especially on the part of the clergy.[74] But there was always a carefully maintained preservation of social distance. The classes might meet on the field, but rarely off it in this illusion of shared social interests. The ruling elite maintained its order and control over the cricket world and its ideological precepts. If anything, the class lines were maintained more rigorously in sport than in most other civic arenas. For example, several exclusive clubs flourished after 1850. Most were created by university graduates and alumni of the public schools. Membership was by invitation only, and some clubs were confined to former students of specific schools. They played among themselves and travelled across the country to do so at their own expense. Others, like Hampstead and Wimbledon, fiercely preserved their respectability by charging high membership fees. This simple expedient allowed them to restrict their teams to upper- and middle-class players.[75]

Labourers were barred from bourgeois and aristocratic teams and were reduced to playing among themselves. They seldom competed, for instance, with the 'respectable' clubs founded by middle-class fami-lies like the Bakers in Canterbury, the Brenchleys in Gravesend and the Graces in Downend.[76] The majority of local cricket clubs, even when funded by publicans, priests and landlords, remained essentially working-class. The Starling Edge XI, so delightfully described by Rich-ard Binns in his popular *Cricket in Firelight*, was typical of the late Victorian (and Edwardian) age.[77]

The political economy of Victorian cricket underlines this class segmentation and the social directives which drove it. Millions of pounds were spent on cricket during the last thirty years of the nine-teenth century when the game underwent explosive growth at village, league and county levels as we now know them.[78] Yet, for all that investment, the economic returns were minimal with many clubs kept afloat by great patrons and local townsmen who provided equipment to the teams and took care of the grounds. Even when clubs were founded as members of so-called professional leagues for the purpose of making a profit, they were sustained by local charity more often than not. Generally speaking, southern clubs did not fare as well as those in the north, but even there it had become necessary for a cricket club to play football or rugby in the winter to balance its books. Given that this was a highly commercialised and profit-oriented 'age of capital', the contin-ued financial support of cricket suggests the strength of its philosophi-cal hold. So, too, was the Victorian refusal to allow the new industrial technology to interfere with the basic tools and implements of the game. By deliberately refusing to apply their new-found engineering skills to the manufacture of bats and balls, the Victorians managed to preserve Georgian cricket in an almost mummified form. Their abid-ing reverence for the eighteenth-century products of Duke & Sons Ltd tells us a great deal about their approach to cricket. To them, it was not a mere sport, like soccer, to be treated as a commercial enterprise. Rather, it was a valued institution to be protected and preserved in the face of rapid industrial and technological shifts.[79] Cricket was a valued resource in the ordering and training of the nation to be supported, not exploited, economically.

This ideological strain and economic downplaying showed up clearly in the relations between amateurs and professionals in national and county teams. If the clubs were important to social leaders, the game was even more so to the majority of its participants. Working-class players viewed cricket as a potential opportunity. If they could play it well enough they might attract a professional contract, and so they therefore took cricket very seriously indeed. This was noticed at the turn of the century by C. E. B. Russell who, in a study of lads in Manchester, lamented the tendency of working-class boys to place too much emphasis on symbols, medals and trophies. They therefore showed none of that *esprit de corps* which so obviously flourished at the public schools. Russell felt that elementary school and Boys' Clubs needed to foster that spirit.[80]

Russell was not the only critic of working-class attitudes towards sport. Many Victorian observers regretted that the proletariat had, in effect, transformed play into work. Cricket competition, especially in the north, had become too fierce and too much emphasis was now being put on winning. Critics feared that sportsmanship departed when cricket was played so seriously. The proletarian approach was revealing, providing a good example of cricket being much more than two teams having fun with bat and ball. Northern cricket, with all its seriousness, was really a mirror of northern life at that time. As Arthur Thomson remarked, life itself was serious business in northern England in the wake of the great cotton slump of the 1860s, and the character of northern cricket was but a reflection of harsher realities.[81] Many club cricketers were often underpaid and sometimes underemployed in the mines and the factories. Their dream was to escape poverty through professional cricket at the highest level. They knew that manifest excellence in the minor leagues could result in more lucrative contracts with a county club. That could lead to invitations to join the ground staff at Lord's or, better still, to travel with England teams abroad. For many workers, therefore, cricket had long ceased to be child's play. Not surprisingly, the northern countries produced the majority of first-class cricket professionals in the later Victorian period.

Professional cricket became regarded as an avenue of escape from the monotony and stigma of industrial labour. It allowed many workers to find and express their individuality more fully and freely than they could have done otherwise. For the majority (as Mandle, Sandiford and Sissons suggest), it provided only temporary relief from poverty but permitted them to earn a living from what they did best. If many of them failed to translate the cricketing opportunity into private fortunes in a financial sense, then it must be remembered that the psychological and spiritual rewards from performing cricket miracles in public, and being exalted (albeit temporarily) by partisan spectators, cannot possibly be quantified. But because of these ideological tensions the social and cricketing elite moved early and quickly to put as much status distance as possible between the proletarian professionals and the privileged amateurs. Class distinctions were so rigidly preserved that professionals and amateurs used different facilities, dressed in different pavilions, used different gates and travelled in different compartments on trains.[82] Even the stands themselves were built with the idea of separating the elite from the multitude. There were members' pavilions, balconies, grandstands, and open areas – each denoting, through price and usage, a certain social status.[83]

The relationship between professionals and amateurs mirrored that between servants and masters. As late as the Edwardian age, the divisions between lower-class professional and upper-class amateur were deep enough to leave men like E. J. 'Tiger' Smith of Warwickshire with very bitter memories.[84] There was considerable snobbery in the bourgeois and aristocratic approach to cricket tempered, at best, by a measure of benevolent paternalism. The wealthy Walkers of Southgate, for instance, gave enormous encouragement and support to the Cricketers' Fund Friendly Society, and Lord Hawke took a fatherly interest in the affairs of his professional players, even though he was a martinet on the field. This social division and tempered benevolence persisted in English cricket well into the twentieth century.[85]

Throughout these formulations of ideology, class relations and institutionalisation of cricket, the printed word was a major vehicle for acculturation. During the last twenty years of the nineteenth century advances in telegraphy and printing spawned a massive sporting press of which cricket literature constituted a major part. Manuals, histories, biographies and match reports all underlined the philosophical objectives of cricket. The *Midland Athlete*, for example, gave wholehearted support to cricket and athleticism: athletics not only built strength but helped produce mental sharpness and spiritual qualities. The editor of the *Athletic News* often expressed the same philosophy. His main concern, shared also by the editor of the *Cricket and Football Times*, was that urbanisation had promoted sedentary life which could prove dangerous to public health, both in a physical and mental sense.[86] By the turn of the century, *Wisden Cricketers' Almanack*, first published in 1864, had become the Bible of cricket and remains so to this day. And as modern textual analysis and literary theory instructs, contextual readings of such works and their contemporary reception suggest just how ideologically imposing they were as indicated in two particular cases, Prince Kumar Shri Ranjitsinhji's *The Jubilee Book of Cricket* and *Cricket* in the Badminton series.[87]

Ranjitsinhji began his first-class career in 1895, the first Indian cricketer of note to play in and for England, and effectively retired in 1905 having scored over 24,000 runs and 72 centuries.[88] He was among the greatest in an age of stars, and all the more so because he demonstrated the power and effectiveness of Victorian cricket ideology. A high-born Indian from the west of the country, he was educated in Rajkot at Rajkumar College, which was set up on English public school lines, and later went to Cambridge. Ranji then returned to India as the Maharajah Jam Sahib of Nawanagar and became a leading prince working, incidentally, on the Montagu–Chelmsford reforms scheme which shifted some power to Indians. He was an indefatigable worker on the Indian Council of Princes as well as the League of Nations, where the cricket ideology seemed to stand him in good stead. He died on the same day as Lord Chelmsford in 1933, the day of the Oxford–Cambridge boat race.

Like Ranjitsinhji himself, his book (even if 'ghosted', as many have suggested, by C. B. Fry) was a sensation and sold thousands of copies in several editions. It contained instruction, sections on public school and university cricket, and action photographs of all the great players. But perhaps its most important chapter was the very last, 'Cricket and the Victorian Era', which captured the depth of contemporary feeling about cricket as social metaphor. Self-control, Ranji argued, was a marked trait among cricketers and their spectators. Physical training was an important preparation for military service, and that gained through cricket was preferable to squad drill whose mental requirements were negligible. Importantly, he noted cricket as an association of ideas in that no matter where it was played, it conjured up pictures of England and traditions English, conventions English, behaviours English. He also stressed its social influence in teaching a balanced approach to life and a sense of social responsibility. Ranji, then, had imbibed the cricket ideology and was now transferring it to his readers.

The Badminton Library volume, written mainly by Alan Gibson Steel and the Hon. Robert Henry Lyttelton (Eton), had a similar impact. Mainly an instruction manual, it is interwoven with philosophical precepts, stressing the importance of the game as an art form and social creed as well as physical activity. The book appeared first in 1889 then ran into several impressions and new editions (as in 1893), so that as late as 1908 the publishers were imprinting a further 1,000 copies.[89] This despite the fact that the book was expensive, over 10s in the 1880s, and aimed at the ruling elite rather than the masses. Like the series of which it was a part, *Cricket* quite consciously sought to maintain and promote a specific social code.

The strength of that code is easily demonstrated by the way in which cricket language passed into general usage. The word 'cricket' became synonymous with fair play, hence the term 'it is not cricket' meaning unacceptable social practice. To be 'caught on a sticky wicket' meant to be in a predicament or a difficult position. To be 'bowled out' meant to be caught in a misdemeanour, while 'playing by the book' implied orthodox dealing. To be 'hit for six' meant to be devastated and to be 'stumped' implied confusion or bafflement. Cricket became synonymous with exemplary moral behaviour and the unwritten conventions of walking from the wicket without waiting for the umpire's decision or reporting non-legal catches simply added to the moral code.[90] Successful players became models for the age, and heroes became the living embodiment of Victorian ideology.

Dr W. G. Grace became *the* great Victorian because of his cricket exploits: 54,896 runs (including 126 centuries), 2,876 wickets and 887 catches in a first-class career that spanned more than forty years (1865–1908).[91] C. L. R. James has argued that cricket was incorporated into

Victorian life by Grace because of his complete mastery over the game and his opponents.[92] His background, upbringing and exploits made him representative of the age while presaging the next. He was both a Victorian and the forerunner of the modern cricketer. He also encapsulated the illusion and reality which polarised the cricket system: an amateur who made a far greater financial fortune from the game than any of his contemporary professionals; the epitome of a game which took pride in fair play, he was an inveterate manipulator of rules who also resorted to gamesmanship (if not chicanery) on occasion; and he was the supreme individualist in a game which stressed team-play and loyalty. But, of course, it was the representational mythology of cricket which counted in Victorian England rather than its detailed actualities.

Cricket, then, was a product of the ruling elite which dominated its growth. It did not bridge the class gaps of Victorian England, was a philosophically rather than economically driven institution, and it emphasised symbolic models rather than realistic ones. It became a national symbol perhaps because the society did not intend it to accomplish any of these miracles. If cricket failed in these respects, so did mainstream institutions like Parliament, Church and Crown. These institutions appealed to Englishmen more because of their Englishness than their ability to fulfil any specific functions. The Crown was revered in England primarily because it had been the first among all the great European monarchies to become constitutionalised. Parliament held a special place in English hearts because it was the first legislative assembly throughout Europe to control the national purse and to dominate the public law. The Anglican Church represented the peculiar English compromise between Roman Catholicism and various European strands of Protestantism. There was no other Church quite like it, even though it had much in common with every other Christian sect. Cricket belonged to the same category. It represented an exclusively Anglo-Saxon contribution to modern civilisation. It stood as further evidence of English cultural supremacy, and if the Scots, Welsh and Irish played the game with less enthusiasm or competence than they did soccer and/or rugby, that was a reflection on their own philistinism rather than any weakness inherent in cricket itself. The cricketing cult prospered during the nineteenth century because it formed part of the wider games ethic then dominant in England. The Victorians were obsessed with the idea that a healthy mind depended upon the development of a robust body. Every good Christian had to be strong and manly. This doctrine of muscular Christianity, supported by so many segments of the society, stimulated the sports explosion.

[28]

There was, of course, a religious base for this complex phenomenon. As R. C. K. Ensor has rightly emphasised, the Victorians were an intensely religious people.[93] Religion dominated their domestic politics to a remarkable degree. Factory Acts, Education Bills, prison reforms, and even Corn Law repeal were all treated in quasi-religious terms. But, as Bruce Haley has demonstrated, the Victorians were even more worried about their bodies than their souls. Good health was uppermost in their thoughts, for the simple reason that it could never have been taken for granted at that time. Even the royal family was not exempt from such hazards as typhoid fever, and the entire society lived in mortal fear of cholera, measles, influenza, pneumonia and an assortment of ailments which lumped together under the general umbrella of 'gout'. No one can read the private correspondence of nineteenth-century English political leaders without being struck by their constant preoccupation with the question of their own health. Physiology and religion became, indeed, the twin pillars of Victorianism. These were skilfully fused together in the philosophy of men as far apart temperamentally as the Arnolds, Carlyle, Hughes, Kingsley, Kipling, Ruskin and Spencer.[94] The result was a fetish for exercise. Physical activity did far more than bodily good: it made men mentally alert and spiritually more adequate. Given these concerns, cricket was the perfect game.

The Victorians revered cricket as an institution because they believed that, like the Church and the Crown, it had a key role to play in English life. Their cultural and political leaders looked upon it as having specific and vital functions to perform. The game was, in their view, a safety valve for the excess energy of Victorian youth as well as those young men who, in a highly mechanised age, had become far more sedentary and physically inactive than their ancestors. The increasing use of industrial technology meant that more work could be done by fewer people in less time than ever before. Machines left society with a surplus of energy and hence the great athletic upheaval, of which the upsurge in cricket formed an important part. Cricket was also seen by many educators as a great training ground for a military career. It taught discipline, self-sacrifice and loyalty to team and country. Indeed, the Victorians came to see cricket as the perfect medium through which a good deal could be learnt about ethics, morals, justice, religion and life itself.

Notes

1 For example, Palmerston to Russell, 1 May 1864, Russell Papers, PRO 30/22/15B, fol. 245: claiming to have scored 'a notch off my own bat', when he had spoken

rather sternly to the Austrian ambassador without the Cabinet's authorisation. Cited in Keith A. P. Sandiford, *Great Britain and the Schleswig-Holstein Question, 1848–64*, Toronto, 1975, p. 103.

2 Ashley Brown, *The Pictorial History of Cricket*, London, 1988; Leslie Frewin, *The Boundary Book*, London, 1962; idem, *The Poetry of Cricket*, London, 1964; and his *The Best of Cricket Fiction*, London, 1966; Norman Gale, *Cricket Songs*, London, 1894; Benny Green, ed., *The Cricket Addict's Archive*, Newton Abbot, 1977, pp. 1–83; James A. Mangan, *Athleticism in the Victorian and Edwardian Public School*, Cambridge, 1981, pp. 141–206; Russell March, *The Cricketers of Vanity Fair*, Exeter, 1982.

3 H. S. Altham and E. W. Swanton, *A History of Cricket*, London, 4th edn, 1948, pp. 27–70; Eric Midwinter, *W. G. Grace: His Life and Times*, London, 1981, pp. 164–8.

4 This point is well developed by Walter E. Houghton in *The Victorian Frame of Mind*, London and New Haven, 1966, pp. 1–89. But it is also noteworthy that although Houghton does refer once (p. 204) to 'muscular' Christianity, he does not have much to say about the cult of athleticism in general or cricket in particular. He belonged to an older generation of scholars who, sadly, neglected or misunderstood the significance of sport in shaping a society's ethos.

5 Keith A. P. Sandiford, *Cricket and the Victorians*, Aldershot, 1994, p. 60; Roy Webber, *The County Cricket Championship*, Sportsmans Book Club, 1958, pp. 14–39.

6 C. P. Snow, *Time of Hope*, in vol. 1 of Omnibus edition of *Strangers and Brothers*, New York, 1972, pp. 12–16.

7 George L. Greaves, *Over the Summers Again: A History of the Harrogate Cricket Club*, London, 1976, pp. 70–2. H. F. and A. P. Squire, *Henfield Cricket and its Sussex Cradle*, Hove, 1949, pp. 74, 121–2.

8 Midwinter, *W. G. Grace*, p. 10.

9 S. Yeo, *Religion and Voluntary Organizations in Crisis*, London, 1976, p. 36.

10 Saltaire Cricket Club, *Souvenir Centenary Booklet 1869–1969*, Saltaire, 1969, p. 3.

11 William F. Mandle, 'The Professional Cricketer in England in the Nineteenth Century', *Labour History*, 23:8 (1972).

12 John Ford, *Cricket: A Social History 1700–1835*, Newton Abbot, 1972, pp. 147–51; Marcus Williams, ed., *Double Century: 200 Years of Cricket in 'The Times'*, London, 1985, p. 22.

13 Ernest W. Swanton, ed., *The World of Cricket*, London, 1966, p. 580.

14 *Wisden Cricketers' Almanack 1870*, London, 7th edn, pp. 17, 66 (hereafter *Wisden*).

15 *Athletic News*, 12 August 1889, p. 1; *Cricket Field*, 7 May 1892, p. 3; G. F. H. Berkeley, *My Recollections of Wellington College*, Newport, 1946, p. 74.

16 *Cricket Field*, 24 August 1895, p. 423.

17 P. Anderson, *Considerations on Western Marxism*, London, 1976, pp. 79–80.

18 Midwinter, *W. G. Grace*, p. 78.

19 *Cricket Field*, 18 June 1892, p. 118.

20 *Cricket*, 15 April 1886, p. 57; 5 August 1886, p. 325.

21 Charles Box, *The English Game of Cricket*, London, 1877, p. 73.

22 See, for example, *Cricketers' and Sporting News*, 25 June 1867, p. 2.

23 Swanton, *World of Cricket*, p. 732; Arthur A. Thomson, *The Great Cricketer: W. G. Grace*, London, 1968, p. 32; James A. Walvin, *Leisure and Society, 1830–1950*, London, 1978, p. 64.

24 Philip Bailey, Philip Thorn and Peter Wynne-Thomas, *Who's Who of Cricketers*, London, 1984, pp. 453; Lord Hawke, *Recollections and Reminiscences*, London, 1924; Derek Hodgson, *The Official History of Yorkshire County Cricket Club*, London, 1989, pp. 41–98; Ric Sissons and Brian Stoddart, *Cricket and Empire: The 1932–33 Bodyline Tour of Australia*, Sydney, 1984, pp. 62–4.

25 Bailey *et al.*, *Who's Who*, p. 1003. See also *Who Was Who*.

26 Quoted in N. G. Annan, *Roxburgh of Stowe*, London, 1965, p. 11.

27 *Ibid.*, pp. 11–13. T. W. Bamford, *Rise of the Public Schools*, London, 1967, pp. 80–3;

A. G. Bradley *et al.*, *A History of Marlborough College*, London, 1923, pp. 250–66; L. H. Cust, *A History of Eton College*, London, 1899, p. 244; Bruce E. Haley, *The Healthy Body and Victorian Culture*, Cambridge, Mass., 1978, pp. 161–8; P. C. McIntosh, *Physical Education in England since 1800*, London, 1952, pp. 9, 62–9; W. S. Patterson, *Sixty Years of Uppingham Cricket*, London, 1909, pp. 51–5; and especially Mangan, *Athleticism*, pp. 68–96.

28 Richard D. Altick, *Victorian People and Ideas*, New York, 1973, p. 143; Desmond Bowen, *The Idea of the Victorian Church*, Montreal, 1969, pp. 213–31; Mangan, *Athleticism*; McIntosh, *Physical Education*, pp. 26–103.

29 *Cricket Field*, 1 June 1895, pp. 141–2; Sir Henry Leveson Gower, *Off and On the Field*, London, 1953, p. 139; Patterson, *Sixty Years*, pp. 48–97.

30 *Ibid.*, pp. 7–10.

31 Leveson Gower, *Off and On the Field*, pp. 17, 35–6.

32 Altham and Swanton, *History of Cricket*, p. 120.

33 *Cricket Field*, 28 January 1893, p. 10.

34 *Athletic News*, 17 June 1895, p. 1; *Cricket*, 8 May 1884, pp. 104–5; *Cricket Field*, 31 December 1892, p. 429; Altham and Swanton, *History of Cricket*, p. 120; Arthur Haygarth, *Scores and Biographies*, 15 vols, London, 1862–76, vol. X, p. 194; Leveson Gower, *Off and On the Field*, p. 139. W. H. D. Rouse, *A History of Rugby School*, London, 1898, p. 327.

35 Bailey *et al.*, *Who's Who*, pp. 960–1; Benny Green, ed., *The Wisden Book of Obituaries*, London, 1986, p. 845; Ernest W. Swanton, George Plumptree and John Woodcock, eds, *Barclays World of Cricket*, London, 1986, p. 234.

36 Altham and Swanton, *History of Cricket*, p. 120; *Cricket*, 20 September 1900, p. 417; *Cricket Field*, 10 November 1894, p. 485; and 6 April 1895, p. 49.

37 McIntosh, *Physical Education*, p. 53.

38 Mangan, *Athleticism*, p. 180.

39 Annan, *Roxburgh of Stowe*, p. 11.

40 Berkeley, *Recollections of Wellington College*, pp. 44–51, 63–79.

41 A. K. Boyd, *The History of Radley College 1847–1947*, Oxford, 1948, p. 89.

42 Bradley *et al.*, *History of Marlborough College*, pp. 166–72.

43 For example, A. C. Ainger, *Memories of Eton Sixty Years Ago*, London, 1917; Berkeley, *Recollections of Wellington College*; Cust, *Eton College*; Rouse, *Rugby School*.

44 *Cricket and Football Times*, 11 March 1880, p. 249; *Cricket Field*, 6 April 1895, p. 47.

45 Bailey *et al.*, *Who's Who*, p. 1002.

46 For details of the 1890 game and information on its participants, see *ibid.*, *passim*; Geoffrey Bolton, *History of the O.U.C.C.*, Oxford, 1962, pp. 133–5; A. C. M. Croome, ed., *Fifty Years of Sport at Oxford, Cambridge and the Great Public Schools*, London, 1913, vol. 1; Green, *Wisden Obituaries*, *passim*; the relevant editions of *Who Was Who*.

47 Haygarth, *Scores and Biographies*, IX, pp. 525–6.

48 McIntosh, *Physical Education*, p. 47.

49 Haley, *Healthy Body*; idem, 'Sports and the Victorian World', *Western Humanities Review*, 12 (1968), pp. 115–25; McIntosh, *Physical Education*, pp. 40–103; David Newsome, *Godliness and God Learning: Four Studies on a Victorian Ideal*, London, 1961.

50 J. W. Diggle, *Godliness and Manliness*, London, 1887; Thomas Hughes, *Tom Brown's Schooldays*, London, 1857; idem, *The Manliness of Christ*, London, 1894; McIntosh, *Physical Education*, p. 41.

51 Haley, *Healthy Body*, pp. 68–119; Charles Kingsley, *Health and Education*, London, 1874.

52 N. G. Annan, *Leslie Stephen: His Thought and Character in Relation to his Time*, London, 1951, p. 29.

53 Peter C. Bailey, *Leisure and Class in Victorian England: Rational Recreation and the Contest for Control, 1830–85*, London, 1978, pp. 18–20; K. S. Inglis, *The*

Churches and the Working Classes in Victorian England, London, 1963, pp. 75–9.
54 P. Scott, 'Cricket and the Religious World in the Victorian Period', *Church Quarterly*, 3 (July 1970), pp. 134–44.
55 Bolton, *History of the O.U.C.C.*, pp. 8–9; Green, *Wisden Obituaries*, pp. 727–8; Revd James Pycroft, who contributed regularly to the cricket journals of the period also wrote such well-known classics as *The Cricket Field*, London, 1851; *Cricketana*, London, 1863; and *Oxford Memories*, London, 1886.
56 Green, *Wisden Obituaries*, p. 984.
57 Swanton, *World of Cricket*, pp. 175–6.
58 *Cricket*, 1 August 1895, 312; *Wisden 1893*, p. xxxiii.
59 *Cricket Field*, 27 January 1894, p. 10; Green, *Wisden Obituaries*, p. 534.
60 Bailey *et al.*, *Who's Who*, p. 593; *Wisden 1893*, pp. xxxv–xxxvi.
61 Noel Stone, 'The Rise of Worcestershire', *Wisden 1963*, p. 125.
62 Altick, *Victorian People and Ideas*, p. 143; Bowen, *Idea of Victorian Church*, p. 231; McIntosh, *Physical Education*, pp. 26–103.
63 Bailey *et al.*, *Who's Who, passim*; R. C. K. Ensor, *England 1870–1914*, Oxford, 1936, pp. 164–7; Edward Grayson, *Corinthians and Cricketers*, Sportsmans Book Club, 1957, p. 18; John Lowerson and John Myserscough, *Time to Spare in Victorian England*, Brighton, 1977; Robert W. Malcolmson, *Popular Recreations in English Society, 1700–1850*, Cambridge, 1973, pp. 11–20; G. M. Young, ed., *Early Victorian England: 1830–65*, Oxford, 1934, vol. I, pp. 236–7.
64 Peter C. Bailey, 'A Mingled Mass of Perfectly Legitimate Pleasures', *Victorian Studies*, 21 (Autumn 1977), pp. 7–28.
65 W. G. Grace, *Cricketing Reminiscences and Personal Recollections*, London, 1899, repr. 1980, pp. 183–4.
66 Cited in R. H. Lyttelton *et al.*, *Giants of the Game*, with an introduction by John Arlott, Newton Abbot, repr. 1974, pp. 117–18.
67 Albert E. Knight, *The Complete Cricketer*, London, 1906.
68 G. J. Chester, *The Young Men at Rest and at Play*, London, 1860, p. 7.
69 Box, *English Game*, p. 73.
70 *Ibid.*
71 McIntosh, *Physical Education*, p. 62.
72 Altham and Swanton, *History of Cricket*, p. 134. Cited also in Helen Meller, *Leisure and the Changing City, 1870–1914*, London, 1976, p. 230.
73 R. Binfield, *George Williams and the YMCA*, London, 1973, p. 306; Hugh Cunningham, *Leisure in the Industrial Revolution*, London, 1980, pp. 27–8, 44, 114, 179, 181–2; Meller, *Leisure and the Changing City*, pp. 161–236.
74 For example, Greaves, *Over the Summers Again*; George Harbottle, *A Century of Cricket in South Northumberland 1864–1969*, Newcastle upon Tyne, 1969; Gerald Howat, *Village Cricket*, London, 1980; J. L. Hurst, *Century of Penrith Cricket*, Penrith, 1967.
75 F. R. D'O. Monro, *The History of the Hampstead Cricket Club*, London, 1949; B. J. Wakley, *The History of the Wimbledon Cricket Club 1854–1953*, Bournemouth, 1954.
76 Midwinter, *W. G. Grace*, p. 11.
77 Richard Binns, *Cricket in Firelight*, Sportsmans Book Club, 1955, p. 39.
78 Keith A. P. Sandiford and Wray Vamplew, 'The Peculiar Economics of English Cricket before 1914', *The British Journal of Sports History*, 3 (December 1986), pp. 311–26.
79 Keith A. P. Sandiford, 'Victorian Cricket Technique and Industrial Technology', *The British Journal of Sports History*, I (December 1984), pp. 272–85.
80 C. E. B. Russell, *Manchester Boys*, London, 1905, pp. 82–7.
81 Arthur A. Thomson, *Cricket: The Wars of the Roses*, Sportsmans Book Club, 1968, p. 13.
82 Christopher Brookes, *English Cricket: The Game and its Players Through the Ages*, Newton Abbot, 1978, p. 138; Mandle, 'The Professional Cricketer', pp. 1–16; Keith

A. P. Sandiford, 'Amateurs and Professionals in Victorian County Cricket', *Albion*, 15 (Spring 1983), pp. 32–51; Ric Sissons, *The Players: A Social History of the Professional Cricketer*, London, 1988.

83 Midwinter, *W. G. Grace*, p. 117.

84 Patrick Murphy, *E. J. 'Tiger' Smith of Warwickshire and England*, Newton Abbot, 1981, pp. 4–13.

85 Sir Home Gordon, *Background of Cricket*, London, 1939, pp. 115–18; J. M. Kilburn, *A History of Yorkshire Cricket*, Sportsmans Book Club, 1971, pp. 25–8; Sir Pelham Warner, *Long Innings: An Autobiography*, London, 1953, pp. 42–3; *Wisden 1885*, p. 106; and 1887, p. xix.

86 *Athletic News*, 30 July 1876, p. 1; 14 October 1876, p. 4; and 19 November 1879, p. 4; *Cricket and Football Times*, 24 February 1881, p. 205; *Midland Athlete*, 4 May 1881, p. 395; and 11 May 1881, p. 423.

87 K. S. Ranjitsinhji, *The Jubilee Book of Cricket*, London, 1897; A. G. Steel and R. H. Lyttelton, *Cricket*, London, 1888.

88 Ashis Nandy, 'Ranji: Cricket, Nationalism, Politics and Person', *Frontline*, 3–16 May 1986, pp. 108–18; Alan Ross, *Ranji: Prince of Cricketers*, London, 1983; Roland Wild, *Ranji*, London, 1934.

89 For some details on the publishing history of cricket, see *Archives of the House of Longman*, Cambridge, 1978; microfilm reels 58 (Impression Book) and 33 (Statement Book, 1902–13).

90 W. J. Lewis, *The Language of Cricket*, Oxford, 1938; Michael Rundell, *The Dictionary of Cricket*, London, 1985.

91 *Wisden 1995*, pp. 122, 140, 147.

92 C. L. R. James, *Beyond a Boundary*, London, 1963, ch. 14. See also William F. Mandle, 'W. G. Grace as a Victorian Hero', *Historical Studies*, 19 (1981), pp. 353–68.

93 Ensor, *England*, p. 137.

94 Haley, *Healthy Body*; Anthony S. Wohl, *Endangered Lives: Public Health in Victorian Britain*, Cambridge, Mass., 1983, pp. 1–2.

CHAPTER TWO

Australia

Richard Cashman

More than any other sport, cricket has exemplified the colonial relationship between England and Australia and expressed imperialist notions to the greatest extent. This was because cricket was viewed as the most 'English of English games', the game which epitomised 'Englishness'. For British settlers, playing cricket in an alien and seemingly hostile environment was a way of establishing normalcy, creating 'Englishness' in the Antipodes. Cricket, and village cricket in particular, had been constructed as a potent symbol of pastoral England from the eighteenth century.[1] During the nineteenth century, cricket symbolised the cultural unity of the nations of the British empire and what some referred to as the 'Anglo-Saxon race'.

The cricket relationship between England and Australia became a defining one in terms of both Australian sport and world cricket, since Australia by the nineteenth century was Britain's senior 'white' colony. Cricket was one of the most popular sports in Australia for this reason, players participating in a wider game steeped with imperial meaning. Cricket was also the prism through which the changing relationship between a colony and its mother country was viewed.

Cricket was the first team game exported to Australia as British settlers brought with them a love of English sports, including cricket, horse-racing and boxing. Although there were few facilities for cricket in the early decades of penal settlement, the game was played in Sydney from 1803 and club cricket was organised from the 1830s in New South Wales and other colonies, several decades before other team sports were established. Some of the first cricket clubs in Australia adopted English names, such as the Mary-le-Bone Club in Sydney in 1832, and copied English cricket constitutions word for word. The Campbelltown Cricket Club, formed in 1832, based its rules on *Lambert's Game of Cricketing*, first published in England in 1816. Some of the leading cricketers were compared to the star English players: J. Rickard, a leading Sydney bowler of the 1840s, was acclaimed as the colonial [James] Lillywhite while batsman W. C. Still was referred to as the Australian [Fuller] Pilch, after two of the leading English players of this era. Letter-writers to newspapers even adopted British pseudonyms, one critic signing himself as 'Beauclerck [sic]', after prominent English administrator Lord Frederick Beauclerk. The first lengthy match report, which Jas Scott regards as the beginning of Australian cricket journalism, appeared in a letter published in the *Australian* of 6 July 1832 by a self-appointed critic who referred to himself as 'Etonian'.[2] Visiting British regiments also provided competition for local teams helping to develop cricket in Australia and matches between military and civilian teams were popular in the 1830s. Australian cricket and sport remained deeply imitative of British models at least until the 1850s. The first sporting newspaper to appear in Australia in 1845, *Bell's Life in Sydney and Sporting Chronicle*, was based on a British newspaper with a similar name, first published in 1816.

Cricket was also associated with imperial nostalgia. Some of the first cricket grounds attempted to replicate the English rural environment, with English rather than indigenous trees encircling them. By the 1870s the Melbourne Cricket Ground (MCG) was 'a pretty ground with nicely ornamented surrounds',[3] being fringed by imported elm trees. The Melbourne Cricket Club Minute Book for 1862 noted that Dr Mueller of the Botanical Gardens and a Mr Moore of Sydney provided the Club with at least 400 'choice' English trees planted between the outer and chain fences.[4] The footballers initially played outside the MCG in parkland where native rather than imported trees dominated. At Sydney's Albert Ground, which operated from 1864 to 1879, each member of George Parr's touring side of 1863–64 planted a tree (undoubtedly an imported tree), each taking the name of the English tourist who had planted it.[5] So English players were active agents in the development of the Australian cricketing landscape and some early cricket illustrations, such as a lithograph of a match between New South Wales and Victoria played on the Sydney Domain in 1856–57, were nostalgic. The artist depicted an English rural scene with the grassy sward flanked by tents, trees and a church in the background.

Another motivation for the establishment of cricket in Australia was to prove that English culture could flourish in an alien environment. Later in the century, when racial notions became even more prominent with the development of Social Darwinism, the success of Australian cricket was taken as proof that British stock could flourish in the Antipodes and that 'Anglo-Saxon' blood had not been thinned in hot sun as many feared. The victories of Australian teams were taken

[35]

as proof that British stock could thrive there. The success of sportsmen in the late nineteenth century affirmed the strength and vitality
of British culture in an alien environment. *The Bulletin* of 29 May
1880 hailed the success of the sculler Trickett on the Thames because
'we all feel that British pride in the physical powers of our race which
has prompted many a glorious martial deed'. Throughout the nineteenth century there was a continuing attempt to prove that the
colonial-born were the physical equal of, if not superior to, the parent
'stock'.

From the 1830s, cricket also played a role in defining the evolving
relationship between the colonies and the mother country. In the
1830s membership of some clubs was confined to the colonial-born
who developed a healthy rivalry with clubs based on the British-born.
The native-born played for clubs such as the Australian, and their flag
was the cornstalk,[6] whereas the British-born played for other clubs
such as Union which flew the Union Jack over their tents.[7]

From the beginning of club cricket in the 1830s, the game became
central to debates on colonial society and its merits, the character of
British culture in the colonies and the relationship of the colonies
with the mother country. The success of Australian cricketers from
1878 inspired much debate in England and Australia about both
the character of colonial society and the nature of the imperial
relationship.

The London *Punch* of 10 August 1878, for instance, published
an extended imaginary dialogue between *Mr Punch* and the touring
Australian cricketers. The conversation started with cricket but extended to discuss the merits of colonial society:

'Australia is a magnificent country', returned *Mr Punch*, with enthusiasm. Then, he added, with a little hesitation, 'and it's famous for all sorts
of things.'

'What things?'

'Oh, gold and Australian beef, and kangaroos – and 'possums, wombats,
and ornithorhyncusses, black swans, black fellows, and bushrangers,
and –' then *Mr Punch* came to a full stop.

'I thought so', said the spokesman, with a smile; 'your ideas about
Australia are of the most zoological Gardenish character. Are you aware,
Sir, that our cities are full of magnificent buildings? Are you aware, Sir,
that trade and commerce are nowhere more prosperous than they are in
our quarter of the globe? Are you aware, Sir, that with us all the learned
professions are represented by the ablest men, and that our Public
Schools and Universities are patterns which are imitated with advantage
in every quarter of the globe?'

[36]

Significantly this conversation was reproduced in full in the 1878 tour report published by P. E. Reynolds.[8]

The social configuration of colonial cricket differed from cricket in Britain at a number of points. Australian cricket, from its earliest days, was far more egalitarian and had a wider geographical spread: it was equally strong in city and country and in the various colonies. British cricket by the late Victorian era was a more middle-class game than soccer and, as Keith Sandiford has noted, 'failed to compete with soccer as a money-making enterprise'. Sandiford identifies the fundamental cause of English cricket's 'relative decline as a sport spectacle' in the 'deliberate refusal of its administrators to modernize it'. The game remained a 'leisurely and protracted affair geared to meet the needs of pre-industrial gentlemen-farmers'.[9] British cricket gained popular support in some parts of the country, such as Yorkshire but was (and is) stronger in some parts of the British Isles than others. Cricket in Britain is relatively weak towards the periphery, such as Wales, Scotland or Cornwall for instance. While Wales developed a national rugby team, there is no Welsh cricket team as such, the Glamorgan county side (which is just one of some seventeen county sides in the 'English' competition) is the closest to a Welsh representative side.

The Australian Cricket Club was founded in 1826 and was the most powerful and successful club in Sydney in the 1830s and 1840s, and demonstrates the social mix of colonial cricket. Publican Edward Flood, one of the founders, became a successful self-made man and politician, was the illegitimate son of an Irish convict and had little schooling. Other members of the club were Edward Gregory (scion of a famous dynasty), a mechanic, and Mountford Clarkson, a cabinet-maker. The club also attracted men of trade and some from the colonial establishment such as solicitor Francis Stephen and Cambridge-educated J. R. Hardy.[10]

By the 1850s there were various clubs in Australia. Some were based on suburbs or voluntary associations, others on institutions such as schools and universities, parts of the civil service or the fire brigade, and some were occupation-specific and work-based. During the 1850s and 1860s cricket teams were composed of professionals (such as barristers), or tradesmen and artisans (drapers, carpenters) or labourers (bricklayers).

However, egalitarianism in Australian cricket must not be exaggerated. It is also true that while cricket attracted male players from a variety of social backgrounds and regions, the dominant clubs and the men who ran cricket came from a more narrow and exclusive social band. The Melbourne Cricket Club, established in 1838, became the most powerful club in the country. Its founders represented an 'inner circle' who 'by default were the actual leaders of Melbourne society'.[11]

Women, on the whole, were not encouraged to play, either. If cricket was the English and imperial game par excellence, it was very much for men. The ideal of manliness was a core notion from the 1830s and along with this ideal were sexism and criticism of women who attempted to play cricket. The comment that Hardy, an 1830s player, was a 'lady batsman'[12] was later echoed by a well-known television commentator of the 1980s who was known to comment that a male player was performing 'like a girl'. Although women have been keen to play cricket for more than a century, and women's test matches between Australia have been played since 1934–35, there has been constant criticism of women who dared trespass in male territory. Women have been accepted as spectators, tea persons and even as scorers, umpires (in grade cricket) and commentators, but women playing cricket have been persistently ridiculed or marginalised.

While there has been greater acceptance of women playing cricket since the 1970s, the Denise Annetts affair in the 1990s demonstrated media interest in a 'leso scandal' which seemed to confirm a widespread public perception that women cricketers were 'closet males', lesbians.[13] However, the success of Zoe Goss, who dismissed West Indian Brian Lara in a charity match, helped counter a negative perception of women playing cricket.

There has been an increase in the number of women playing cricket in the 1990s, but it is ironic that there has been much greater growth in modified forms of cricket, such as vigoro, which was more popular than cricket in New South Wales in the 1920s and 1930s. It is also ironic that a modified American game, softball, grew spectacularly from the time it was introduced in the 1940s. Women playing softball escaped the criticism levelled at women playing cricket.[14]

Some scholars have argued that racial and class barriers were important factors in preventing most talented Aborigines from appearing in the top echelons in cricket.[15] Aborigines were prominent in Australian cricket in the mid-nineteenth century and an Aboriginal cricket team toured England in 1868. There were a number of talented Aboriginal fast bowlers in the late nineteenth and early twentieth centuries, but their careers were cut short by the issue of 'chucking' in particular and a lack of acceptance in general. While Aborigines have been overrepresented (in terms of their numbers) at the top level of many sports – such as boxing and various football codes in recent decades – they have been under-represented in cricket. No Aboriginal male has represented Australia in cricket and only one Aboriginal female, Faith Thomas, has achieved this honour.

While British settlers brought cricket to Australia initially, there were other methods by which the game was promoted as the century progressed. International tours were powerful expressions of empire, performing many cultural and educative roles in addition to advancing cricket-playing. Brian Stoddart noted that 'during the nineteenth century, the cricket tour was perhaps the major popular cultural vehicle for bonding between England, the imperial parent, and Australia, the colonial child'.[16]

Tours were also important because they created popular images of empire. James Bradley notes that 'cricket created a dialogue about the nature of the colonial relationship' and in the process Australians were 'invented' for an English audience.[17] A similar image-making process took place in Australia where the image of the cricketer representing the motherland underwent refinement. The primary aims for the professionals on the first two tours in 1861–62 and 1863–64 were to make money and have a good time. However, tours also had an educative role extending the market for cricket and spreading the imperial game. Tours confirmed the superior status of English cricket and the inferior, deferential status of colonial cricket and society. A number of English cricketers remained in Australia as professionals to help educate Australian cricketers and to develop the Australian game.

English cricket tours of Australia from 1861–62 did much to promote the popularity of the game in Australia. From the start they were immensely popular and profitable. Australian crowds flocked to watch the tourists, in part because they were the best players in the world, and the 1873–74 visit (and some later ones) included one of the best-known Englishmen of the nineteenth century, the charismatic and controversial W. G. Grace.

However, cricket's great nineteenth-century advantage was that, more than any other sport, it demonstrated the evolving relationship between Australia and the mother country as the first stirrings of nationalism developed, the love–hate relationship of a youthful colonial society attempting to define its identity and a greater sense of nationhood. Contests against England took on special significance because as the century progressed Australians developed a keen desire, as Bill Mandle put it, 'to thrash the motherland'. Tours also provided, as Stoddart noted, a 'kind of cultural growth barometer in that the win versus loss records were interpreted as signs of either imperial decline or colonial development'.[18]

Australian cricket tours to England represented a form of cultural pilgrimage providing players with an opportunity to visit English cricket shrines. Much importance was placed on playing against the Marylebone Cricket Club (MCC) at Lord's, and the defeat of the MCC team in the second match of the 1878 tour was more highly regarded by Australians than the success in what was later defined as the first test match at Melbourne in 1877. Australians have always had a deep reverence for Lord's, and this great sense of reverence is one explanation why they have performed so well there (particularly in the twentieth century), having a vastly superior record to that of England at the ground.[19] For English players, who play county matches there regularly, Lord's has far less mystique.

During the second half of the nineteenth century, North American cities provided alternative models for the development of sport and popular culture. Several forms of American popular culture proved popular in Australia in the late nineteenth century including vaudeville, minstrel shows, amusement parks (such as Coney Island and Luna Park) and the American circus. From 1875 to 1900 no fewer than six large American circuses visited Australia.[20] However, there was far less interest in American sport, particularly baseball, which was a potential challenger to cricket. Albert Goodwill Spalding organised a missionary tour of Australia in 1888–89 to promote baseball. While the tour was well organised and promoted, it achieved limited long-term success.[21] An American game had far less appeal than an English one, particularly because cricket addressed the central social and political issue of the day, the relationship between the motherland and colonial Australia. There was no compelling cultural reason why 1880s Australians should discard British sports for American ones, because the Australian-American relationship did not assume major proportions until well into the twentieth century. The new sports which did become popular, such as surf-board riding, were not in competition with British ones.

Australian baseball since that time has had an interesting relationship with cricket, and for most of the past century it has been viewed in a complementary rather than competitive light. By defining itself as a winter game from the late 1930s to 1973 – letting cricket rule in the summer – baseball accepted a subsidiary role. The participation of many cricketers in winter baseball has sharpened the fielding techniques of Australian players. Cricketers, in turn, have nurtured Australian baseball as typified by Norman 'Norrie' Claxton (1877–1951). Claxton represented South Australia both at cricket and baseball and contributed significantly to both sports. His name was perpetuated in baseball circles when he donated the Claxton Shield for inter-state baseball competition in 1934.

Believing that cricket was becoming less dominant as a summer sport by the 1960s, Australian baseball authorities declared that the game was a summer sport in 1973, thereby directly challenging the status of cricket.[22] Baseball administrators were encouraged by the American cultural penetration of Australia to that point through film, television, consumer goods, and by the altered geopolitical balance between Australia and England. With the growing popularity of American sports, and the impressive rise in popularity of basketball in the 1980s, baseball has advanced its claims by the 1990s as a genuinely popular summer sport.

Contemporary Australia is a less hostile environment for baseball. Throughout the twentieth century, and particularly since the Second World War, the relationship between Australia and the United States has gradually assumed greater importance while the Australian–British link has steadily declined. The attractive salaries paid in the American baseball leagues, which are many times larger than the remuneration for representing Australia at cricket, has also encouraged many young Australians to turn to baseball. Available statistics in the 1990s suggest that baseball is not a direct competitor to cricket or a threat to its popularity in the short term. While baseball has attracted larger crowds in the 1990s and basketball has been the fastest-growing sport in the country, cricket has also enjoyed a boom in popularity in the mid-1990s.

Publicans, more than any other group, were prominent in cricket organisation in the 1830s and 1840s. The first cricket clubs were linked with public houses and publicans were the first patrons of cricket. Gambling and drinking associations were accepted without question as a central part of the game in this era. Cricket achieved greater status in Australia from the 1850s by which time regular inter-club competition was organised, intercolonials were first played and, by the following decades, international tours took place. Cricket clubs were also established in schools and universities and colonial associations were set up to provide necessary organisation of the game. With its enhanced status, cricket attracted middle-class and professional men who dominated the cricket associations which ran the game from the 1850s. From that time on, the game was seen as too important to be left in the control of publicans.

The men who ran Australian cricket from the 1850s did much to elevate the ideological status of the game, to promote it as a superior game by virtue of its English associations, a manly game which built character, and an imperial game which expressed the bonds of empire. The English amateur tradition was another ideal which was much admired, though amateurism remained a different concept in Australia largely because Australia never developed a cadre of professional cricketers. Because of its earlier associations with gambling and drinking, many middle-class officials believed that there was a need to purify

Australian cricket in the second half of the nineteenth century. This move to promote cricket as a morally pure game received a boost when gambling was considered the root cause of the celebrated riot at the Sydney Cricket Ground (SCG) on 8 February 1879. Lord Harris, captain of the visiting English team and an apostle of amateurism, had no doubt that the presence of bookmakers in the grandstand was a critical factor in the riot. While some of the Harris claims were disputed by local officials, the Harris view prevailed in the longer term and colonial administrators, following the advice of a leading English administrator, made concerted attempts to clean up the game of empire.

While cricket attracted players from all social backgrounds, those who ran the game were pro-imperial, mostly Protestant and Masonic as well. Philip Derriman has noted that Masons were influential in Australian cricket until the 1960s at least and from the 1930s until the 1960s Catholics complained that they were 'kept out of senior positions' on the New South Wales Cricket Association (NSWCA) believing that 'the Masons had formed a ruling clique within the Association'.[23] A recent biography of Bradman has revealed that he was a Mason.[24] Such views dominated cricket circles well into the twentieth century. Sydney Smith Junior (1880–1972), who was an influential administrator, was a man who believed in imperial connection. Smith was a long-serving administrator involved with NSWCA from 1907 to 1966, its president from 1935 to 1966, and honorary secretary to the Australian Board of Control from 1911 to 1926 and treasurer as well for most of this period. Philip Derriman described Smith as 'conservative and rather strait-laced. He did not drink or smoke and was never heard to swear' and was a Mason.[25]

Many prominent players and officials of this era were clerics and Muscular Christians. The Waddy brothers of the King's School were devoted both to their church and cricket. Principal L. A. Adamson, a prominent educator and Muscular Christian, was the first president of the Australian Board of Control of 1905. Canon E. S. Hughes, who was known as the 'sporting parson', was president of the Victorian Cricket Association from 1932 to 1942.

Sissons and Stoddart have noted that the 'philosophical views on cricket' of Eric P. Barbour 'reveal the power of the imperial ethos in the Australian game at the time of bodyline'. Barbour argued that 'cricket encouraged cleanness of mind and thought, and was a vital antidote to idleness induced by unemployment. As a team game it taught individual unselfishness in the collective interests of the community. It taught discipline, and moral and physical self-control. Above all, "the regular arrangement of Test matches promotes, not only a healthy feeling of rivalry, but what is more important, a healthy feeling of friendship and unity between the Dominions and the Mother Country".[26]

The appeal of cricket for Prime Minister Robert Menzies in the 1950s and 1960s was that, more than any other game or activity, it expressed his Anglophile and pro-imperial outlook. Although Menzies was no great cricket ability, he associated himself with the game in various ways, attending test matches and supporting a Prime Minister's XI match when touring sides visited Australia. He also contributed an article in the 1963 *Wisden* annual in which he valued cricket as part of Australia's British inheritance for 'Great Britain and Australia are of the same blood and allegiance and history and instinctive mental processes'.[27]

While cricket before the 1970s was run by men who were mostly conservative and favoured the imperial connection, Australian administrators did not blindly imitate English precedent. In fact, they developed distinctive Australian traditions. While class and ethnic concerns were undoubtedly a factor in the mindset of Australia's ruling cricket elite – their dominance provided them with social and political power – they developed a more pragmatic and more commercial view of cricket from the nineteenth century onwards. Unlike British cricket administrators who had limited interest in promoting cricket as a mass game and even discouraged working-class participation at times,[28] Australian cricket officials took steps to modernise the game. They were prepared to accommodate and even welcome a working-class presence in cricket. They developed larger and more commodious grounds (though this was partly achieved because cricket shared ovals with the major football codes), more modern scoreboards, and accepted league competitions in which winning was a central element. Australian administrators kept costs of gate entry to a reasonable level,[29] whereas Keith Sandiford has recorded instances where higher gate entry charges were levelled in English cricket to reduce the size of crowds at major matches.[30] It appears that the comment made by Keith Sandiford in regard to English cricket administrators is less applicable to Australian administrators:

> By refusing to tamper with the traditional rules and tools of the game, the Victorians preserved Georgian cricket in a more or less mummified form . . . This reactionary approach on the part of cricket's administrators was accompanied by an almost dogged refusal of the leading county cricket club committees to sell the game to the rising urban proletariat as aggressively and as effectively as the first division soccer clubs so obviously did.[31]

The Mandle thesis, on 'cricket and Australian nationalism',[32] has dominated writing on late nineteenth-century cricket. A seminal article published in 1973, it has only been challenged on one major point, that it understated the continuing intercolonial jealousies which plagued Australian cricket at the turn of the century.[33] The Mandle thesis argues that cricket provided a vehicle for an emerging Australian nationalism, in that teams representing Australia (against England) appeared well in advance of Federation in 1901. The success of the Australian XI against the motherland provided 'a symbol of what national co-operation could achieve – the best example of Federation yet'.[34] Mandle also traces the evolution of a hesitant and tentative nationalism of the 1860s to a more confident assertion of national worth in the 1880s and 1890s when Australian cricket teams were able to match and beat the best English teams in Australia and in England itself.

The Mandle thesis also suggests two other related themes. Success against England was the ultimate yardstick of measuring colonial advance and because England was the focal point of world sport (and civilisation), success against England on even terms in England itself was regarded as the ultimate achievement, proof of progress and the worth of colonial society. Then, from the 1860s and 1870s, when touring cricketing parties visited England and Australia on a regular basis, there was a continuing discourse about what constituted an Australian and an Englishman.

This process occurred in several ways. James Bradley has suggested that English cricket writers helped to define images of Australian cricketers which evolved as Australian cricketers became a more regular and familiar part of the English summer. At the time of the first English tours there was great ignorance about Australians and Australian society, with many English spectators being surprised that the 1878 team was 'white'. By the 1920s Neville Cardus depicted a distinctive Australian batsman as a 'conquistador' with 'murderous intents'. While some English batsmen, like Spooner, batted with 'courtliness', 'batting not for the contest's prize but simply for beauty's sake', for some Australian batsmen like Charlie Macartney 'every innings was a scherzo – in a battle symphony; there was a touch of the macabre in the way that he led bowlers along the dancing track to their ruin'.[35] There were continuing echoes in later decades of these judgements of the Australian cricketer as pragmatic (and occasionally uncouth) and too determined to win.

Englishmen who visited Australia also helped to define images of colony. W. G. Grace published his reminiscences (in 1899) giving credence to popular images of Australia as a rough and exotic country where playing conditions were primitive, umpires inexperienced and players less skilled than their English counterparts. It was also a common practice of nineteenth-century Australian newspapers to reproduce large sections of the English press so that Australians could read both what their own journalists thought of England and English cricketers, and also what the English journalists said about Australia and Australian cricketers. That practice perpetuated an Australian 'cultural cringe' in cricket which placed great importance on opinions emanating from Fleet Street.

While the Mandle thesis provides valuable insights into cricket and Australian nationalism, the focus underplays one important ingredient of Australian cricket nationalism. Although Australian cricket nationalism of the late nineteenth century did become confident and even strident and cricket success was loudly acclaimed, it was in another sense a very deferential and pro-imperial expression of nationalism. It can be contrasted with a more indigenous, radical, populist nationalism which found expression in journals such as *The Bulletin* in the 1880s and 1890s. While *The Bulletin* 'foundered in a mass of contradictions', as Manning Clark pointed out, it encouraged the native-born to take pride in all things Australian – their language, culture and environment – and satirised Anglophiles who attempted to become 'pale' imitations of 'polite Englishmen'.[36] Cricket administrators, and many of the leading players and journalists of the 1880s and 1890s, were deeply Anglophile and had a great reverence for the imperial connection and the cricket shrines of England. A cricket annual produced by P. E. Reynolds, in conjunction with the *Argus*, referred to the journey to England as 'The Trip Home'.[37] Many Australian cricketers of this era defined themselves as Anglo-Australians, or Englishmen who happened to be living in Australia.

From 1877 to 1900 five Australians represented both Australia and England, and a sixth expressed his willingness to appear for England against Australia. The five included Jack Ferris (eight tests for Australia, one for England), Billy Midwinter (eight for Australia, four for England), William Murdoch (eighteen for Australia and one for England), Albert Trott (three for Australia, two for England) and Sammy Woods (three for Australia, three for England).[38] Fred Spofforth, who played eighteen tests for Australia, declared that he would be happy to represent England (against Australia) after he migrated there. In the absence of international qualification rules, these Australians were able to act out Anglo-Australian ideals.[39]

There was an interesting exchange at a farewell dinner to Spofforth in Melbourne in 1888 before he set out for England. With his scheduled arrival in England in late July, Murdoch noted that Spofforth would arrive in time to be of assistance to the 1888 touring Australians, and added that 'whatever his [Spofforth's] success in England, [he] would never be found opposing an Australian eleven'. While agreeing with Murdoch that he would be pleased to assist the Australians, in a peculiar twist of logic Spofforth declared that he would even play against Australia if picked by England and 'if as a member of an English team he was instrumental in beating an Australian eleven, he would feel all the more proud of it for the sake of Australia'. His comments were cheered by the audience who believed fervently in Anglo-Australian ideals.[40]

The Bulletin, which expressed a more radical and populist form of nationalism, was less impressed by this effusion of Anglo-Australian ideals. In its issue of 9 June it made several sarcastic comments about Spofforth's ability and decision to live out Anglo-Australian ideals:

> Spofforth, the erstwhile demon bowler, having come in for money, leaves next month to take up residence in England. If Turner keeps up his present form with bat and ball the Britishers will forget all about Spofforth who was at his best only a one-part demon.

Billy Murdoch was another who believed in Anglo-Australian ideals. Unlike Spofforth he did represent England in a test but not against his country of birth. Murdoch and Jack Ferris gave an imperial dimension to the English team which toured South Africa in 1891–92. Born in Australia, Murdoch lived most of his life there and was a celebrated and successful Australian captain in the 1880s, but returned permanently to England in 1891 to reclaim his English birthright. When he died while watching a test in Australia in 1911, his body was embalmed and he was buried at Kensal Green, London.

While cricket was undoubtedly linked with Australian nationalism in the late nineteenth century, it was largely a very deferential nationalism which reinforced pro-imperial links. This remained a dominant perspective of many of the leading cricketing administrators of Australia until the 1970s, by which time a more pragmatic and corporatist ethic helped dilute pro-imperial sentiments leading to some divergence between English and Australian cricketing authorities.

However, even in the late nineteenth century and certainly in the twentieth there were other voices of Australian cricket which articulated alternative values less sympathetic to Anglo-Australian ideals. Many of the cricketers who played for Australia after 1900, particularly those from working-class backgrounds, regarded Australia as 'home' and the idea of representing both Australia and England was remote. Victor Trumper was one such player.

Another voice was that of Irish-Australian cricketers. While Irish-born Australians were under-represented in Australian cricket before the Second World War,[41] many second- and third-generation Irish took up the game. Irish-Australians, according to Patrick O'Farrell, chose to participate in 'Australian' sports, such as cricket and rugby, opting to 'Australianise rather than perish' in an Irish sporting ghetto.[42] By the twentieth century there were considerable Irish and Catholic cricket organisations. While Protestant groups created leagues such as the New South Wales Churches Competition (founded in 1902), there was also the Catholic Young Men's Cricket Association in New South Wales (1908). By the 1930s Australia had significant number of Irish-Australian cricketers including Lindsay Hassett, Stan McCabe, Chuck Fleetwood-Smith, Leo O'Brien and Bill O'Reilly. O'Reilly has written of a celebrated incident when sectarianism reared its head in Australian cricket in the 1930s, when four of these five cricketers were hauled before the Board and it was implied that they were 'representatives of an insubordinate and disloyal team of slackers and boozers'.[43]

Although cricket attracted working-class cricketers, including Irish-Australians, and has found powerful supporters in the Labor Party – including Prime Ministers John Curtin and Bob Hawke and Leader of the Opposition, Dr H. V. Evatt – there was no left attack on cricket as an imperial agent of British influence. Possibly the answer was that by the 1930s Australian cricket had become so recognisably Australian and the national sport by the time of Bradman, that it attracted politicians both of the left and the right. It could appeal in different ways to both Menzies and Evatt who, while political antagonists in the 1950s, were both deeply involved in cricket. Although Menzies publicly paraded his love for cricket, Evatt had greater direct involvement as a player and an administrator. Captain of the Sydney University Second XI Evatt was later club secretary and active in the New South Wales Cricket Association for more than two decades. Evatt contributed three articles to *Wisden* on the control and organisation of Australian cricket (1935); an appreciation of Bradman (1938); and the role of cricket in the British Commonwealth (1949). In the last of these, he agreed with Menzies that cricket served a great moral purpose for both Commonwealth and Australian society:

> Since the re-establishment of Test cricket after World War II, a most heartening fact has been its very firm hold on all peoples throughout the British Commonwealth and Empire . . . Looking back over a vista of forty years of Test cricket, one is deeply impressed with the fact that cricket has no equal in its sustained contribution not only to the dignified leisure but to the happiness of our countrymen. In the blackest months

of the last war, memories of the great Tests and the great cricketers who participated in them were often a solace, always holding out a sure and certain hope for the future.[44]

The Australian cricket crowd also developed its own oppositional traditions of barracking, particularly its working-class sections which were located in the outer sections, such as the Sydney 'Hill'. Australian crowds were criticised from time to time by middle-class administrators and by some touring Englishmen, such as Andrew Stoddart, who dismissed the crowd as 'intimidating' and even 'evil'. While many commentators viewed the crowd as colourful and 'playful', many saw their comments as insidious and failing to grasp the higher ideals of cricket. In more recent decades Australian cricket crowds (particularly those at Limited Overs games) have been castigated by some English commentators as boorish and jingoistic. John Woodcock, editor of *Wisden*, was disturbed by the crowd behaviour at a match between Australia and England at the SCG on 11 January 1982:

> England was drowned in a sea of jingoism in yesterday's World Series Cup . . . The sounds of fury, the beating of the boards, and the booing of English batsmen were orgiastic. This was not so much sport as jingoism. But there it was . . . The scenes of mass hysteria as Australia surged to victory were, to me at any rate, discordant and unattractive.[45]

David Frith in 1996 was critical of 'rabidly patriotic' Australian supporters in recent decades:

> When Australia wins the Ashes in a Test series against England, it hardly proves that the younger country is thereby a greater force politically, militarily, artistically and in terms of virility than the older country – or vice versa. Yet to judge from some of the catcalls emerging from the outer at the MCG, SCG or the WACA [Western Australian Cricket Association ground], one might suppose this to be true.[46]

Australian cricket nationalism has assumed many different forms: a deferential pro-imperial nationalism was more prominent before 1970, but a populist, indigenous and even jingoistic nationalism has been expressed by crowds in recent decades.

While alternative perspectives of cricket and Australian nationalism had been articulated by the 1930s, Australian cricket was still very much dominated by a deferential pro-imperial perspective. Certainly this was the accepted view of those who ran the game so that the tactics of Bodyline, which seemed to elevate winning at any cost above the notion of 'sportsmanship', was regarded in Australia as a great betrayal as noted by Brian Stoddart: 'For Australians, the English approach was a betrayal of the best traditions of the game which

[48]

reflected the general imperial attitude towards the Antipodes at the time'.[47]

Sissons and Stoddart have demonstrated that the Bodyline crisis strained the Anglo-Australian relationship at a difficult time of imperial relationships and it was a rare occasion when cricketing issues were discussed in the highest political circles.[48] While the Bodyline crisis appeared a damaging one, which threatened not only Anglo-Australian cricketing and broader relations, by itself it did not weaken the imperial cricketing relationship in the long run. This occurred, first of all, for cricket reasons. Although the MCC rejected the Australian cable that the tactics were 'unsportsmanlike', the tactic of Bodyline was effectively banned. Criticism of the tactic was focused on Douglas Jardine, who was depicted as the architect and villain and, to a lesser extent, on 'Plum' Warner who was regarded as the Pontius Pilate who washed his hands of the whole affair. The chief instrument of Bodyline bowling, Harold Larwood, was forgiven by Australians and even helped to settle in Australia by Jack Fingleton. Bill Woodfull, the Australian captain, was viewed as upholding the best British traditions of the game which Australians came to believe had been temporarily forgotten by the extremist Jardine. When England next toured Australia it was captained by a more acceptable person, 'Gubby' Allen, who had refused to bowl Bodyline in 1932–33.

Teams involving services in the 1940s and dominions in the 1950s demonstrated that many regarded cricket as the game which could be used for imperial purposes. The idea of a services tour was supported in high circles (including Labor Prime Minister John Curtin) because the resumption of cricket, more than any other game, demonstrated a return to normalcy. When he watched an Australian team play at Lord's in May 1944 Curtin expressed his deep reverence for the imperial game and its shrines: 'Australians will always fight for those twenty-two yards. Lord's and its traditions belong to Australia just as much as to England'.[49] By touring in many countries (England, South Africa, India and Australia) the teams also demonstrated that cricket had a continuing imperial role. The concept was extended by the practice of sending out mixed teams to tour the dominions, such as India and Pakistan, so as to provide additional competition for emerging cricket countries, to provide fringe test players with international experience and to enhance the imperial links.

However, it is ironic that while Australian officials of this era were concerned to nurture the imperial relationship, and to maintain British-Australian links, they were strangely reluctant to encourage the growth of cricket in other parts of the empire where cricket was less developed. While England did much to encourage the growth of cricket in India, playing a number of test series against India in the 1930s, Australian Board officials were reluctant to allow any of its senior players to embark on a private tour organised by the Maharaja of Patiala in 1935–36. Australia did not tour India until 1956, more than two decades after England, and this tour was tacked on to the end of an English tour. There was even more paternalism (and condescension) involved in Australia's relationship with near neighbour, New Zealand. Greg Ryan has concluded that 'regrettably much of NZ's long-standing low profile must be traced to the attitudes held by successive generations of Australian administrators, who were quick to identify the weaknesses of NZ cricket but slow to assist in their remedy'.[50] Before the 1973–74 New Zealand tour of Australia, the two countries had only played one test, in 1945–46.

The 'revolution' that was World Series Cricket, from 1977 to 1979, represented a watershed in Australian cricket which affected every aspect of how the game was organised and perceived in Australia. Such a momentous change had profound implications for the imperial relationship. Although World Series Cricket ended in May 1979, when there was a truce between the Establishment and the Packer cricket forces, Packer cricket agendas were prominent in Australian cricket over the next decades. Australian cricket, from the late 1970s, became more market-driven than before. Central to the cricket planning was an extensive programme of Limited Overs day-night internationals each season, because these matches drew the largest crowds and greatest television audiences. Along with the changed programming, PBL Marketing (cricket marketing division of Channel 9) introduced new marketing strategies such as coloured clothing and new television techniques.

During the 1980s Australian cricket officials moved away from English models and became far more independent of English authorities. Possibly for the first time Australian cricket administrators became leaders – rather than blind followers of English cricket precepts – in world cricket. David Frith has noted that Australian administrators in time even received a grudging acceptance from authorities at Lord's:

> A peace settlement was reached [in Australia] in 1979, but traditionalists resented the increased commercialism which resulted. It was no small irony that much of the English resentment at what was seen as an Australian assault on the old order gradually turned to resigned acceptance, the authorities at Lord's actually becoming more commercially minded themselves in the years that followed.[51]

Packer cricket helped turn Australian cricket further away from English models. In the interests of greater commerical penetration it promoted a more indigenous and populist Australian culture.[52] Channel 9 commentators, such as Bill Lawry, were more distinctively and unashamedly Australian than their Australian Broadcasting Corporation (ABC) counterparts. Australian cricket also drew greater inspiration from American models of sports promotion, which were becoming popular in Australia in the 1980s. The gap between the culture of Australian and British cricket widened during this period.

World Series Cricket swept aside the old official cadre which fervently believed in the imperial ideals and amateurism, replacing it with a more corporatist and pragmatic group who were no longer antagonistic to the commercial and professional penetration of cricket. Whereas the pre-World Series Cricket administrators were complacent about the continuing dominant role of cricket in the Australian sporting firmament, cricket administrators in the 1980s and 1990s realised that they were operating in a far more competitive and difficult sporting environment.

Another significant change in Australian officialdom in this period was that it became both more independent (of Britain) and internationalist in perspective. Recognising that English cricket was in a state of temporary, or permanent, decline, Australian administrators such as Fred Bennett and Alan Crompton developed closer ties with cricket in other parts of the world, notably the subcontinent. This was part of an Australian discovery of Asia in cricket, which was part of a wider discovery in trade, politics and education. Officials such as Bennett and Crompton recognised that subcontinental cricket represented a vibrant cricket culture of great future potential. Bennett played an important role in lobbying for the admission of Sri Lanka to test status.

Since the Second World War, and particularly since the 1970s, the British presence in Australia has declined, politically, economically and culturally. America and Asia have progressively taken over the cultural role once the exclusive preserve of the British. The development of a more multicultural society – with many post-1950 immigrants coming from non-English-speaking backgrounds – has further diluted a colonial culture which drew inspiration from its British-Irish roots.

Despite the Australian move away from things British and the relative weakness of English teams in the past decade, the Ashes remains one of the most popular cricket contests. Possibly because of weight of tradition, many cricket followers have a deep love of contests which have a distinctive and lengthy past. Perhaps the continuing strength of Anglo-Australian contests exists because it is a way of measuring how far Australia has diverged from the British models. There has been a long tradition of defining Englishmen as the 'other' – from Douglas Jardine as the 'stiff upper-lip Englishman' to Mike Brearley as the 'archetypical upper-class Englishman' – which was been drawn upon even more in the past two decades.

Although the Ashes remains *the* popular contest the gap is closing with other countries such as the West Indies, Pakistan and even Sri Lanka, appearing to offer tougher competition. It is likely that the mystique of the Ashes will be insufficient to retain public interest in Anglo-Australian contests if England continues to decline as a cricket force.

The development of a more multicultural (global) society in Australia has implications for the future of Australian cricket. There is a possible danger that cricket may be typecast as the old 'imperial' game for English-speaking Australians of British and Irish descent and not a game for all Australians. There is also the danger that cricket may be labelled the game of 'old empire' and therefore less appealing than basketball, the sport of 'the new [American] empire'. Cricket has also lagged behind other sports, particularly the football codes, in its penetration of ethnic communities.

It remains to be seen whether the game of cricket can reinvent itself to continue to appeal to a more multicultural and republican-leaning Australia. To retain its status as the premier team sport in the country, it appears necessary that cricket divest itself of some of its imperial legacies and define itself in more global terms.

Notes

1 James Bradley, 'Inventing Australians and Constructing Englishness: Cricket and the Creation of National Consciousness', *Sporting Traditions*, 11, 2, May 1995, pp. 35–60.
2 Jas Scott, *Early Cricket in Sydney 1803 to 1856*, ed. R. Cashman and S. Gibbs, Sydney, 1991, pp. 13, 15.
3 Richard Christen, *Some Grounds to Appeal: The Australian Venues for First-Class Cricket*, Sydney, 1995, p. 59.
4 Quoted in Kristen Thornton, 'The MCG: 1953–1990', MA thesis, Monash University, 1990.
5 Christen, *Some Grounds to Appeal*, p. 119.
6 A symbol of the colonial-born.
7 Richard Cashman, 'The Rise and Fall of the Australian Cricket Club 1826–1868', *Sporting Traditions*, 5, 1, November 1988, pp. 112–30.
8 P. E. Reynolds. *The Australian Cricketers' Tour through Australia, New Zealand and Great Britain in 1878*, Sydney, 1878, pp. 93–4.
9 Keith A. P. Sandiford, *Cricket and the Victorians*, Aldershot, 1994, pp. 121–2.
10 Scott, *Early Cricket in Sydney*, pp. xi–xii.
11 Paul de Serville, *Port Phillip Gentlemen and the Good Society in Melbourne before the Gold Rushes*, Oxford, 1980, p. 58.
12 Scott, *Early Cricket in Sydney*, p. 47.

13 Angela Burroughs, Leonie Seebohm and Liz Ashburn, 'A Leso Story', *Sporting Traditions*, 12, 1, November 1995, pp. 27–46.
14 Richard Cashman and Amanda Weaver, *Wicket Women: Cricket and Women in Australia*, Sydney, 1991.
15 Colin Tatz, *Obstacle Race*, Sydney, 1995.
16 Brian Stoddart, 'Tours', in R. Cashman *et al.*, eds, *The Oxford Companion to Australian Cricket (hereafter OCAC)*, Melbourne, 1996, pp. 536–7.
17 Bradley, 'Inventing Australians', p. 35.
18 Stoddart, 'Tours'.
19 The Australian Test record at Lord's in the twentieth century has been astonishing. Since 1902, Australia has won ten tests against England at Lord's as against only one loss (in 1934).
20 Richard Waterhouse, 'Popular Culture and Pastimes', in Neville Meaney, ed., *Under New Heavens: Cultural Transmission and the Making of Australia*, Melbourne, 1989, pp. 238–85.
21 Bruce Mitchell, 'Baseball in Australia: Two Tours and the Beginnings of Baseball in Australia', *Sporting Traditions*, 7, 1, November 1990, pp. 2–24.
22 *Ibid.*; W. Vamplew *et al.*, eds, *Oxford Companion to Australian Sport*, Melbourne, rev. edn, 1994, pp. 54–6.
23 Philip Derriman, *True to the Blue: A History of the New South Wales Cricket Association*, Sydney, 1985, p. 177.
24 Roland Perry, *The Don: A Biography*, Sydney, 1995.
25 Derriman, *True to the Blue*, p. 174.
26 Ric Sissons and Brian Stoddart, *Cricket and Empire: The 1932–33 Bodyline Tour of Australia*, Sydney, 1984, pp. 36–7.
27 *Wisden 1963*, pp. 67–73.
28 Sandiford, *Cricket and the Victorians*.
29 Richard Cashman, *Australian Cricket Crowds: The Attendance Cycle*, Sydney, 1984, p. 27.
30 Keith A. P. Sandiford, 'English Cricket Crowds during the Victorian Age', *Journal of Sport History*, 9, 3, Winter 1982, p. 12.
31 *Ibid.*, p. 16.
32 W. F. Mandle, 'Cricket and Australian Nationalism in the Nineteenth Century', *Journal of the Royal Australian Historical Society*, 59, 4, December 1973, pp. 225–45.
33 David Montefiore, *Cricket in the Doldrums: The Struggle between Private and Public Control of Cricket in the 1880s*, Campbelltown, 1992.
34 Mandle, 'Cricket and Australian Nationalism'.
35 Neville Cardus, *Cardus on the Ashes*, London, 1989, p. 5, quoted in Bradley, 'Inventing Australians', p. 51.
36 C. M. H. Clark, *A History of Australia*, vol. 4, *The Earth Abideth for Ever 1851–1888*, Melbourne, 1982, pp. 363–4.
37 Reynolds, *The Australian Cricketers' Tour*, p. 12.
38 R. Cashman, 'Symbols of Unity: Anglo-Australian Cricketers 1877–1900', in J. A. Mangan, ed., *The Cultural Bond: Sport, Empire, Society*, London, 1992, pp. 128–41.
39 Richard Cashman, *The 'Demon' Spofforth*, Sydney, 1990.
40 Cashman, *The 'Demon' Spofforth*, pp. 193–4.
41 Philip A. Mosely, Richard Cashman, John O'Hara and Hilary Weatherburn, eds, *Sporting Immigrants: Sport and Ethnicity in Australia*, Sydney, 1997, p. 176. Calculates proportions of Irish-born.
42 Patrick O'Farrell, *The Irish in Australia*, Sydney, 1993, pp. 185–7.
43 W. O'Reilly, *'Tiger': Sixty Years of Cricket*, Sydney, 1985, pp. 157–60.
44 *Wisden 1949*, pp. 111–12.
45 *Sydney Morning Herald*, 13 January 1982.
46 *OCAC*, p. 171.
47 Stoddart, 'Tours'.
48 Ric Sissons and Brian Stoddart, *Cricket and Empire: The 1932–33 Bodyline Tour of Australia*, London, 1984.

49 Ed Jaggard, 'Forgotten Heroes: The 1945 Australian Services Cricket Team', *Sporting Traditions*, 12, 2, May 1996, pp. 68–9.
50 Greg Ryan, 'New Zealand', in *OCAC*, p. 383.
51 David Frith, *OCAC*, p. 171.
52 Richard Cashman, 'Packer Cricket', in David Headon, Joy Hooton and Donald Horne, eds, *The Abundant Culture: Meaning and Significance in Everyday Life*, Sydney, 1995, pp. 80–5.

CHAPTER THREE

South Africa

Christopher Merrett and John Nauright

In the study of the transfer of imperial cultural forms, South Africa provides one of the most fascinating case studies. In many respects, South Africa encompassed the full range of social, cultural, political, gender and racial problems which existed throughout the British empire. Distinct cultural groups had emerged by the late nineteenth century to include two groups of whites, mixed race people or 'Coloureds', migrant workers brought to Natal from the Indian subcontinent, and indigenous African peoples. Among whites, the main division was between Dutch and, later, Afrikaans-speaking whites descended from Dutch, German and French Huguenot settlers, and English-speakers from the British Isles and other parts of the white Western world. From 1806, the British controlled the region of the Cape and, with that control, began to introduce elements of imperial culture. Soon, from 1820, English-speaking settlers began to arrive as did missionaries who sought to convert Africans to Christianity and to submit them to the ultimate authority of the British empire.

Cricket has long been part of the imperial dimension in South African history. It was imported by military personnel, administrators and settlers from Britain: the coastal towns in particular 'received assistance from the members of the Military garrison'.[1] Instrumental use was made of sport by missionaries at stations such as Healdtown, Lovedale and Zonnebloem, in their attempt to inculcate 'respectability' in the emergent black middle class, and by blacks demonstrating their acceptance of Victorian values. Organised sport including cricket, tennis, croquet, soccer and rugby was particularly well developed in the Eastern Cape: Africans were reported to be playing cricket in Queenstown in 1862;[2] the first African cricket club was founded in Port Elizabeth in 1869; and by 1887 *Imvo Zabantsundu* (the King William's Town newspaper) had a sports edition.[3] The Eastern Cape showed high levels of black political organisation and an important part of that mobilisation was the visibility of political leaders through their involvement in sports clubs. Throughout many areas of Africa, sporting clubs provided the initial location for interaction between different groups of African elites within a colony as educated Africans gravitated to administrative, professional and educational posts in colonial capitals and large regional towns.

In 1885, a black team beat the local whites at King William's Town, and in the same year blacks from Port Elizabeth defeated the whites of Cradock. Matches between whites and blacks were a feature of imperial public holidays.[4] J. T. Jabavu, editor of the newspaper *Imvo*, a churchman and educationalist involved in cricket and tennis, supported a Cape Bill of 1891 designed to outlaw tribal amusements. Black cricket clubs frequently had imperial-sounding names and in Kimberley the highlight of the annual social calendar in the mid-1890s was a Christmas Day cricket match.[5] This emulated the social role of cricket in the white community. During the nineteenth century, matches at the Western Province Cricket Club (WPCC) at Newlands in Cape Town were accompanied by military bands and the presence of the Governor and his staff.[6] A simplistic analysis of the use of imperial names by black teams would suggest a form of cultural mimicry. The real issue, however, was one of proving respectability. The ideology of respectability was crucial for the aspirations of middle-class blacks. Colonial and later South African governments would only converse with those men who behaved in a 'European' manner, even if they denigrated them at the same time in discussions with other whites. Many middle-class blacks through the 1940s believed that behaving 'respectably' was the key to advancement. White missionaries promoted notions of respectability in their attempts to 'uplift' and Christianise Africans.[7]

This paternalistic, assimilationist approach characteristic of Cape liberalism gave way, however, to concerns about the competitiveness of blacks which manifested themselves in segregationist policy. By the early twentieth century, social institutions were adapted to play a role not only of social control but also for purposes of exclusivity. If the proper place for blacks was in the working class, to which they were increasingly consigned by exclusion from the franchise, landownership and commercial opportunity, and by general immiseration, then their removal from middle-class sport was a natural concomitant. Jarvie emphasises that 'sport must not be understood abstractly or simply in the context of ideas about racial prejudice, but rather in the context of the ensemble of social relations characterizing the South African social formation'.[8] Cricket in South Africa represented British imperialist ideology and, increasingly, a racist exclusivism.

[56]

White cricket was entrenched in segregated schools and clubs (often based on old boys' associations) whose purpose was to demonstrate solidarity, superiority and apartness. Elitism and racism were dominant except for the occasional mixing on special, usually imperial, holidays.[9] The South African Cricket Association (SACA), set up in 1890 to 'foster and develop cricket throughout South Africa',[10] had no need to include racial barriers in its constitution as social custom achieved the necessary ends. Significantly, one of the clauses in its constitution specified its managerial role in relation to tours to and from England. SACA originally included a union for Portuguese East Africa while ignoring the aspirations of South Africa's black cricketers; and the 1886–87 intercolonial tournament included a white team from Bechuanaland. The Currie Cup, instituted as the prize for inter-provincial white cricket in 1888, was presented by Donald Currie, diamond and gold magnate, of Castle Mail Packets Ltd which provided the sea link between South Africa and England.[11] Rhodesia was admitted to the Currie Cup competition for one match in the 1904–05 season but did not play again until 1930.[12]

From 1864 an important (and for a while the premier) fixture in South African cricket had been the match between mother country and colonial-born. Implicit in this contest was a deference to 'home' origins and the significance of cultural ties to England. Though not unique to South Africa, links to English culture were even more important in a setting where whites were surrounded by a large local population.[13] The ability to appropriate and dispense English culture as the measure of social acceptability gave English-speaking whites and those they chose to include a real sense of cultural and moral power and superiority.

The way in which blacks experienced English culture, however, became increasingly fraught with contradictions as the push for rigid segregation increased. King William's Town's black cricketers were rewarded for their 1885 victory by being banned from the pavilion.[14] Segregation became the norm by the 1890s, although white facilities were made available to Coloureds as in the case of the Malay tournament[15] played at Newlands in Cape Town during the 1889–90 season involving teams from Cape Town, Johannesburg, Port Elizabeth and Claremont (a Cape Town suburb).[16] In 1892, W. W. Read's England side played a Malay XVIII at Newlands, but the amateurs withdrew rather than play against blacks. An alternative interpretation, that the match was played for 'the benefits of the professionals',[17] amounted to the same disdain for black cricketers. Two years later, Krom Hendricks, a Coloured fast bowler thought to be among the fastest in the world of his era,[18] who had taken 4–50 in 25 overs in the Newlands match, was named in the fifteen from which a tour party to England was to be chosen. His selection was, however, declared 'impolitic'[19] and after pressure he was omitted, as he was from the colonial-born team. Thus it was not South Africa who invented notions of racial exclusivity in sport and other social activities, but rather the English who refused to mix with 'racial inferiors'.

Black cricket went into gradual decline by the early 1900s and mixed matches became the exception, although there are records of Coloured players in Cape Town hired to take part in practice sessions with white teams;[20] and white farmers (ex-British soldiers) playing the BaRolong of Thaba Nchu in the Orange Free State.[21] On the other hand, a British army officer who included his servant in a team was told that this defied local custom.[22] The Barnato cricket tournament was instituted in 1904 as a segregated, national black competition, its trophy having been presented by Sir David Harris, director of De Beers and a politician and soldier, to the Griqualand West Coloured Cricket Board in 1897. This was endorsement by imperial capitalism of cricket segregation.

Cricket was the imperial game *par excellence*, the epitome of British culture, morality and manners (and racism),[23] and this dimension served to alienate Afrikaners. In 1854, a match at the Cape involved 'Hottentots' versus 'Boers' (won by the former),[24] but towards the end of the century, and in particular after the South African War (1899–1902), it found little favour in the Afrikaner community and its imperial characteristics limited its reconciliatory potential. Before the South African War, a number of Afrikaners represented South Africa: Arthur Ochse and Nicolaas Hendrik Theunissen in the first test of 1888; Jacobus François du Toit and Charles Gustav Fichardt in the 1891–92 series; and Fichardt again in 1895–96. The fast bowler Johannes Jacobus Kotze, a 'Boer . . . who preferred cricket to war',[25] went on tour with South Africa to England in 1901 while the war was still being fought, although his five tests were played later. While it is unwise to assign community on the basis of language, it would appear that after 1907 no Afrikaner appeared in a test for South Africa until Jacobus Petrus Duminy in 1927–28. Cricket, as the epitome of empire, was unlikely to attract those who considered themselves dispossessed by the South African War. In addition, the British had won the war only after placing Afrikaner women and children in concentration camps so as to force Afrikaner men out of the bush and into a settlement. Afrikaners viewed the concentration camps as a British attempt to wipe them out and fed into emerging explications of Afrikaner nationalism and the Afrikaners as a 'besieged people'. Just before the

Second World War it was reported that 'The Boer element in South Africa is not vastly taken up with the game, although some of the papers do print reports of it in Africaans [sic]'.[26] It thus became a symbol of divisions among the whites of South Africa, as well as separateness from the rest of the population, until 1948 after which it increasingly functioned as a totem of white national unity. Cricket never achieved the same status as rugby during the apartheid years. The relative insignificance of cricket to some Afrikaners is evidenced in a story about Prime Minister John Vorster. He was told that 'die Engelse' had lost three wickets for 42 runs in the test between South Africa and England. Upon being given the information, Vorster replied 'Hulle Engelse of ons Engelse?' ('their English or our English?').[27]

There is some evidence, however, of a belief in the reconciliatory potential of cricket between the whites of South Africa. Another match involving Afrikaners illustrated the imperial use of cricket. In 1901, Boer prisoners of war interned at Diyatalawa in Ceylon played a match against Colombo Colts at the Nondescripts Ground. A report in the *Ceylon Independent* described the match as 'a sporting event . . . no other significance need be attached to it . . . The men are on parole; they have given their word that they will not enter into the discussion of any controversial subjects'. The captain of the prisoners of war was P. H. de Villiers of the WPCC in Cape Town[28] and at least two others had played club cricket, though they lost the match by 141 runs. Contrary to the newspaper report, the match was significant in at least two ways. First, the Governor attended, the prisoners were given lunch at the Galle Face Hotel and after the match Commandant van Zyl called for three cheers for His Excellency, which were 'heartily given, with great waving of hats and a display of the utmost cordiality'. Second, when a 'native' crowd, described as over-excited, invaded the pitch, the police made 'free application' of canes to control them.[29]

This match was thus characterised by white sporting solidarity,[30] deference to the imperial representative and brisk treatment of the unruly locals. In its way, although played thousands of miles away, this match captures some of the essence of South African cricket at the dawn of the twentieth century. The notion of 'over-excited natives' who then had to be punished pervaded white international social thought at the turn of the century. Thus, the playing of cricket juxtaposed with the caning of 'natives' reinforced central notions of white superiority. On a social Darwinist hierarchy cricket was believed to be the most moral of games and one that demonstrated the inherent superiority of the English over other 'races'. As Will Whittam proudly wrote in 1884, '. . . No German, Frenchman, or Fijee can ever master cricket, sir, Because they haven't got the pluck to stand before the wicket, sir'.[31]

The role of Anglo-South African commerce was crucial to the survival of early tours. Donald Currie funded the first touring team in 1888–89 put together by Major Warton, an official at the Cape.[32] The 1895 team to England (frequently referred to as the 'Africans' in *Wisden*) was described condescendingly as 'commonplace', attracting gate receipts of only £500 compared with £3,500 worth of expenses. Someone evidently felt the need to maintain the link since 'a collapse was only avoided by the advance of money by South African friends in England'. Maybe they were the 'several gentlemen connected with South Africa' invited to the opening match versus Lord Sheffield's XI.[33] It is not without significance that the 1901 touring side left for England before the end of the South African War.[34] The link with South Africa failed to rouse the English public, however, and 'The whole expenses of the trip were defrayed by Mr Logan [of Matjiesfontein], with whom the whole idea of the enterprise originated'.[35] Logan has been described as 'the second of the three great patrons of their cricket',[36] the others being Currie and Bailey.

The political leanings of visiting cricketers were not hard to discern. C. B. Fry maintains that the 1896 England touring team was sent to Johannesburg at the time of the Jameson Raid 'as an antidote to the inflamed melancholy of that distant city';[37] a motive supported by Lord Hawke who said he was 'telegraphed . . . to go to Johannesburg to play there to turn people's minds from the raid'.[38] Three of the team (Lord Hawke, Sir Timothy O'Brien and Charles Wright) dined and played cards with the captives in Johannesburg Prison. Nevertheless, a match was played against a predominantly Afrikaner team in Pretoria, although entertainment by, and a polo match with, the 7th Hussars in Pietermaritzburg was more typical of the tour. The touring team promoted both game and empire: the teams of the 1890s may accurately be described as 'Imperial Wanderers' including as they did the Australians J. J. Ferris and W. Murdoch (1891–92), S. M. J. Woods (1895–96) and Albert Trott (1898–99).[39] The South African viewpoint was reciprocal. It was said of the 1894 touring team to England that 'it cannot fail to have a beneficial effect as forming one more link between the Old Country and ourselves . . . one that especially influences the youth of both lands', adding that 'indirectly, our team . . . will accomplish as much good as would the visit of a Minister or the efforts of an Agent-General'.[40] Lord Hawke's team played two matches at Bulawayo in March 1899 (versus eighteen of Bulawayo and fifteen of Rhodesia) at a time when it was merely 'a town in the making'.[41] Cricket as well as trade closely followed the flag.

The insecurity of colonial society was counteracted by invoking the imperial connection and elevating Britain as the source of all light.[42] Cricket was the training ground for life and service to the British empire.[43] At the turn of the century, the tone of writing on cricket was deferential in the extreme: Lord Hawke's team to South Africa in 1895–96 was described as 'the men from the Homeland',[44] while 'cricketing teams from all parts of the Empire look to Lord's as the home, and to MCC as the head of the game'.[45] Lord Harris (who believed that the MCC was the most venerated institution of the empire) commenting on the same tour described it as 'a strand in the elastic which unites the colonies and the Mother Country'.[46] South Africa's cricket, cricketers and spectators were routinely referred to as 'colonial' and by implication as of a lesser standard than those of the 'Mother Country'.[47] For example, H. H. Castens's team to England in 1894 was described as 'of the calibre of a second-class county' even though it managed to beat the MCC at Lords in one day by 11 runs;[48] but by 1905 'her education was almost complete'.[49] When, in January 1906 at Johannesburg, South Africa beat England for the first time, this was attributed by Pelham Warner to 'that grit and courage which we are so proud of saying are inherent in the British race'.[50] Nevertheless, England continued to send sides of less than full strength (10 tours in 50 years) to South Africa until 1938.[51] This generally deferential attitude to English cricket was not at all in conflict with a will to beat England, as such events reinforced South Africa's worth to the empire.

British military influence in South African cricket was pronounced. Included in South Africa's first test team that played at Port Elizabeth in 1888 was Major R. Stewart. A number of cricketing British soldiers settled in South Africa after the 1899–1902 war, such as A. D. 'Dave' Nourse and Frank Mitchell.[52] The military influence on the game is illustrated by the ranks named on scorecards: Brigadier-General Reginald Montagu Poore is a good example of this connection. An officer in the 7th Hussars who served in India and South Africa, a noted shot and polo and tennis player, he played cricket for Bombay Presidency from 1893 to 1895 (while ADC to Lord Harris, Governor of Bombay) and for Natal and South Africa (three tests) in 1895 and 1896.[53] Another is Captain C. O. H. Sewell who 'unfortunately for Colonial cricket, remained in the Old Country'.[54] Natal cricket was interrupted in 1906 by the 'Native Rebellion' (Bambatha Rebellion), but on 9 May the Durban Light Infantry played the Composite Regiment at Mapumulo, where Dave Nourse took 10 for 11.[55]

The whites of Natal, in particular, saw themselves as a beleaguered, homogeneous group, the consequence of which was the gross stereotyping of others. 'White attitudes towards Africans at the turn of the

[61]

century were a curious blend of paternalism, fear and contempt.' White and black were seen as opposites in which the latter occupied a place as minors and were made to understand that 'the presence and pre-dominance of the white race will be preserved at all hazards'.[56] While attitudes towards Africans implied that they were 'non-persons', the threat of urbanised, free immigrants of Indian origin (as opposed to indentured Indians) gave rise to virulent racism. Their main transgression was that of effective commercial competition and their presence was countered by racist laws concerning immigration (the 'Natal for-mula'), the franchise and licensing. Indians were legally declared 'un-civilised' and described in the Natal legislature in 1880 as 'the scum of Madras and Calcutta'. Other racist epithets such as 'Asiatic curse' were common and Indians were sometimes pushed off pavements. Their competitiveness 'aroused the petty bourgeois establishment that held sway in Natal's towns and cities' as they failed to 'wait patiently, hat in hand, outside the shrine of Victorian Anglo-Saxonism'.[57] South African white society consistently displayed fron-tier behaviour insisting upon 'religious, moral, and cultural barriers between itself and its neighbours'.[58] Sports in general and cricket and rugby in particular were important means used to create social unity among English-speaking whites and to maintain social distance from the rest. In the words of J. A. Mangan, cricket contributed a 'cultural bond of white imperial fraternity'[59] of instrumental use to the domi-nant male elite.

In the context of cricket, the opinion of the arch-imperialist Pelham Warner, who had a quasi-religious approach to the game,[60] was highly valued: 'Mr Warner says the position of South Africa in the cricket world is largely due to the munificence and sagacity of Mr Abe Bailey'.[61] Warner himself wrote that 'For South African cricket [Bailey] did much, as he put his hand deeply into his pocket to further its interest and development, as did the great Rhodes . . .'[62] Sir Abe Bailey was interested in South African cricket from the early 1890s, under-wrote the South African cricket tours of England in 1904 and 1906, funded the 1902 Australians and provided Transvaal with a guarantee for the MCC match of 1905.[63] Bailey was an imperialist, Rand magnate (with real estate, farming and mining interests throughout southern Africa) and politician who had captained Transvaal in the Currie Cup, belonged to the Reform Committee in 1896 at the time of the Jameson Raid, served as an intelligence officer in the South African War, and raised an irregular corps in that conflict 'continuing his support of imperial interests in South Africa'.[64] He identified strongly with the philosophy of Cecil John Rhodes, whose constituency at Barkly West he took over from 1902 to 1905. A racist who opposed the rights of

Indian immigrants in Natal and the Transvaal (by 1922 he was arguing for their expulsion), he worked for the union of the South African colonies (financing *The State*, a journal started by Philip Kerr, one of the 'Milner kindergarten', who advocated it) and promoted imperial preference. A contemporary writer observed that 'There was no racialism in his composition . . .'[65] By this it was meant that Bailey valued highly good relations between South Africans of British origins and Afrikaners:[66] the idea of not being racist with regard to Indians and Africans was not even considered and explains their absence from the world of South African cricket.

Leveson Gower maintains that cricket was so important to Bailey that he was moved to greater nervousness over a tight test match than in matters of high finance.[67] His writings on cricket scale the heights of imperial, purple prose:

> Sport has played a great part in creating a balance between the two great white races of this Country and . . . the Sportsmen of the Empire have responded in a most gallant manner to the call of their King and Country . . . The part Imperial cricket has played in the past is known to all. It has added to the union of hearts, it has strengthened the bonds of Empire, it has brought closer together our immense family, and to-day the cricketers of our vast Empire who played with us in the time of peace, are fighting with us in a greater game for liberty.[68]

Cypher (H. E. Holmes), writing at the same time about Natal cricket, also used the imperial image when he wrote 'nothing less than a German occupation of the Province will kill the spirit of cricket which prevails'.[69] Cricket as a moral metaphor and imperial symbol was ideally suited to the social anxieties and political allegiances of English-speaking whites of the era.

Cricket tours by the MCC were intimately connected with the imperial social scene. On the 1905–06 tour, Pelham Warner stayed with Godfrey Lagden, the Basutoland administrator and Lord Cobham, ADC to the Governor-General, Lord Selborne.[70] When the MCC met Natal at Pietermaritzburg in January 1910 they found room in the side for R. Ponsonby, Secretary to ex-Governor Sir Matthew Nathan.[71] The 1909–10 tourists were also entertained by Lord Methuen at Government House, Pietermaritzburg, and after their win in the third test at Cape Town he sent an encouraging telegram. At the end of the tour in March 1910, L. S. Jameson, an imperial visionary who shared Rhodes's dream of British territory stretching from Cape to Cairo and who had been an agent for the British South Africa Company, and Abe Bailey invited the team to Rhodesia, an offer accepted by the amateurs.[72] This social serenity appears to have been mildly inconvenienced during the

1913–14 tour which was 'marred by the labour troubles in Johannes-burg, and owing to an unfortunate misunderstanding, there was a little unpleasantness in Bloemfontein'.[73] Of the match between MCC and a Transvaal XI at Vogelsfontein on 14–15 January 1914 *Wisden* reported 'The Labour troubles were at their height and the match excited very little interest'.[74] Local concerns had clearly eclipsed the imperial con-nection, if only briefly. The English players made their political loyal-ties plain by volunteering as special constables.[75]

The suggestion in 1909 of an imperial cricket conference was initi-ated by Abe Bailey. Two meetings of the British Colonial Cricket Conference were held in London on 15 and 20 July at which the term 'Imperial' was adopted. Bailey represented South Africa at the second meeting; fellow representatives were G. W. Hillyard and H. D. G. Leverson Gower. Figures with closer ties to the MCC than Newlands routinely represented South Africa at the Imperial Cricket Conference (ICC): Leverson Gower at the meeting on 16 July 1912 (with the South African G. Allsop); Leverson Gower (again) and Pelham Warner at the June 1921 meeting. The power of South African gold was instrumental in setting up the 1912 Triangular tournament,[76] 'which was brought about through Sir Abe Bailey's efforts'.[77] *Wisden* describes it as 'the first trial of Sir Abe Bailey's ambitious scheme',[78] implying that he saw it setting a new trend. Unfortunately for Sir Abe the South African side was no stronger than the average English county side and the weather was abysmal. Nevertheless, this was the imperial tournament *par excellence* and, to an extent, resisted by the Australians who saw it as a threat to the primacy of their relationship with England. The found-ing of the ICC tied South Africa firmly into the international fixture list, which at the time was Australia, England and South Africa, so much so that with the outbreak of the First World War South Africa asked that the 'Imperial programme' be advanced by one year to allow Australia to tour in 1915–16. This was turned down by the Australians pending 'the wishes of the MCC'.[79] The Australian Impe-rial Forces team visited South Africa in 1919–20 and the mining mag-nate S. P. Joel sponsored the England second team to South Africa in 1924–25.[80]

In 1929, at a British Empire League dinner in London for visiting South African cricketers, Eric Louw emphasised the role of sport in bringing together the whites of South Africa and asserting their iden-tity in the eyes of the British.[81] This also extended to white kith and kin north of the Limpopo. In 1935, D. S. Tomlinson was the first Rhodesian to represent South Africa and included on the same tour was R. J. Crisp of Western Province, who had grown up in Rhodesia.[82] The image was created of a small cricketing nation manfully struggling to keep up standards: 'It is not surprising that in a country so vast and with so scattered a white population as exists . . . there should have been innumerable difficulties to overcome in the organisation and harnessing of the cricket potentialities that existed'.[83] Clearly only white potential counted. During the 1920s 'White society became more acutely conscious than before of its numerical inferiority, against which neither natural increase nor immigration from Europe showed any promise of prevailing'. Ties with the mother country were strengthened by 'A belief in an innate and invincible white superiority . . . [which] became a faith, and racial and social segregation a creed'.[84] At this point, South African whites took British racial attitudes further in promoting full segregation down to the detail of which jobs each race could hold. The entrenchment of white attitudes was evidenced in the 'swart gevaar' or black peril election of 1929 when a fear of Africans overrunning whites in the cities became the central election issue.

In line with the colonial attitudes of the time, blacks were treated like children, if their presence was acknowledged at all. Thus the Newlands scoreboard was operated 'by a team of Coloured enthusiasts'.[85] During the match between MCC and Natal at Durban in 1938 'a small army of bare-footed non-Europeans periodically sall[ied] forth, armed with brooms, to sweep away the water from the wicket covers . . .';[86] while on the last day of the Timeless Test (Durban, 1938), 'At 3.15 pm an Indian came out with a tray of cool drinks . . .'[87] Louis Duffus, writing in 1947, aptly summed up the attitudes of the 1930s. He opens his book with a daydream about a cricket match on the Reef: 'Out in the centre of the oval Sixpence, the ground boy is methodically rolling up the mat. As he wheels away the pitch he chants a tune of his kraal-land, a low-toned drawling song that his proud ancestors were wont to sing as night fell over the rolling hills of Zululand'. In another passage, about schools cricket, he describes 'The native, Jim Fish . . . pulling up the last strip of matting'.[88]

These cameos are very revealing. The only proper place for a black on a cricket field used by whites was as a labourer (unless he was Indian, in which case he would naturally be a waiter) and his real identity was camouflaged by a nickname intelligible to and imposed by whites. In any case, Sixpence, it is implied, really belongs hundred of miles away, not in a white urban area. The use of these signifiers: 'native', 'boy', 'bare-footed non-Europeans' and links to primeval singing or dancing based in the rural areas continually reminded whites of the difference between themselves and the black 'others' in the country. Eventually, such signifiers helped draw whites closer together as a social collectivity that was different from, and, as they viewed it, culturally and morally superior to, blacks. The overwhelming reliance on race as social signifier served to submerge the real and distinct class differences within each grouping. Members of the educated black middle class were far more likely to support 'respectable' British cultural values and play cricket than were the members of the Afrikaner working class that began to arrive in the cities in large numbers after 1907. Racial separation and perceived distinctiveness was so powerful that even in the early 1990s, many whites believed that blacks had only taken to the 'white' sports of cricket and rugby in the previous ten to twenty years!

The supposed 'excitability' of black South Africans was also used by whites to keep them in isolated sections of grounds or away altogether. Coloured, Indian and African cricket culture developed its own forms in opposition to the dominant white culture. Defensive batting was not supported and quality of stroke play and shot making was paramount. Most matches lasted one day or less as that was the limit of available time free from work. The quality of the pitches also made playing 'safe' a potentially dangerous proposition. Many teams were based on areas within communities or by ex-school old boys or occupation, so they were firmly rooted in local community culture. Matches took on a communal atmosphere and food and drink was shared among members of the crowd. While patronised by the black middle classes, cricket took place within communities dominated in numbers by the urban working class and thus reflected many of the values of working-class urban culture – a far cry from the concerns of many white cricket supporters for whom cricket embodied pastoral images of rural England and peaceful isolation from the tensions of life outside the grounds.

The separateness of black cricket in the 1920s and 1930s was illustrated by the first known overseas tour by a team from the Indian community to India in 1922.[89] In the inter-war period, cricket survived precariously as an activity for middle-class blacks with social aspirations and on special occasions whites played black teams; for instance, at the opening of the Bantu Sports Club in 1932 when 15,000 turned out to watch. In the Eastern Cape, some mixed cricket survived in matches between Rhodes University and the University of Fort Hare.[90] There is also a record of a Malay XI playing a White XI including Dave Nourse and Xenophon Balaskas (presumably in the 1920s); while tourists such as Clarrie Grimmett came into contact with, and commented favourably upon, aspects of black cricket.[91] But unified black cricket ceased due to 'divergent opinions among the cricket administrators'[92] under the centrifugal pressure of segregationist policy. In 1926 the South African Independent Coloured Cricket Board broke away from the South African Coloured Cricket Board and by the time the South African Bantu Cricket Board had departed (in 1932) and the South African Indian Cricket Union had deserted (in 1940) it was effectively the Malay Board. The Malay Board ran a strong competition in Cape Town that produced a number of players of high quality. A. J. 'Dol' Freeman, for example, regularly scored centuries as well as being rated as the best black rugby player of the inter-war period. Many in the Coloured community, and some whites, believe he could have played for the Springboks in either rugby or cricket. Salie Abed, a wicket-keeper, also played in Cape Town and most agree that he would easily have been selected for the South African team if he had been classified white. Later, Basil d'Oliveira came out of this competition.[93] In some parts of South Africa (Transvaal and the Cape Province) inter-race bodies kept alive links between the different groups and there is evidence that in the Transvaal whites were included.

In 1939 Lord Nuffield, at a function to welcome the visiting England team, announced a donation of £10,000 to be used to further white schoolboy cricket. After the inaugural 1940 tournament, an opinion was ventured that 'tournaments of this nature will make the boys of South Africa just one big family, regardless of considerations of race or birth'.[94] The 'one big family' referred, of course, to white hegemony. Even after the election of a National Party government in 1948 and the implementaion of apartheid, the status quo survived. The Governor-General was the President of SACA until South Africa left the Commonwealth in 1961; and the cricket literature of the time was redolent of imperial linkage. SACA's annual report of 1955 noted the death of Lady Warner, widow of Sir Pelham; but when C. B. Llewellyn, South Africa's only black international cricketer, died in June 1964, it was five years before this was recorded in South Africa's white cricketing annual, and no obituary appeared.[95]

The post-war period was, however, one of resistance to the prevailing social orthodoxy and the imperial inheritance. Within black and liberation politics inter-racial alliances were made and this was reflected gradually in cricket. From 1945 the South African Cricket Board of Control (SACBOC) worked to reunify black cricket, first through an umbrella body and inter-race tournaments (the first was at Natalspruit, Johannesburg, in March 1951). This initially involved Indian, coloured and African boards with the 'Barnato Board' (South African Coloured Cricket Board) changing its name to the South African Malay Cricket Board and joining in 1952. Race classification was increasingly ignored, particularly when faced with the issue of selecting provincial sides to play the touring Kenyans in 1956; and from 1958 SACBOC operated as one unified body. By 1961 it was organised purely along provincial lines. Integration was often forced by players against the conservative inclinations of officials. The Malays abstained from the vote on the united body but joined it nevertheless while the Africans, who voted for it, broke away as the South African African Cricket Board (SAACB). Its position was redolent of the social order and residual paternalism, suspicious of Indian and Coloured bodies and more comfortable with a role as protégé of the South African Cricket Association, a position it occupied for the next decade.

This raises the question of the demoralisation of many sectors of the South African community which was a legacy of the colonial order and had been a major concern of the African National Congress (ANC) Youth League in the immediate post-war period. Cricket as a whole by the late 1950s adopted a relatively conciliatory stance in the spectrum of opinion represented by black sportspeople: SACBOC was viewed with some scepticism by the radical South African Sports Association (SASA), formed in 1958. For instance, in 1959 SACBOC made plans to invite to South Africa a strong West Indian side under the captaincy of Frank Worrell. Although supported by none other than C. L. R. James, it was condemned by SASA as unhelpful to the cause of black cricketers and supportive of the colonial order.[96] Conditions for the use of Kingsmead in Durban included the erection of extra dressing rooms and toilets made out of corrugated iron so that the white facilities would not be 'contaminated'.[97] Clearly cricket was still used to create space between the elite and the masses in South Africa.

From 1950 onwards, SACBOC looked to develop ties with India and Pakistan. A tour of India was thwarted by financial problems but would probably have been vetoed by the ICC in deference to SACA.[98] Pressure from SACBOC and later SASA to recognise the position of black South African cricketers caused India, Pakistan and the West Indies to question the position of white South Africa in the ICC, creating, for the first time, cracks in the traditional assumptions of that body. This cleavage was to characterise the ICC from the late 1950s and throughout the 1960s. Appeals to the MCC in the early 1950s fell on deaf ears and no challenge was made to SACA. In spite of demonstrations against the 1960 cricket team in England and pressure from within South Africa on New Zealand to cancel its 1961–62 tour, traditional ties persisted.[99]

In fact, the aims of SACBOC in the 1950s were extremely limited. In 1955 it applied to join the ICC, but was told to prove its ability to conduct tours and attract sponsors.[100] Its request for a match against the 1956–57 MCC tourists, which was rejected, would simply have turned the clock back to 1892. Limited international contact opened up for black South African cricketers within a segregationist framework. India and Pakistan refused to tour South Africa for political reasons, but in 1956 the Kenya Asians lost a three-match series 2–0 to a team captained by Basil d'Oliveira and including Salie Abed, thought by then to be as good a wicketkeeper as any in the world. In 1958, the black South African team visited East Africa and Rhodesia, beating Kenya (three times), Uganda, Tanganyika and Zanzibar as well as a Rhodesian Indian XI. Tom Reddick described d'Oliveira in the Hartleyvale (Cape Town) test of 1956 as 'a really good player',[101] but much comment still dwelt on solidarity between the white groups: 'until the Afrikaner takes his place on our cricket fields no Springbok team can be said to be truly representative of our country's cricketing ability'.[102] In 1959, a South African cricket magazine carried a front page picture of d'Oliveira above the ironic caption 'South African cricket captain'.[103] The basis of black cricket was explained by Abe Adams: 'All cricket under the aegis of the SACBOC is played on matting over gravel pitches. They do not possess one ground which is even remotely up to international standard.'[104] D'Oliveira recalls the twenty-five pitches at the Cape Town municipal ground whose out-fields overlapped one another;[105] while Lenasia had pitches evocatively named Gravel 1 and Gravel 2.[106] Ray Robinson, writing in 1949, de-scribed pitches that 'no first class player would normally have set foot on, even if his life insurance was doubled'.[107] It is therefore amazing that Freeman, d'Oliveira and others could score half-centuries and centuries with regularity on such pitches. There was clear understand-ing in black cricket circles that, in the absence of clarity in the law, sports apartheid was maintained by governing bodies that invoked 'tradition' to protect white cultural separateness.[108]

The opinion of blacks on this situation was illustrated at the test match at Johannesburg in December 1957 between South Africa and Australia when the South Africans were booed by black spectators. The Transvaal Cricket Union threatened to raise the price of tickets (a common strategy in the 1990s) or exclude blacks altogether.[109] At Johannesburg black spectators were corralled in a wire netting com-pound; at Newlands in Cape Town in space under the trees with a separate entrance.[110] Attempts to prevent the 1960 tour of England were mirrored by small demonstrations in England. Charles Fortune described one gathering condescendingly as 'a tattered and bleak little conglomeration of chilly looking adolescents . . . no more than the cats-paws of certain churchmen who seized on the visit of the cricket-ers as an opportunity to gain for themselves some public notice'.[111] This shows a complete lack of understanding that the certainties of the imperium were beginning to crumble, accentuated by the fact that it was written shortly after the shooting at Sharpeville. Louis Duffus considered what he described as the introduction of politics into South African cricket as 'sinister, ignorant and illogical'.[112] The affiliation concept championed in 1961 by Eric Rowan for the Transvaal Cricket Federation was already out of date. Non-racial bodies would not countenance the idea of racially defined unions affiliating to white national controlling bodies with the same status as a white province, and pushed for amalgamation or equality.[113]

Between 1888 and 1970, South Africa participated in 45 series and 172 test matches; but the only opponents were the white-dominated countries of England, Australia (from 1902–03) and New Zealand (from 1931–32). Until 1958, England, Australia and South Africa had two votes each on the ICC, ensuring the dominance of the larger white dominions. The survival of South African whites in international competition in the 1960s was underpinned by 'a pattern of social, political and business relationships',[114] which owed a great deal to lingering imperial bonds. In the words of Derek Birley, 'South Africa had always occupied a special place in the affections of the cricket establishment'.[115] An editorial in The Times welcomed the 1960 South African tourists to England, describing them as 'old friends'.[116] Such characterisation survived the period of sporting boycotts and apartheid and reappeared in advertisements for the 1993–94 series between South Africa and Australia, the first series between the two countries for twenty-three years. Although South Africa had been instrumental in the setting up of the ICC and its representative, Foster Bowley, argued in July 1961 for continued test status, South Africa was required to leave the ICC on departing from the Commonwealth, after which all matches played with the remaining members were technically unofficial. SASA and elements in the government of India pushed for total exclusion, but the ICC solution was a system which permitted the continuation of the status quo while giving an impression of grappling with changed geopolitical circumstances.[117] The Australian cricket authorities strongly supported South Africa and made it clear that they would regard all their matches as official.[118] A report in the South African press assessed the situation astutely: 'all countries showed sympathy with the MCC view that nothing should be done which would be detrimental to the interests of South African cricket'.[119] The imperial old boy network was alive and well in the 1960s.

The myopia of the times in establishment cricket circles is illustrated by Geoffrey Chettle, editor of the South African Cricket Annual, who explained in an editorial of 1963 that South Africa's future in international cricket depended upon positive, attacking cricket and good performances in forthcoming encounters with the Australians and New Zealanders.[120] Jackie McGlew, writing at much the same time, emphasised similar concerns adding his worry about the nature of pitches.[121] The view persisted that traditional bonds could be maintained if performances were good enough. Thus Chettle was able to write in 1964: 'After being discarded as a member of the [ICC] and relegated to the position of sharing a tour with another country, the Springboks returned from their fourth visit to Australia and New Zealand having restored the country's prestige as a major cricketing power'.[122] He added that the core of the South African test side had been set for the next ten years and after the 1965 tour of England he stated, 'This is the dawn of a new era'.[123] The black cricketers of South Africa remained invisible. During the mid-1960s, however, some white cricketers were growing increasingly worried about the loss of long-standing ties with the white Commonwealth nations and the effect this would have on their sporting careers. They were thwarted in their desire to diversify South Africa's international cricket links by the National Party government's insistence on 'traditional policy' and attacks on those, individual and corporate, who sought to amend it. While ironic, this was historically logical growing as it did out of the instrumental use of cricket throughout the twentieth century. At this stage of South Africa's cricket history, the basic issue (as in other sports) was that of mixed national trials. Although master of the ambivalent statement and policy of variable interpretation, the South African government was consistent in its rejection of mixed trials. In May 1970 when the South African cricket tour of England was called off, Vorster made it clear that cricket relations with the rest of the world were white relations.[124]

The attitude of the MCC over the d'Oliveira affair of 1968 was one of turning a blind eye to the realities of South Africa, trying not to embarrass the South African government, above all maintaining contact; an approach made easier by the fact that this had underlain relations between South Africa and her traditional cricketing partner all century. Hain describes the MCC's approach as one of 'feudal absolutism'[125] which sat well with the imperial inheritance. Billy Griffith, MCC Secretary, took the line that South Africa was too important to be left out of world cricket, that South African teams abroad would play anyone, that within South Africa teams were subject to the law (which he, like so many others, confused with government policy) and that there was no colour bar in the constitution of SACA.[126] Much was made of 'traditional links' and 'essential communications'. Dennis Brutus was able to make use of these bland phrases after the election of Sir Cyril Hawker as President of the MCC, asking him if his position as Chairman of Standard Bank had anything to do with these links and communications.[127]

[71]

An MCC call for volunteer stewards to protect the threatened 1970 South African cricket tour of England evoked a colonial image of loyalists putting down an uprising of dissident natives. Lord Monckton, quoted in the *Guardian* of 6 December 1968, described a Conservative Cabinet as a group of left-wingers by comparison with the committee of the MCC.[128] Right-wing British support for the South African status quo was plain to see and later manifested itself in the private prosecution of Peter Hain for his role in the Stop the Seventy Tour campaign. The problem for more rational right-wing elements was that continued support for the remnants of imperialism threatened the unity of the contemporary Commonwealth and confounded the MCC's claim that it was acting in the long-term interests of cricket. English-speaking South African cricketers blamed the National Party government and the 'stench of politics',[129] seemingly oblivious to the fact that segregationist politics had governed the game since the end of the nineteenth century. The imperial family image was invoked by one commentator who accused the MCC of committing 'cricket fratricide upon a younger brother in the prime of life, a brother who has never been . . . better equipped to perpetuate the best aspects . . . Because of one cricketer the great players produced in this country and the game itself have both been victimized'.[130] In an extraordinary attack on the MCC the same writer accused it of conspiracy to break South African law. His confusion about law, social custom and government policy was revealed in the statement that 'England knew the law when a much greater cricketer, K. S. Duleepsinhji, could have been chosen to tour this country'. But his admission of the tacit agreement between SACA and MCC was clearly revealed in the rider 'He was not selected and nothing was ever said about it'.[131] Duffus claims that he received a torrent of supportive mail after these sentiments were printed in the Johannesburg *Star*. No doubt he would have been supported by many English cricketers. Wilfred Wooler, for instance, pillar of the British sporting establishment, clearly articulated traditional attitudes when he wrote to Brutus, 'We have no sympathy with your cause in any shape or form and regard you as an utter nuisance . . . I personally suspect your motives and your background'.[132] The traditionalist view that cricket relations between South Africa and the white Commonwealth should remain unchanged frequently invoked images of the Second World War. Wilfred Isaacs mentions his fighter pilot experience and the bonds of friendship created by that conflict in justifying the organisation of tours in his name to England.[133] John Vorster's bitter claim that the 1968 MCC team to South Africa was that of his political opponents was extraordinarily misdirected given the effort MCC had made to keep his country in the international fold.[134]

It was at this point that SACA set up a trust fund of R50,000 for black cricket out of tour profits, an offer predictably spurned by SACBOC as a bribe but accepted by the SAACB to fund a schools week. By 1970, with the advent of isolation, it had dawned on some of the SACA establishment that South Africa's customary way of life was ruining her international cricket future and there was a need to 'modernise our way of thinking'.[135] SACA's decision to invite SACBOC to nominate two names for consideration for the Australian tour was vetoed by the South African Government on 26 March 1971 and led to the famous walk off at the Republic Festival match and final trial at Newlands on 3 April 1971. For the first time a significant body of white South African cricketers had accepted that 'merit [should be] the only criterion on the cricket field'.[136] Ironically, while the republican Prime Minister of South Africa had now taken on an imperial role as selector-in-chief, 'The final link of the chain connecting South Africa to her traditional rivals [had] been severed'.[137]

Clearly, by the early 1970s, South Africa was out of step with her old imperial partners and the loss of sporting ties emerged as one of the most potent psychological pressure points in international campaigns to oppose apartheid. Imperial links involving common ideology and long-standing relationships gave way to commercial expediency. The significance of cricket within white society and the willingness of English, Australian and later even West Indian cricketers to travel to South Africa led government and big business to underwrite the cost of mercenary tours. Supporters of the status quo and entrepreneurs found common cause in defying international sanctions. At the same time, internal protest continued. In sport this was aided in 1973 by the formation of the South African Council on Sport (SACOS) which at the time was one of the new effective opponents of the apartheid regime (together with the emergent trade unions, the universities and the churches). Non-racial sporting competitions developed, attracting a handful of white players such as André Odendaal in cricket and Cheeky Watson in rugby union, who gave up potential fame in white sport in the hope of contributing to the foundation of a democratic, liberated South Africa.

The fault line in South African sport until the late 1980s was between democrats with a non-racial vision for society and the establishment with a self-serving and limited understanding of the role of sport. In international terms this was reflected in support for and against the sports boycott of South Africa. After the unbanning of the

ANC in 1990 and the release of long-term political prisoners, the international cricket boycott was speedily (and some would argue unjustifiably) abandoned. South Africa was reinstated at the ICC and in mid-1994 readmitted to the Commonwealth. Traditional links had been restored, but the ideological bond was now sealed by commercialism rather than racial superiority and political, social and economic power.

Notes

1 H. P. Swaffer, ed., *South African Sport*, Johannesburg, 1914, p. 29.
2 Robert Archer and Antoine Bouillon, *The South African Game: Sport and Racism*, London, 1982, p. 79.
3 André Odendaal, 'South Africa's Black Victorians: Sport and Society in South Africa in the Nineteenth Century', in J. A. Mangan, ed., *Pleasure, Profit, Proselytism: British Culture and Sport at Home and Abroad, 1700–1914*, London, 1988, pp. 197–8.
4 Odendaal, 'South Africa's Black Victorians', p. 199.
5 Archer and Bouillon, *The South African Game*, p. 89.
6 H. S. Altham, *A History of Cricket*, vol. 1, London, 1962, p. 294.
7 For more on this ideology, see John Nauright, ' "Black Island in a White Sea": Black and white in the Making of Alexandra Township', unpublished PhD thesis, Queen's University, Kingston, Ontario, Canada, 1992, pp. 44–81; Alan Gregor Cobley, *Class and Consciousness: The Black Petty Bourgeoisie in South Africa, 1924–1950*, Westport, CT, 1990; for links between whites and blacks in the provision of sporting facilities and opportunities, see Alan Gregor Cobley, 'A Political History of Playing Fields: The Provision of Sporting Facilities for Africans in the Johannesburg Area to 1948', *International Journal of the History of Sport*, 11, 2, August 1994, pp. 212–30.
8 Grant Jarvie, ed., *Sport, Racism and Ethnicity*, London, 1991, p. 182.
9 Archer and Bouillon, *The South African Game*, pp. 85–6.
10 G. A. Parker, *South African Sports: An Official Handbook*, London, 1897, p. 47.
11 Louis Duffus, 'South Africa', in E. W. Swanton and J. Woodcock, eds, *Barclays World of Cricket: The Game From A–Z*, London, 2nd edn, 1980, p. 934. Currie presented three other cups for interprovincial rugby, soccer and swimming. Cricket was, however, the first.
12 Louis Duffus, *Play Abandoned*, Cape Town, 1969, p. 28.
13 In examining rugby in colonial Natal, Robert Morrell provides an excellent analysis of the use of British culture in an environment where whites were a small minority in 'Forging a Ruling Race: Rugby and White Masculinity in Colonial Natal, c. 1870–1910', in John Nauright and Timothy Chandler, eds, *Making Men: Rugby and Masculine Identity*, London, 1996, pp. 91–120.
14 Odendaal, 'South Africa's Black Victorians', pp. 203–4.
15 Malay referred to the group of 'coloureds' who were brought to South Africa as slaves from Malaysia and Indonesia in the seventeenth and eighteenth centuries who had kept their Muslim religion and culture. Most of the 'Malays' lived in the inner city suburbs of Cape Town and Port Elizabeth.
16 R. Bowen, *Cricket: A History of its Growth and Development Throughout the World*, London, 1970, p. 297.
17 S. E. West, comp., and W. J. Luker, ed., *Century at Newlands, 1864–1964: A History of the Western Province Cricket Club*, Newlands, 1965, p. 21.
18 André Odendaal, ed., *Cricket in Isolation: The Politics of Race and Cricket in South Africa*, Cape Town, 1977, p. 325.

19 B. Bassano, *South Africa in International Cricket, 1888–1970*, East London, 1979, p. 17.
20 One, C. J. Nicholls, was also coach and organiser of cricket for the South African forces in France, baggage master to the Australian Services team in South Africa, 1919–20, and served touring teams in the 1920s: see Odendaal, *Cricket in Isolation*, p. 326.
21 Odendaal, 'South Africa's Black Victorians', pp. 210–11.
22 Archer and Bouillon, *The South African Game*, p. 90.
23 V. Pakenham, *The Noonday Sun: Edwardians in the Tropics*, London, 1985, p. 174.
24 Archer and Bouillon, *The South African Game*, p. 79.
25 Christopher Martin-Jenkins, *The Complete Who's Who of Test Cricketers*, Johannesburg, 1980, p. 265.
26 W. Pollock, *Talking about Cricket*, London, 1941, p. 121.
27 Related in Donald Woods, *Black and White*, Dublin, 1981, p. 46.
28 According to one story, de Villiers was captured on the Natal front wearing a cricket kit: see West and Luker, *Century at Newlands*, pp. 28–9.
29 In M. W. Luckin, ed., *The History of South African Cricket*, Johannesburg, 1915, pp. 803–6.
30 Ironically, the Boers were forced to play against a number of Singhalese in the Colombo side.
31 Will Whittam, *Modern Cricket and Other Sports*, Sheffield, 1884, p. 54, quoted in John Nauright, 'Colonial Manhood and Imperial Race Virility: British Responses to Post-Boer War Colonial Rugby Tours', in Nauright and Chandler, *Making Men*, p. 130.
32 H. S. Altham and E. W. Swanton, *A History of Cricket*, London, 4th edn, 1948, p. 311; Parker, *South African Sports*, p. 3.
33 *Wisden 1895*, pp. 333, 336.
34 Altham, *A History of Cricket*, p. 295. One of its members, J. H. Sinclair, it is said, had escaped from a prisoner of war camp in time to join the tour, see Martin-Jenkins, *The Complete Who's Who of Test Cricketers*, p. 282.
35 *Wisden 1902*, p. 467.
36 Altham and Swanton, *A History of Cricket*, p. 311. Logan also had an unspecified stake in the second of Lord Hawke's tours, 1898–99.
37 C. B. Fry, *A Life Worth Living: Some Phases of an Englishman*, London, 1986, p. 109.
38 M. B. Hawke, *Recollections and Reminiscences*, London, 1924, p. 151. The team was held up by an armed group of Transvaal men at Vereeniging who were given two cricket bats as a peace offering.
39 Malcolm Tozer, 'A Sacred Trinity: Cricket, School, Empire: E. W. Hornung and his Young Guard' and Richard Cashman, 'Symbols of Unity: Anglo-Australian Cricketers, 1877–1900', both in J. A. Mangan, ed., *The Cultural Bond: Sport, Empire and Society*, London, 1992, p. 39 and pp. 135, 137.
40 *Cape Illustrated Magazine*, 4 October 1984, p. 370.
41 Hawke, *Recollections*, p. 160.
42 C. L. R. James, *Beyond a Boundary*, New York, 1984, pp. 38–9.
43 Tozer, 'A Sacred Trinity', p. 17.
44 H. V. Dorey, *The Triangular Tests, 1878–1912*, London, 1912, p. 187.
45 J. T. Henderson, *South African Cricketers Annual 1905–1906*, pp. 1, 5.
46 *Ibid.*, p. 5.
47 T. Routledge, 'The Third English Team in South Africa, 1895–6', in Luckin, *History of South African Cricket*, p. 521.
48 Dorey, *The Triangular Tests*, p. 184.
49 Swaffer, *South African Sport*, p. 31.
50 P. F. Warner, *The M.C.C. in South Africa*, London, 1906, p. 68.
51 Swanton and Woodcock, *Barclays World of Cricket*, pp. 287, 289.
52 Nourse, although from a military background, had settled in Natal in 1896 before the outbreak of war and joined the Natal Police.

53 His team solidarity was somewhat elastic: after playing for Natal he tried to transfer to Lord Hawke's side only to have permission refused by the Army: Hawke, *Recollections*, p. 152. Poore was born in 1866 and died in 1938. He played county cricket for Hampshire from 1898 until 1906 and in 1899 scored 1,309 at an average of 115.58 including three consecutive centuries.

54 Henderson, 'Early cricket in Natal', p. 97.

55 Henderson, *South African Cricketers Annual 1905–1906*, p. 106.

56 Shula Marks, *Reluctant Rebellion: The 1906–8 Disturbances in Natal*, Oxford, 1970, pp. 11, 13; see also Morrell, 'Forging Ruling Race', on insecurity in colonial Natal.

57 R. A. Huttenback, *Racism and Empire: White Settlers and Colored Immigrants in the British Self Governing Colonies, 1830–1910*, Ithaca, 1976, pp. 197–8.

58 C. W. de Kiewiet, *A History of South Africa: Social and Economic*, London, 1941, p. 211.

59 Mangan, *The Cultural Bond*, p. 6.

60 James Bradley, 'M.C.C., Society and Empire: A Portrait of Cricket's Ruling Body, 1860–1914', in Mangan, *The Cultural Bond*, p. 39.

61 Henderson, *South African Cricketers Annual 1905–1906*, p. 120.

62 P. F. Warner, *Long Innings: The Autobiography*, London, 1951, p. 135.

63 Bassano, *South Africa in International Cricket*, p. 31; Henderson, *South African Cricketers Annual 1906–1907*, p. 174.

64 *Dictionary of South African Biography*, vol. II, p. 19.

65 L. E. Neame, *Some South African Politicians*, Cape Town, 1929, p. 167.

66 Phyllis Lewsen, 'A Complete South African', *Lantern*, January 1954, p. 296.

67 H. Leveson Gower, *Off and On the Field*, London 1953, p. 160.

68 Foreword to Luckin, *History of South African Cricket*.

69 Cypher, 'History of Natal Cricket', in Luckin, *History of South African Cricket*, p. 81.

70 Warner, *Long Innings*, p. 71.

71 *Wisden 1912*.

72 Leveson Gower, *Off and On the Field*, pp. 159–64.

73 *Wisden 1915*, p. 477.

74 *Ibid.*, p. 491.

75 L. Tennyson, *Sticky Wickets*, London, 1950, p. 73.

76 Bowen, *Cricket*, p. 150. A major anxiety for Britain in the years leading up to the First World War was a shortage of gold reserves, making all relations with South Africa of crucial importance: see R. Alley, *Gold and Empire: The Bank of England and South Africa's Gold Producers, 1886–1926*, Johannesburg, 1994, pp. 18–20.

77 H. W. Taylor, 'South African Cricket, 1910–1924', in Cape Times, *Sports and Sportsmen: South Africa*, Cape Town, 1925, p. 125.

78 *Wisden 1913*, p. 230.

79 *Wisden 1915*, p. 208.

80 Bassano, *South Africa in International Cricket*, pp. 57, 71.

81 Alan Paton, *Hofmeyr*, London, 1964, p. 159. Eric Louw was a neo-Nazi who later became Minister of External Affairs, 1955–63.

82 Duffus, 'South Africa', p. 938.

83 A. C. Webber, 'The Control of Cricket in South Africa', in M. W. Luckin, *South African Cricket, 1919–1927*, Johannesburg, p. 21. A similar sentiment was expressed in Bisset, p. 106.

84 De Kiewiet, *A History of South Africa*, pp. 222, 226.

85 West and Luker, *Century at Newlands*, p. 114.

86 Pollock, *Talking about Cricket*, p. 116.

87 *Ibid.*, p. 152.

88 Louis Duffus, *Cricketers of the Veld*, London, 1947, pp. 5–6, 11.

89 Bowen, *Cricket*, p. 329.

90 Archer and Bouillon, *The South African Game*, pp. 121, 151.

91 Odendaal, *Cricket in Isolation*, p. 328.
92 S. J. Reddy, 'South African Non-European Cricket', in Swanton and Woodcock, *Barclays World of Cricket*, p. 950.
93 Interview with 'Meneer' Abdullah Adams, 'Meneer' Effendi and Goosain Emeran by John Nauright, Cape Town, 19 December 1994.
94 *South African Cricket Annual*, 1, 1951–1952, p. 208.
95 *South African Cricket Annual*, 4, 1955; 16, 1969, p. 45. *Wisden* carried an obituary in 1964, p. 968.
96 Letter from Dennis Brutus (SASA) to Rashid Varachia (SACBOC) dated 28 February 1959; and to West Indies Cricket Board of Control dated 20 March 1959 in *The Brutus Papers*, Borthwick Institute, University of York, England (CAS MF 15 and Box II).
97 *Post*, 4 May 1969.
98 Odendaal, *Cricket in Isolation*, p. 332.
99 *Ibid.*, p. 4.
100 *Ibid.*, p. 335.
101 *South African Cricket Review*, 1, 2, December 1956, p. 11.
102 *Ibid.*, p. 34.
103 S. J. Reddy, ed., *South African Cricketer: The National Cricket Journal of Southern Africa*, 1, 1, 1959.
104 Reddy, *South African Cricketer*, 2, 2, 1960, p. 3.
105 Basil d'Oliveira, *The D'Oliveira Affair*, London, 1969, p. 22.
106 Odendaal, *Cricket in Isolation*, p. 237.
107 D'Oliveira, *The D'Oliveira Affair*, p. 34.
108 Peter Hain, *Don't Play with Apartheid: The Background to the Stop the Seventy Tour Campaign*, London, 1971, p. 42.
109 Richard Lapchick, *The Politics of Race and International Sport: The Case of South Africa*, Denver, 1973, p. 72.
110 D'Oliveira, *The D'Oliveira Affair*, p. 32.
111 C. Fortune, *Cricket Overthrown*, Cape Town, 1960, p. 2.
112 Duffus, *Play Abandoned*, p. 164.
113 Odendaal, *Cricket in Isolation*, p. 24.
114 Richard Thompson, *Race and Sport*, London, 1964, p. 67.
115 Derek Birley, *The Willow Wand: Some Cricket Myths Explored*, London, 1979, p. 154.
116 Quoted in Lapchick, *Politics of Race*, pp. 84–5.
117 *Ibid.*, p. 91.
118 South African Institute of Race Relations, *Survey of Race Relations 1962*, p. 220; *South African Cricket Annual*, 10, 1963, p. 5.
119 *Rand Daily Mail*, 18 July 1962.
120 *South African Cricket Annual*, 10, 1963, p. 5.
121 Jackie McGlew, *Cricket in Crisis*, Cape Town, 1965.
122 *South African Cricket Annual*, 11, 1964, p. 5.
123 *South African Cricket Annual*, 12, 1965, p. 5.
124 Lapchick, *Politics of Race*, p. 345.
125 Hain, *Don't Play with Apartheid*, p. 105.
126 D'Oliveira, *The D'Oliveira Affair*, p. 83.
127 Letter from Dennis Brutus to Sir Cyril Hawker, chair of MCC Council, 29 May 1969, in Brutus Papers.
128 Lapchick, *Politics of Race*, p. 254.
129 *South African Cricket Annual*, 15, 1968, p. 5.
130 Duffus, *Play Abandoned*, p. 173.
131 *Ibid.*, p. 172. Duffus is presumably referring to the 1930–31 tour by England to South Africa when a less than full strength side was sent (*Wisden 1932*). There is also the possibility that Duleep was left out of the England team *in England* during the 1929 season because of the South African attitude (Hain, *Don't Play with Apartheid*, p. 75). The act of playing mixed cricket has *never* been unlawful at any

stage of South African history. E. M. Wellings also suggested that d'Oliveira's selection was a deliberate MCC provocation (d'Oliveira, *The D'Oliveira Affair*, p. 106).

132 Letter from Wilfred Wooller, Glamorgan County Cricket Club secretary to Dennis Brutus, 31 December 1968, in Brutus Papers.

133 Letter from Wilfred Isaacs to Dennis Brutus, 26 May 1969, in Brutus Papers.

134 *Survey of Race Relations*, 1968, p. 300.

135 *South African Cricket Annual*, 17, 1970, p. 7.

136 Part of the statement released by all the players in the match to SACA, *South African Cricket Annual*, 18, 1971, p. 53.

137 *Ibid.*, p. 52.

CHAPTER FOUR

West Indies

Brian Stoddart

Unlikely though it is that he had cricket in mind when noting that 'terms of cultural engagement, whether antagonistic or affiliative, are produced performatively', Homi Bhabha might well agree that the West Indies game bears out his maxim perfectly. After all, his comments on the 'social articulation of difference' and the struggle for recognition, along with the affiliated challenge to tradition, encapsulate the social evolution of cricket in the Caribbean.[1] From its beginnings in semi-organised form through its unfolding into a contemporary internationalised structure, Caribbean cricket has both marked and been marked by a tight affiliation with complex social processing in the islands and states which make up the West Indies.[2] For that very reason, of all global cricketing traditions the Caribbean one has produced the deepest analytical writings and the sharpest academic attention.[3] To write of Caribbean cricket is to write of Caribbean history, culture, politics and economy in addition to the great playing tradition established during the past 150 years. It has been so from the outset.

Not surprisingly, the earliest regional forms of the game were played by the military in the immediate aftermath of the abolition of slavery.[4] As the sugar barons sought to maintain their sway in a setting where the forms of labour were altered radically after 1834 and 1838, the military became an important symbol of deterrence throughout the region in the desperate search for a new social stability (as it was seen through the eyes of the socially dominant, anyway). The coalition between European planters and the forces of authority were frequently seen on the cricket field which itself, very often, was a central physical feature of the garrison. It was but a short step from there to the social segmentation of the game which became a hallmark of the West Indian tradition.

The original carriers of cricket were from the monied classes, either those coming out from England to create a fortune (even during sugar's waning prosperity in the second half of the nineteenth century) as producers or as part of the service industries, or members of the local economic power elite who had gone 'Home' to England for an education or other such social enlightenment.[5] Some notable personalities in cricket history appeared among these names including those of (Sir) Pelham Warner, born into a Trinidadian family of prominence and who became one of the great English cricket bosses.[6] The importance of all this was underlined by the involvement of Great Britian's official regional representatives who, along with donating the important competitive trophies, also promoted the uptake of the game. As elsewhere in Britain's colonies, the Oxbridge-educated civil servants of empire spread both the play and the philosophy of cricket in the belief that it created a cross-cultural bond amongst members of an artificial political entity who had little else in common.[7] Of course, this was not universal bonding.

People of African descent were playing cricket among themselves at a very early point, as the missionary Greville John Chester pointed out in the mid-nineteenth century.[8] What is clear, however, is that those players were cut out of the earliest competitive forms of the game organised at island level across the Caribbean. The major clubs first established – like Queens Park in Trinidad and Wanderers in Barbados – all consisted of whites drawn from the upper social echelons such as the planters, financiers, clergy, lawyers, doctors and commercialists. These clubs guarded their exclusivity with great zeal, and deviations from the accepted norms occasioned much debate. Cricket matches were leisure time meetings of the rich and powerful and, as such, a significant adjunct to the power culture. The patrons and administrators were drawn from the elite social sections as the game became the pre-eminent passion of the ruling culture.[9] By the turn of the twentieth century, leading clubs were also premier social institutions with a major role in the process of social and institutional reproduction so well chronicled elsewhere by Pierre Bourdieu.[10]

At the same time, however, other groups and clubs came along to contest the field, literally and figuratively, as sketched out by Homi Bhabha. And as he suggests, the results were not so simple as analysts once believed: 'the borderline engagements of cultural difference may as often be consensual as conflictual . . . and challenge normative expectations of development and progress'.[11] While social elevation from the ranks of slavery began, in limited ways, well before the advent of emancipation among small pockets of people, that process escalated in the generation which followed so that by the later nineteenth century there were noticeable numbers of non-white teachers, clerks, clerics and even business people and professionals attempting to find a place in the social constellation.[12] Their natural reaction was to set up social clubs, and prominent among those were cricketing ones. One of the most famous sections in C. L. R. James's classic work describes the minute social marking which categorised the Trinidadian cricket clubs early in the twentieth century: white the shade for the power elite, off-white next and grading through to the blackest in descending order of social leverage, and with all of the colour coding cross-referenced by associated economic and social standing.[13]

What emerged was a complex mixture of accommodation and resistance rather than, as the raw form of the subaltern studies project would have it, domination and subordination.[14] There were as many struggles over boundaries within and between the lower ranked social groupings as there were within the white elite. The key was that all groups were seeking continuity of identity and existence. One marvellous illustration concerned the Empire Club in Barbados founded by Herman Griffith, a highly talented international player who himself suffered the slings of structured inequality. His club, however, could be as exclusionist as any other – one player recalled his application being rejected with his declared occupation being downgraded from 'delivery officer' to 'ice carrier'.[15] Because of this formulation, then, there appeared all over the Caribbean clubs based on status quality. There were clubs for all colours, all economic levels, all occupational categories, and every variation in between. Many district clubs were held together by their socio-economic profiles rather than by their geographical location. This was most striking in the vastly under-privileged areas of the type recalled in George Lamming's iconic novel about the Bajan underclasses.[16]

Predictably, these different cultures drew on their own experiences and predilections in order to react to the game and, in turn, that flowed through into governance which was as much about style and form as about the substance of playing. The white elites of the Caribbean territories behaved as they thought befitted the local equivalents of the county cadres back in England.[17] They built elegant (for the day) club-houses with dining and (especially) drinking facilities. They took afternoon tea as in England, dressed as in England, and applauded politely as in England. At the other end of the scale the poor blacks packed the outer regions of the grounds, drank hard, shouted hard and saw spectating as a direct form of involvement, as another variation of carnival.[18] Needless to say, these extreme forms of cricket culture packed into the same tiny physical arena often had little understanding of each other and, sadly, sometimes little tolerance of each other. Because of the cricket-as-an-education-for-life approach taken over

[81]

from England, the white elite frequently took black crowd behaviour as a sign of non-social progress with all the consequences of that for education, commerce and politics[19] in the wider realm.

Much of this was reproduced in and by the social institutions, most notably the schools.[20] Again, though, it was not a straightforward matter. It is true that most of the white elite in Barbados, for example, went to Harrison College, the plantocracy to Lodge with elements of the non-white elite eventually getting into Harrison and the bulk of the emergent middle class (and some intellectually talented) non-whites going to Combermere. When they left school, however, the players 'knew' which club they should gravitate towards: the white elite to Wanderers and the next layer to Pickwick, with the non-white elite moving to Spartan and the next echelon to Empire. One black batsman from the 1930s recalled playing through school with a particular white opening partner, but literally parting at the school gates the day they left en route to different clubs.[21] While the schools taught the moral uplift theories of the game inherited from England, they also instilled social self-categorisation.

All these groups had an exclusionist role in that substantial sections of the communities were either discouraged from participation, or forced into playing within an ascripted social setting. In Trinidad, for example, separate leagues were established for the Indian and Chinese communities, while in Guyana (or British Guiana as it was known pre-independence) the Indian community also had to set its own course.[22] All over the Caribbean, the poorest elements of the black communities were barred from the mainstream competitions, and that led to the establishment of working-class leagues in some locations.[23]

Wherever the game originated, however, the clubs formed very strong centres for social activity and the reaffirmation of group ties. In Barbados, for example, the Windward and Leeward clubs were the focus for planter activities, renowned for the food, entertainment and sense of occasion when they met each other in play. Similarly, Empire became known as a very strongly bonded group. In Barbados, it became a common social shorthand to describe a man by his cricket affiliation to denote his standing, as in 'a Spartan man', for example.[24]

One major section of society, however, had very different roles in this social environment. Women became renowned as 'hailers' (club supporters and spectators), but, as with the game around the globe, their main function was as auxiliary to the male players. Women provided the food and all the other support required: childrearing and minding, home support, psychological buffering. In both non-white society where marriage was not a norm, and in white society where it was, the cricket ground also provided a venue for the building of social relationships. While some women dared to become players in the very early days, it was towards the end of the twentieth century before a concerted effort was made to promote the game among Caribbean women. For the most part, women played the supporting roles in this social drama.[25]

All sections of Caribbean society, then, had some relationship to cricket, even if in some cases it was to be rejected by the game. Cricket had become a hallmark of Caribbean society by the turn of the twentieth century but, of course, the major question is why? While the answers are complex, there are some reasonable starting points.

For the white elite, cricket was a substantial bond with the culture of 'Home'.[26] Even though many families had been in the Caribbean for two or three hundred years, their cultural affiliations were still with England rather than with any emergent hybridity. The spoken form of their English might have become very different from that of the home counterpart, but these people still thought of themselves as English. Their rhetoric was filled with references to cricket as the game of empire, as a bond between like-minded people, as a moral force in the patterning of lives, as a reminder of home and as a game where means were significantly more important than ends. Concomitantly (although the rhetoric was much quieter on this), the game was seen as a way of separating the elite from other social orders.

For second-level whites the story was slightly different.[27] In many locations the ends, the results, became more significant for a group which had no real natural social sway, but which needed to establish an identity even more than did their white social superiors. Matches between these two groups turned into titanic struggles not only for playing superiority but also for group recognition and satisfaction. For Pickwick to beat Wanderers became a matter of significant social triumph, the service classes beating the monied classes. Alternatively, it was as important to beat the non-white elite and lower middle-class teams in order to take comfort in the continuation of a preferred set of social relations. In cricket there was really no such thing as just another match, because meetings between different teams were about the representation of and struggle over cultural evolution.

For that reason, the power of representation, it is interesting that the one C. L. R. James work to escape Edward Said's attention in his provocative *Culture and Imperialism* was *Beyond a Boundary*.[28] Indeed, beyond a reference to J. A. Mangan and a mention that James was, among other things, a cricket writer, sport gets no reference at all. Yet the evidence is now quite clear on just how central a social institution sport was in the development of British colonial rule, in particular, and in the post-colonial reformulations of former British possessions.[29] Nowhere are the inner contradictions better described than in James, the Marxist who loved a game which, theoretically, represented much of what he wanted to eliminate and, so, had to find a resistance strain within. Many years later Malcolm Caldwell, the radical historian of south-east Asia (murdered in Cambodia for his views) exhibited the same love–hate relationship for the game in discussing his membership of the Sussex County Cricket Club.[30]

For non-white Caribbean clubs the struggle for recognition and social positioning was as intense, if not more so. It was more than simple emulation. Rather, it was a rich combination of accommodation and reconstitution: accommodation in some quarters, that is, in that it led to social acceptance (albeit in limited senses) from the white sections.[31] That acceptance might take psychological form, as in a fleeting meeting at a common venue, or a more practical one, as in the provision of work as recognition for achievement. For players at the lowest levels of the social order, cricket often represented an economic escape route which was outside the Caribbean geographically. In the later nineteenth century, for example, a significant number of Caribbean players found work in professional leagues in North America while, from the 1920s onwards, Caribbean players were a major presence in English league cricket.[32] But that escape need not always be in the playing arena, because many black players found other work through cricketing contacts within the white commerical elite.

It must be remembered, however, that there was as much a struggle for level within the non-white communities as there was with and within the white ones. Matches between the socially different black teams were contested as fiercely as those in the white community with, again, the stakes being about respect as well as simple match result. That social contest guaranteed the sheer size of the crowds at what in other cricket cultures would have been seen as mere club games. Supporters of the respective sides had invested considerable amounts of emotional capital in the outcome.[33] Therein lies one of the key strains of Caribbean cricket, the emotion and the passion.

That became transferred into the international arena and, again, in complex ways. The background, of local specificity in practice and the interweaving of cricket and cultural evolution, helps explain the intense intra-regional struggles which developed in the selection of early representative sides.[34] There were, for example, territories which refused to select black players for their teams which, consequently, meant that those players could not gain regional status and, so, had a possible line of economic development cut off. C. A. Ollivierre of St Vincent, for example, toured England at the turn of the twentieth century, stayed on to play for Derbyshire and made a later career in

English club cricket and, even later, in coaching in the Netherlands.[35] But there were many players as talented who never won that opportunity.

Then there was the struggle between the then colonies for representation in what became the regional sides. While the individual territories had grown up under the general banner of the British West Indies they had, as noted already, very early on developed their own traditions and characteristics which meant that, despite a superficially common heritage, they were in competition with each other. Put (perhaps too) simply, respect was often gained by demonstrating superiority over other entities involved in the same quest for recognition. Until well into the 1920s there were fierce debates over the correctness, or otherwise, of selections into the regional sides.[36]

The next issue, of course, concerned the culturally layered and coded nature of the representative side, and it is important to recall the significance of that representative function, with officials and others forever emphasising the importance of national teams and tours as the symbol of progress. Most spectacularly, that was seen in the practice of every West Indian team up until 1957 having a white captain who, increasingly, might have been the only non-black in the side. The struggle over that issue is well recorded and well known.[37] Even so, the significance of Frank Worrell's elevation to the leadership cannot be overestimated. Symbolically, perhaps, it was more significant than the coming of political independence to the islands and territories, because at the level of popular culture and passion the black man had arrived at the end of at least one great struggle. In one logic, at least, the next stage came with the awesome success of the all-black sides of the late 1970s into the early 1990s led by Clive Lloyd, Viv Richards and Richie Richardson: in their victories over the cricket powers, England in particular, they demonstrated a real change in the social order. In a Saidian sense, perhaps, they suggested a shift in power from the metropolitan world to the Other. In so doing, they laid the way for the international successes of India, Pakistan and, spectacularly at the 1996 World Cup, Sri Lanka.

In the meantime, the actual playing of the game took several forms throughout the region with 'big cricket', as we might call it, the elite and obvious form, being just one of a myriad of expressions in which local conditions were adapted to social circumstances. In England, clearly enough, cricket was a summer game played on grass strips which, although usually on the soft side, had a consistency of playing surface. The weather was more or less fine so that players and spectators alike could express their sentiments in a mellow atmosphere; hence all the romantic rhetoric about cricket 'the summer game' in which writers waxed lyrical about long evenings, the smell of freshly cut grass, long shadows and cool drinks. That was all very different in the Caribbean.

There, the distinction was not so much winter and summer as wet and dry, the periods when rain did or did not usually occur. While logically the dry would have been the time to play, that did not always follow. In many parts of the West Indies the dry was also the time when the sugar cane crop was harvested, and during that time the demand for labour was high with very long working hours. For that reason cricket, above all a time-intensive game, was often played not during the dry but in the wet.[38] That had a profound effect on the game, and on the social patterns of its dramatic performance. In places like Barbados, games came to be played over three days spread over three successive weekends and on uncovered pitches. Clearly, the weather became a major feature of the game. What any side desired was a spell of fine weather while it was batting, so that its batsmen enjoyed hard and fast pitches, followed by rain which softened the pitch while the other side was batting and, so, gave advantage to the bowlers. Meteorological intervention was rarely so ordered, compliant and helpful. In most locations, players learned to maximise the moment. During one Barbados club match in the late 1950s, for example, the genial and big-hitting test player Cammie Smith hit over three hundred runs in an afternoon taking advantage, as he recalled later, of perfect conditions for batting which did not come along all that often.[39] Almost thirty years later I watched as one of my team-mates blasted at everything in an attempt to beat the rain which was soon to fill a nearby canal in less than an hour. On another occasion during the same season, we played the day following a downpour of six inches of rain, trying to bowl on a pitch which moved every time you stepped on the surface.[40]

Because of that, many experts have argued, the game took on distinctive playing characteristics in the Caribbean: good drivers of the ball and great fast bowlers loved dry conditions, while good pullers and cutters of the ball came from areas where softer conditions prevailed as did medium pacers and the spinners who disappeared from the West Indies sides from the 1970s onwards as the all-pace attack prevailed. There is some mythology in all this because exceptions to the rule are numerous in all the Caribbean settings. Even so, there is something to the idea that conditions produce a form: it may be coincidence that over the past thirty years the great off-spinners of successive generations (Lance Gibbs, Roger Harper and Cark Hooper) all came from Guyana where the conditions are very different from elsewhere in the region.

Beyond that level of cricket, Caribbean supporters invented numerous variations to the game accommodating playing area, equipment and personnel limitations. The most famous form, perhaps, is beach cricket from which many visiting international stars have retreated in defeat after an initial dalliance. Because the game is played on the edge of the ocean with a soft ball, the impression is of a gentle practice. However, a combination of ball, hard sand and total physical involvement leads to a lot of bruising with bowlers coming at batsmen from a few yards shorter than the normal pitch. It is an exhilarating form played with great enthusiasm. Lesser known forms include tapeball, in which a shaved tennis ball is wound in electrical tape with the pitch, again short, being a car park or similar space. An intriguing version is kneeball in which players kneel for all aspects of the game, reducing the power in line with a reduced playing area. All of these forms, and numerous others found throughout the Caribbean, help feed the following for cricket and the game's skills, adding to the general permeation of the sport through the culture.

It is more difficult and culturally fraught, however, to link playing style with underlying social and psychological preconditions. Thus commentators have, subconsciously, linked aggressive fast bowling with a deep-seated desire to beat the former colonial masters, 'flashy' and irresponsible batting with a devil-may-care irresponsibility created by the instant gratification circumstances of slavery.[41] Again, this is overstretching the evidence even if it is possible, as Ashis Nandy believes, to claim national cultural sovereignty over and ownership of the game.[42] While there has always been an effervescent streak in the Caribbean game, it is too easy to overlook the technical competence of a great many of the early players, not to mention the 'professional' approach displayed in English league and county cricket. The problem with the interpretation has been a tendency to link vigorous style with irresponsibility when the two, in fact, are not automatically linked. Worse, vigour and dash were valued when displayed by players like Keith Miller in Australia and Ian Botham in England: the cultural and racial undertones were all too obvious.

Because of that intermix of post-colonialism, passion for the game, layered meanings and mass popularity, cricket became an inextricable part of political culture in the former British West Indies territories.[43] The drive towards self-government in Guyana helped spark a major cricket riot (at the Georgetown test against England in 1954), former test players aplenty have gone into politics as a post-career activity (Wes Hall and Roy Fredericks spring immediately to mind), the politics of regionalism have often been caught up with cricket (after the collapse of federalism in the early 1960s, only cricket and university

[87]

education have carried the tag of unity and even the university system excluded Guyana) and, above all, cricket was the prime vehicle by which the Caribbean communities demonstrated to the world their abhorrence of apartheid in South Africa. Because of the increasing significance of the West Indies in the cricket world from the 1960s onwards, its administrators could hold the line within an International (formerly Imperial) Cricket Council which, otherwise, might have been more lenient and precipitant in the readmission of South Africa to the fold. While West Indian players played in the banned republic, they were punished much more severely for doing so than were their counterparts elsewhere. At home in the Caribbean, cricket was frequently held up as an example of what unity might achieve, the circumstances of various intra-regional squabbles conveniently forgotten. In many of the territories cricket, along with other sports in some cases, was seen as a tool for fixing youth problems and for physical nation-building in general.[44]

Not surprisingly, cricket entered other forms of Caribbean popular culture.[45] Edward Kamau Braithwaite has written some famous poetry, Gary Sobers had a play written about him, calypso and other musical forms have often taken a cricket turn, what might be termed folk writing has often contained references to cricket and, above all, popular discourse in rumshops and other public places has long employed cricket as the common meeting ground.[46] Visions of the Caribbean for such diverse purposes as tourism and commerce have employed cricket and cricketers as the lures. An extension of that has been the proliferation of 'Cricket Weeks' around the region which attract large numbers of playing visitors mainly, but not exclusively, from England. The game has been an economic factor, then, in addition to its other cultural roles.

None of that should be allowed to persuade, however, that change and contestation have been absent as both the game and its cultural hosts move more into a global world while, at the same time, becoming more comfortable in a post-colonial environment. Some of it has been contentious. There is still a white population in the Caribbean, but it is now twenty-five years since someone from that community played for the West Indies.[47] Earlier on, some critics felt that there were whites good enough to play but that the immediate post-independence period made it difficult for them to be selected. Since then, though, the white playing population has dwindled, a natural result of outflow as younger generations seek their fortune and futures outside the region in which they were born.

Social change has not been limited to the tiny white population, either, as the Caribbean has been drawn more into a wider than British network. There were always strong links with, say, Canada and the United States during colonial days, but that connection has strengthened considerably since the 1950s and 1960s through migration, trade (as in the North American Free Trade Agreement), politics and security (as in various treaties and spectacular actions such as the invasion of Grenada), finance (as in the World Bank and the International Monetary Fund), mass tourism and a massive exposure to outside popular cultures (mainly American) via satellite television. While some changes have been superficial, others have been more serious where cricket is concerned.

For example, while cricket remains a popular youth activity there have arisen serious challenges to its once unquestioned primacy. In Trinidad, for example, basketball has become a quite significant sport with its own specific sociological condition.[48] The importance of Patrick Ewing as a former Jamaican, now NBA (National Basketball Association) star, further suggests the importance of this change. Then, where cricket seemed once the only way out of the ghetto for physically talented young men, over the past decades the sports scholarships of North American colleges have become equally, if not more, attractive – even if the numbers of graduating students is not automatically that high, the financial rewards for sporting success certainly are. The rise of the Afro-Caribbean athletes has been a notable social feature in recent years. And socio-economic change within the region itself has led to a widening of sports choice in the more middle-class range: windsurfing has become very popular, while golf is spreading quite quickly (Stephen Ames of Trinidad and Tobago has won on the European PGA Tour).

Ironically, the agency which has stimulated much of the change (television) has not served cricket all that well. Until very recently, few West Indian home series were broadcast to the outside world, and that had a detrimental effect on income which, in turn, had an effect on development programmes. (Not that those were all that prevalent – one of the major debates has been about whether there should be more coaching in the Caribbean to augment the 'natural' evolution of talent. After the West Indies slid out of the 1996 World Cup, the under-pressure captain Richie Richardson bemoaned the absence at home of the coaching which was bearing fruit elsewhere.) While technical deficiencies provided part of the reason for this non-coverage, there was also the problem that cricket did not appeal to the culture behind the major regional television systems, that of the United States. While radio continued and continues to be an important purveyor of cricket, there can be little doubt that television-inclined youth have been exposed to little cricket but a lot of other sports.

[89]

Ironically, the Afro-Caribbean influence, in particular, has become particularly prominent at county and test level in England, and the rise of talented players there leads to idle speculation of what might have happened if... Beginning in the 1920s with players like George Francis who went to the leagues, and boosted over the following years by players like Learie Constantine, Everton Weekes and a host of others, the presence changed character from the 1950s onwards with the rise of Caribbean migration. Eventually, home-grown or -developed players began to emerge so that by the 1980s and 1990s players like Devon Malcolm, Chris Lewis and Dean Headley (the grandson of a famous and son of a not-so-famous Caribbean player) were only the most prominent of a myriad of players. Sadly, though increasingly British-born they were not immune from the inherent racism which marked and continues to mark sport in Britain. In many cases, selection policies and comments seemed to say as much about colour as they did about ability.[49] And all this was a long way from the Caribbean itself.

Caribbean cricket has always been marked by its social trends and its interactions with other powers, England most notably. What the newer circumstances suggest is that as the Caribbean policies and cultures change, so, too, does cricket in ways that are not always comfortable or acceptable. That in itself is the continuation of the long and troubled Caribbean tradition.

Notes

1 Homi K. Bhabha, *The Location of Culture*, London, 1994, p. 1 for the specific reference and the Introduction generally for the overall ideas.
2 The terms 'West Indies' and 'West Indian' here are used as shorthand references to the independent states which succeeded the former British West Indies political jurisdiction. It is important to remember that the traditions and make-up of cricket in the different states carry quite separate benchmarks which signify their distinctive histories.
3 The most convenient reference for the range of this literature is to be found in Hilary McD. Beckles and Brian Stoddart, eds, *Liberation Cricket: West Indies Cricket Culture*, Manchester, 1995.
4 An indication of this may be seen in Clayton Goodwin, *West Indians at the Wicket*, London, 1986, p. 3.
5 See Brian Stoddart, 'Cricket, Social Formation and Cultural Continuity in Barbados: A Preliminary Ethnohistory', *Journal of Sport History*, 14, 3, Winter 1987, reprinted in Beckles and Stoddart, *Liberation Cricket*.
6 For the Warner story in this context, see P. F. Warner, *Cricket in Many Climes*, London, 1900.
7 For an example, see Sir G. William des Voeux, *My Colonial Service*, London, 1903, 2 vols.
8 Greville John Chester, *Transatlantic Sketches in the West Indies, South America, Canada and the United States*, London, 1860, p. 99.

9 See T. Marshall, 'Race, Class and Cricket in Barbadian Society, 1800–1970', *Manjak*, 11 November 1973.
10 See Pierre Bourdieu, 'Sport and Social Class', *Social Science Information*, 17, 1978, for his first foray into the social world of sport.
11 Bhabha, *The Location of Culture*, p. 2.
12 For the background, see Jerome S. Handler and Arnold Sio, 'Barbados', in David W. Cohen and Jack P. Greene, eds, *Neither Slave nor Free: The Freedmen of African Descent in the Slave Societies of the New World*, Baltimore, 1972.
13 C. L. R. James, *Beyond a Boundary*, London, 1963.
14 For the 'map' of this project see Ranajit Guha, 'The Prose of Counter-Insurgency', conveniently reprinted in Ranajit Guha and Gayatri Chakravorty Spivak, eds, *Selected Subaltern Studies*, Oxford, 1988, which also indicates the range of work in the opening phase of this line of analysis.
15 See *The Empire Club Book, 1914–1989*, Bridgetown, 1989.
16 George Lamming, *In the Castle of my Skin*, Ann Arbor, 1991.
17 For some views, *Queen's Park Cricket Club Diamond Jubilee*, Port of Spain, 1956; *Wanderers Cricket Club Centenary, 1877–1977*, Bridgetown, 1977; Herbert G. MacDonald, *History of the Kingston Cricket Club*, Kingston, 1938.
18 See, for some points here, R. D. E. Burton, 'Cricket, Carnival and Street Culture in the Caribbean', *British Journal of Sport History*, 2, 1985, reprinted in Beckles and Stoddart, *Liberation Cricket*.
19 For some elements of this, Orlando Patterson, 'The Ritual of Cricket', *Jamaica Journal*, 3, 1969, reprinted in Beckles and Stoddart, *Liberation Cricket*.
20 See Keith A. P. Sandiford and Brian Stoddart, 'The Elite Schools and Cricket in Barbados: A Study in Colonial Continuity', *International Journal for the History of Sport*, 4, 1987, reprinted in Beckles and Stoddart, *Liberation Cricket*.
21 Interview material.
22 In British Guiana, widespread social segregation included cricket club organisation.
23 For the Frame Food Competition story in Barbados, see Stoddart, 'Cricket, Social Formation and Cultural Continuity in Barbados'.
24 Interview material.
25 For an overview, see Hilary McD. Beckles, 'A Purely Natural Extension: Women's Cricket in West Indies Cricket Culture', in Beckles and Stoddart, *Liberation Cricket*.
26 See, for example, L. S. Smith, ed., *West Indies Cricket History and Cricket Tours to England, 1900, 1906, 1923*, Port of Spain, 1922 [sic], p. 27.
27 For some influences in this section, David Lowenthal, *West Indian Societies*, Oxford, 1972, pp. 82–3.
28 Edward Said, *Culture and Imperialism*, New York, 1993.
29 See Brian Stoddart, 'Sport, Cultural Imperialism and Colonial Response in the British Empire: A Framework for Analysis', *Comparative Studies in Society and History*, 30, 4, October 1988.
30 Interview material.
31 Barbadian white clubs, for example, were scrupulous hosts to visiting black teams.
32 Several West Indians were in the American sides which played against Australia in the 1920s and 1930s.
33 One small club game I observed (and played in) during 1985 attracted at least 1,500 spectators.
34 There were titanic struggles over the selection of even leading players.
35 Goodwin, *West Indians at the Wicket*, pp. 152–4.
36 See James, *Beyond a Boundary*, for the 1920s story.
37 *Ibid.*
38 For this general story, Brian Stoddart, 'Cricket and Colonialism in the English-Speaking Caribbean to 1914: Towards a Cultural Analysis', in James A. Mangan, ed., *Pleasure, Profit and Proselytism: British Culture and Sport at Home and Abroad, 1750–1914*, London, 1988, reprinted in Beckles and Stoddart, *Liberation Cricket*.

39 Interview material.
40 Participant observation with the Maple Club, Barbados.
41 This came through in many radio commentaries over the years.
42 Ashis Nandy, *The Tao of Cricket*, Delhi, 1992.
43 Brian Stoddart, 'Caribbean Cricket: The Role of Sport in Emerging Small-Nation Politics', *International Journal*, 43, 4, 1988.
44 Colin A. Martindale, 'The Role of Sport in Nation-Building: A Comparative Analysis of Four Newly Developing Nations in the Commonwealth Caribbean', doctoral dissertation, City University of New York, 1980.
45 Hilary McD. Beckles and Harclyde Walcott, 'Redemption Sounds: Music, Literature and the Popular Ideology of West Indian Cricket Crowds', in Beckles and Stoddart, *Liberation Cricket*.
46 *Ibid.* I remember, too, making many rumshop friends through discussion of cricket.
47 Interview material.
48 See Jay R. and Joan Mandle, 'Open Cultural Space: Grassroots Basketball in the English-Speaking Caribbean', *Arena Review*, 14, 1, May 1990.
49 The Ray Illingworth–Devon Malcolm fracas during and after the 1996 England tour of South Africa was a case in point. See also Mike Marqusee, *Anyone but England: Cricket and the National Malaise*, London, 1994, pp. 141–5 and 170–5.

CHAPTER FIVE

New Zealand

Greg Ryan

New Zealand holds a distinctly ambiguous position among major cricketing countries. Until at least the mid-1890s cricket was the 'national' game. Thereafter, in common with South Africa, rugby union superseded it and has remained dominant. But, unlike South Africa, the secondary position of New Zealand cricket produced only sporadic moments of international respectability before the mid-1980s. Whereas the South Africans achieved first victories over England in 1905–06 and Australia in 1910–11 and consolidated as a major cricketing power during the 1960s, New Zealand did not achieve a test victory until 1956 (West Indies), Australia were not defeated until 1974 and England until 1978.[1]

New Zealand rugby demonstrates many of the themes central to cricket in other countries. Rugby became, first, an assertion of New Zealand's strong contribution to empire, and later a component of a more independent emergent nationalism during the early twentieth century.[2] But to substitute rugby for cricket in the New Zealand case is to miss the point. It is precisely the retarded development of New Zealand cricket which reinforced a strongly deferential imperial ideology. The metaphors applied to it lingered within a narrower conception of imperialism than those applied to rugby – as a reminder that the colony was still very much dependent on Britain. This ideology forms the core of what follows.

Yet New Zealand's most frequent cricketing contacts, and calamities, were not against England – the 'mother country' – but against Australia, her nearest colonial neighbour and a land with which parity was otherwise maintained in an economic, political and social context.[3] While much may be said of cricket and empire, in New Zealand it is also important to place cricket within late nineteenth-century conceptions of intercolonial and imperial federation.

Central to the prevailing ideology in New Zealand was a middle-class infrastructure which subscribed to a conventional English form and conception of cricket far more determinedly than was the case in Australia. A summary of the quite different histories of the game in the four main provinces – Auckland, Wellington, Canterbury and Otago – reveals that this was strongest in Canterbury. That most English of New Zealand provinces early assumed the mantle of cricket's spiritual home, and Christchurch has remained its administrative centre. Likewise, Christ's College, its leading private school, was the centrepiece of an elite education system which diligently replicated the educational and sporting ideals of the English public school system. From this base emerged an unyielding symmetry between the administration of New Zealand cricket and the political and economic elite of the colony, with the result that the game never lacked for articulate appreciation of its wider implications.

Yet there were factors in New Zealand's social and geographical structure which posed severe obstacles to the determined cricketing idealist. When combined with the middle-class anglophilia of leading administrators and commentators, the narrower conception of New Zealand cricket was reinforced. Nothing occurred on the field to justify emulating the assertive barracking tradition of Australian spectators. Change and expansion were approached more with caution than confidence, and there was little to inspire an enduring sense of local tradition. Despite proximity to Australia, New Zealand shaped a cricketing idyll based firmly on that of England.

New Zealand's origins owe most to the principles of 'systematic colonisation' and their strongest proponent, Edward Gibbon Wakefield. Like Karl Marx, Wakefield saw the inevitability of a class war as the tensions of rapid social change and the Industrial Revolution came to a head in Britain during the early 1830s. His solution to the problem, however, lay not with a wholesale changing of the social order but with the creation of a safety valve through colonisation for the existing order. His essential mechanism was a 'sufficient price' on land – set at a level to limit the number of colonial landowners and simultaneously regulate class relationships by creating a subservient workforce from among those without means to purchase. With population distribution confined in this way, Wakefield sought to prevent the perceived chaos and dislocation of 'frontier' settlements in Australia and North America.[4] His was a conservative recreation of eighteenth-century rural England, described by Keith Sinclair as 'a vertical section of English society excluding the lowest stratum. It would form not a "new people", but an "extension" of an old, retaining its virtues, but eliminating its poverty and overcrowding'.[5]

In reality the theory provided unsolvable problems, not the least of which was: what was a sufficient price for land? Many aspects remained untested and its failure came from problems of both conception and application. Nevertheless, the guiding principle has important implications for the English character of New Zealand cricket. As an essential institution of England in general and its leisured class especially, cricket emerged early and naturally when one might normally expect other amenities and causes to have taken priority. Wakefield himself wrote in 1850, 'I tell the boys in summer time to play at cricket and play well, that those who are the best cricketers most likely will be the best readers and writers'.[6] For Wakefield the cricket club, as much as the dialectic society or the Masonic lodge, provided a focal point for like-minded gentlemen to make essential business and social contacts and consolidate their position at the head of the new society.

Canterbury, where the Wakefield ideal was applied with the greatest success, produced the strongest cricketing tradition in New Zealand – both on the field and off. Its first cricket club, formed in June 1851 under the Presidency of John Robert Godley, leader of the Canterbury Association colonists, epitomised Wakefield's emphasis on social delineation and a cultivated 'leisured class'. Of the forty-one reasonably regular players during the years 1851–56, fifteen were at some time members of the Canterbury Provincial Council, and nine served in the New Zealand General Assembly. Most were prominent landowners and public figures. None of them was an artisan. Membership was by nomination with an annual subscription ranging from 10s 6d in 1851 to a preclusive £2 in 1867.[7] Deriving from the club's status, Canterbury cricketers had little difficulty overcoming the perennial colonial problem of limited funds and a shortage of suitable playing fields. 'English liberality in support of an English game' ensured the club had a ground, groundsman and pavilion by 1854.[8]

Elite domination remained long after the Wakefieldian ideal collapsed. Canterbury's English tradition attracted a disproportionate number of public school and Oxbridge graduates who reached New Zealand in the years 1850–80. The first four presidents of the Canterbury Cricket Association, covering the period 1878–1907, were parliamentarians. The fifth, Frederick Wilding KC, 1907–23, was a prolific sporting patron and father of four times Wimbledon tennis champion Anthony Wilding. With the exception of a select few whose superior playing ability justified inclusion, the Association committee was dominated well into the twentieth century by solicitors and prominent businessman.[9] The local club competition, monopolised by the United Canterbury CC which had direct lineage to the club of 1851, contained a much higher proportion of white-collar players – professionals, major proprietors, clerical staff – than were to be found in the other main centres between 1880 and 1914.[10]

Christ's College provided continuity between generations of Canterbury cricketers. The school employed a succession of headmasters and masters devoted to the principles of public school and Oxbridge athleticism.[11] Most notable was Charles Carteret Corfe, headmaster from 1873 to 1888. Educated at Cambridge, where he accumulated a formidable athletic record, Corfe assured his students that the winning and losing of games were entirely secondary to their correct 'form' and purpose. As his obituary recorded nearly fifty years after he left the school:

> He had a keen sense of his own responsibility, and both by example and by precept he created a similar sense in the minds of his boys. He knew what he was doing when he inculcated in his boys the love of games for their own sake and when he taught them that it was the quest and not the quarry that was important.[12]

Corfe and his successor, F. A. Hare, took a missionary role with local cricket. Although the performances of the XI were frequently mediocre, the College *Sports Register* of February 1886 blamed the standard of opponents for stifling the higher purpose of their cricket.

> Now without wishing to speak severely of a style as seen in the ordinary run of second eleven players in Christchurch, it may be safely affirmed that any youngster playing with or against them, will see quite as much to be avoided as to be imitated. Yet it is against second elevens that Christ's College cricket is almost entirely played.

To remedy this problem, matches were instituted between the XI and teams combining leading Canterbury players and aspiring College colts.[13]

Such a reputation was jealously guarded and threats to it not easily tolerated. When the Revd E. C. Crosse succeeded as headmaster in 1920 he attempted to raise the academic standard of the school and reduce its sporting emphasis. Although he remained for a decade, Crosse steadily alienated the Old Boys Association and eventually resigned due to ill health. His successor, R. C. Richards, was an Old Boy and athlete.[14]

The prominence given to correct playing form did not end with Christ's College. Not content that cricket was played in a rudimentary colonial environment, the Canterbury press frequently pontificated on the need for assiduous practice.[15] In August 1878 hope was expressed that Lord Harris's amateur England team might be enticed to New Zealand after touring Australia.

Such a visit would do more real good to the noble game than almost any number of matches with professional players. The character of the game as played by the gentlemen of England and the players is vastly different and our colonial players would derive great advantage from a contest with the former, as their play is of the more brilliant character, combining as it does good defense with grand hitting powers.[16]

The tour did not take place, and numerous other attempts by Canterbury to entice touring teams during the 1880s and 1890s also failed.[17]

No other New Zealand province attained the sophistication of Canterbury cricket prior to 1914. During the early 1840s Wellington cricket displayed the class divisions born of strict adherence to systematic colonising principles. The first cricket club in 1841–42 included several future provincial and legislative councillors, leading merchants and landholders. A separate Albion Cricket Club was established for tradesmen and labourers.[18] But the collapse of Wakefield's scheme in favour of random, unselected migration and a 'levelling' social attitude implicit in the opportunities open to new colonists prompted many of Wellington's original settlers to depart, and its cricket altered accordingly. Clubs functioned sporadically during the late 1840s, and the game was almost extinct during the 1850s. Only when New Zealand's capital shifted from Auckland to Wellington in 1865 did cricket administration attract influential politicians and public figures. Most prominent was Sir F. H. D. Bell, Attorney-General and New Zealand's first native-born Prime Minister, who presided over the Wellington Cricket Association in the period 1893–1936. He was ably assisted by a plethora of solicitors, leading merchants and company managers. Yet the playing strength of Wellington teams remained largely in the hands of minor clerical staff and skilled tradesmen.[19]

Auckland followed a similar pattern, but for different reasons. Without the strictures of systematic settlement, it grew from predominantly Australian commercial and trading interests during the 1830s.[20] There was no deliberately transplanted leisured class, and its earliest cricket clubs struggled under the patronage of a small group of government servants and staff. In addition, vulnerability to Maori attack during the mid-1840s and again during the early 1860s necessitated a strong military presence with obvious advantages for cricket. Almost all Auckland cricket from 1845–65 incorporated garrison players, but the game was virtually extinct when they were stationed elsewhere.

Relative peace after 1865 brought expansion, and for the first time there were more intra-club and inter-club than military matches.[21] By the mid-1870s, consistent patronage was emerging from the business and legal community of Auckland, but the absence of an elite civilian tradition meant that Auckland cricket became more democratic than that in other provinces. Although prominent solicitors and account-ants monopolised the presidency of the Auckland Cricket Association from 1890 to 1945, the body also accommodated a cabinet-maker, saddler and labourer before 1914 and was more willing to vest power in its constituent clubs than a central committee.[22]

Otago cricket was the antithesis to neighbouring Canterbury. Al-though colonised on 'systematic' principles, Otago was a Scottish Presbyterian Free Church establishment. Those who migrated were predominantly working class, small farmers and villagers from remote parts of Scotland not penetrated by cricketing Sassenachs.[23] Such cricket as there was during the 1850s revolved around a small English faction, or 'Little Enemy' as the prevailing Scottish theocracy termed them.[24]

Cricket took root with the discovery of gold in Otago during 1861. The Otago XXII which played the All England XI in February 1864 included at least ten miners, most of them from Victoria.[25] This artifi-cial injection of talent enabled Otago to inflict several defeats on Canterbury prior to 1870. But cricket was as precarious as the supply of gold and once the bulk of the mining population departed, there was no intrinsically English cricketing tradition to foster players and Otago lost ten of eleven fixtures against Canterbury during the 1870s.[26] It remained the least active and least successful of the main cricketing provinces prior to 1914.[27]

By the mid-1890s other New Zealand schools began to match the ethos developed at Christ's College twenty years earlier. With staff drawn largely from the public schools and ancient universities, supple-mented by the first generation of New Zealand graduates, these schools placed cricket close to the heart of their curriculum.[28] This was most pronounced at Wellington College during the headmastership of Joseph Firth, 1891–1920. A product of Nelson College, the University of Canterbury and six years as gymnastics master at Christ's College, Firth transformed a struggling school into one of the best equipped and respected in New Zealand. As his friend and biographer, Sir James Eliott, summarised Firth's educational priorities:

> [He] aimed at the development of the complete man, and would have placed first, character and personality; second, scholarship; and third, sport . . . Firth looked upon games for boys not only as physical exercise but also, and mainly, as moral and mental training . . . He remained all through the days of his manhood a grown-up, game-playing boy, and kept that spirit and outlook.[29]

Together, the elite schools made a disproportionate contribution to cricket and its administration. By 1914 Christ's College had produced at least fifty-seven first-class cricketers – including perhaps a third of all Canterbury representatives. Auckland Grammar School contributed a similar proportion to Auckland teams.[30]

Reinforcing such middle-class domination was a social structure which militated against a significant level of blue-collar participation in first-class cricket. The main obstacle was the urbanisation of the first-class game. Isolated rural areas had little chance to develop the facilities or competitive structures necessary for good cricket. Accordingly, few first-class cricketers prior to 1950 were drawn from outside the main cities of the four leading provinces. Yet these centres constituted only 30 per cent of the European population of New Zealand in 1911 and 36 per cent in 1936. Moreover, the cities contained the vast majority of professional and white-collar occupations. Semi-skilled and unskilled workers were predominantly rural and often transient,[31] and hence they were always likely to be under-represented in the cricket teams of the main centres.

Nor was the urban working class much better placed. Legislation during the 1890s to provide for a weekly half-holiday was not universal.[32] Others were obliged to take their holiday on Wednesday or Thursday rather than Saturday when all senior grade cricket was played. The days or weeks of work leave required to play representative cricket also ensured that it became the domain of those with independent means or most flexible working arrangements. Educational opportunities were also a factor. In 1901 less than 8 per cent of the European population were enrolled in high schools of any description. The majority were never subjected to the ethos, to say nothing of the coaching and facilities, offered at Christ's or Wellington College.[33]

In purely cricketing terms, the greater continuity and status of Canterbury cricket during the nineteenth century has obvious implications. A provincial XV defeated the first Australians in 1878, and undertook the first tour outside New Zealand – playing eight matches against Victorian clubs early in 1879. Always the most consistent opposition for touring teams, Canterbury secured five of only seven first-class victories by New Zealand provinces prior to 1914.[34] Moreover, it was largely on the initiative of Cantabrians that the New Zealand Cricket Council was established in Christchurch at the end of 1894. Its permanent staff, most of them Christ's College educated, were all drawn from Christchurch.[35]

The ideological implications of Canterbury primacy are equally significant. New Zealand cricket possesses a 'geography of interpretation'. That is to say, the extent to which press sources and public figures imbued cricket with notions of moral value, political symbolism and imperial sentiment mirrors the different patterns of development outlined above. By the 1880s none of the main centres lacked informed cricketing patrons, but the most active and articulate were found in Canterbury.

This is most apparent in the visit of Parr's All England XI to New Zealand in 1864. While initiative and finance for the tour came from gold-rich entrepreneurs in Otago, Canterbury devoted the largest column space to proceedings and treated the team with the greatest ceremony. Amid realistic expectations of a heavy defeat, the influential committee of politicians and businessmen who oversaw arrangements for the Canterbury leg of the tour well understood that such a venture meant a great deal irrespective of what it achieved on the field. When the visit was first mooted in October 1863, the Christchurch *Press* cast it in expansionist terms:

> The mere mention of the scheme affords an undeniable proof of the advancement of the colony, and also of the gradual lessening of the distance which separates us from the Mother Country. When last the Eleven came to Australia there was hardly a mention of their coming to New Zealand . . . Such symptoms of the growth of the colony are not to be mistaken, and auger well for the approaching establishment of the Panama route and the great increase to the prosperity of the settlement which will infallibly result there from.[36]

Two months later, when arrangements were confirmed, the same source stressed that the performance of the Canterbury team would determine whether the men of the province were perceived in England 'as a plucky set of fellows who in the midst of the hard struggles of a settler's life, and the incessant grind of money-grubbing, have retained some of the manly tastes of our race', or whether they would be accused of having 'exchanged pluck and activity for bounce and tall talk'.[37]

The Otago *Daily Times*, under the editorship of future New Zealand Premier Julius Vogel, was equally forthright in its view of the tour as a vital strand of Empire:

> [I]t is . . . an absolute certainty that the press of London and the different counties has more encouraging articles on this proof of colonial enterprise, than on the fact of our gold discoveries, for it shows us to be British still in both commercial daring and love of national pastime.[38]

Others felt that the performances in New Zealand would be as keenly viewed by Australians as Englishmen. *The Press* suggested that Canterbury was not so much competing against the England XI as against neighbouring colonies. 'The thing we should aim at is that the twenty-two of Canterbury should leave on record a score which shall show favourably against, if it cannot overtop, the score of any other twenty-two in the colonies.'[39] In the end an Otago XXII, dominated by recently arrived Australian miners, performed rather better than Canterbury. Efforts to entice the England XI to Wellington and Auckland amounted to nothing.

The next English teams in 1877 and 1882, the first to tour the whole country, enabled Auckland and Wellington to demonstrate that they did not lack an appreciation of the issues at stake. At a reception for the 1877 team in Auckland, W. L. Rees, parliamentarian and cousin of the Grace family, declared that 'The common love for these sports was one of the strongest links in the chain which connected the Mother Country with her offspring, a chain which, though light as silk, was strong as steel'.[40] In a long editorial on 25 January 1882, Wellington's *New Zealand Times* echoed earlier sentiments regarding the value of tours as a barometer of colonial quality:

> A vast deal of good has been done by these cricketing visits to and from the Australian colonies. They have been the best advertisement of our prosperity and energy these colonies could have had; they have shown, physically at least, there has been no deterioration in the British subjects of Her Majesty at this part of the world; and the friendly reception of the cricketers sent from either 'end of the earth' to the other has greatly strengthened the sentimental tie uniting England to her colonies and the colonies to England.[41]

For reasons to be explained shortly, this was the last major English visit until Lord Hawke's team arrived in 1902.

Yet the presence of a touring team was not in itself a necessary cue for editors and commentators to expound on the uniquely English characteristics of cricket. In a preview to the 1860–61 season in Canterbury, the *Lyttelton Times* produced a quite xenophobic analysis:

> The Frenchman, the Russian and the German all hunt, shoot and race, and try to carry out their sport after the English model, though they all fail more or less in the attempt; but who ever heard or saw one or other able to handle a bat decently, or send the near stump flying with a rippling round hander, or even catch or throw a ball in any other style than that peculiar one adopted by young ladies when they attempt the game.[42]

Almost half a century later the *New Zealand Herald* was equally forthright in its condemnation of the 'Latin races of Europe' for having 'no national out of door games of mingled skill and endurance in which all classes of the people can join'. Englishmen, on the other hand, looked to cricket to mould both individual characteristics and the destiny of the people.[43] Indeed, as the *Otago Daily Times* declared in February 1884, 'we may say that the lessons which cricket teaches are just those which distinguish the British character in every department of life and have made our national pride not altogether empty'.[44]

With the cessation of English tours during the early 1880s, the focus shifted to Australian teams – of which thirteen visited New Zealand from 1878 to 1914. Although a Canterbury XV aroused interest by defeating the 1878 Australians by six wickets, this was prior to their pioneering tour of England. Once the colonial reputation had been forged at 'Home' in 1878 and 1880, the next Australian visit to New Zealand – by W. L. Murdoch's team in 1881 – drew much greater interest. As the *Otago Daily Times* put it, local spectators wanted to see 'the eleven Colonials who have not only proved themselves "the cricket monarchs of Pacific's main", . . . but very nearly of Atlantic's also'.[45]

At a reception for Murdoch's team in Christchurch E. C. J. Stevens, politician and cricketer, said that Canterbury were glad to play a team who had shown 'the old country that we here in the colonies have not forgotten the manly sports of our fatherland'. John Ollivier, provincial politician and father of a Canterbury cricketing dynasty, expressed pleasure at welcoming a team which had 'achieved such honour as would convince the old country that she had planted in these Australasian colonies men who had determined to show that they intended to develop to the fullest those sports which made the name of England famous'. In reply, Murdoch stressed that in playing for the honour of the Australian colonies his team had always included New Zealand. There was already a South Australian in the team, and therefore no reason why a New Zealander could not also accompany them to England 'so that it might be a thoroughly representative team of Australasia'.[46]

Murdoch hinted at the notions of colonial federation gaining political currency in New Zealand during the last quarter of the nineteenth century. Ideas that New Zealand might federate with the Australian colonies were first aired during the early 1880s, mainly in the consultative Federal Council established in 1886. But aside from a brief revival of interest during the Colonial conferences of 1890 and 1891, and a belated flurry of activity in 1899 after the Australians had committed themselves to Federation, there was little public or political support for the concept in New Zealand. Moreover, New Zealand newspapers did not campaign for colonial federation.[47]

The *Evening Post* suggested that visits by New South Wales athletes and cricketers at the end of 1895 were transcending the contradictions of existing attempts to federate at a political level:

[102]

While politicians are in the same breath talking of drawing closer the bonds of unions between the colonies, and making hostile tariffs to drive them apart, there is a practical federation of the young generation in the field of athletics which will probably do much in moulding the future Federal opinions, and it is for this reason, as well as for the sake of the branches of sport concerned, that we especially welcome at this Christmas season the New South Wales Cricketers and the New South Wales Amateur Athletes.[48]

Ten years later, the *New Zealand Herald* took the visit of the 1905 Australians as an opportunity to remind its readers of an ultimate loyalty among the colonies and with Britain:

The friendliness that is manifested, the common interests that are called forth, the very emulation that is excited between the branches of the same people keeps alive the feeling that we are one people and not strangers. This, more than many more seemingly important things, forms a real bond of union which may at least help to stand the strain which distance, and to some extent, perhaps, conflicting interests, may hereafter put upon the unity of the Empire.[49]

In referring to 'conflicting interests' the *Herald* was, perhaps, mindful of tensions between imperial and national aspirations in such areas as defence and the application of restrictive immigration policies.

As late as 1928, New Zealand Prime Minister Gordon Coates was affirming his faith in the ability of cricket tours to weld closer ties between New Zealand and Australia. In an address to the departing Australian team he said,

Visits such as these do an enormous amount of good. In fact they are essential in order that the representatives of either country can come into closer contact and understand the viewpoints of each other better. You know that in the political world today there is an effort to have some point round which representatives from all parts of the world can meet and discuss international problems . . . It would be difficult to draw comparisons, but, nevertheless, we can not underestimate the good visits of this kind bring with them.[50]

Ironically, this was the last Australian tour of New Zealand for eighteen years.

Clearly a strong sense of imperial and intercolonial symbolism existed within the middle-class stratum which dominated New Zealand cricket, but it gains greater clarity because it was never subsumed by a transition to expressions of assertive imperialism or emergent nationalism. New Zealand retained an attachment to Britain far longer than Australia, Canada or South Africa. In part this reflects the later growth of New Zealand compared to eastern Australia, which meant that an immigrant rather than native-born population predominated longer. Moreover, there was no convict transportation to New Zealand, nor a dominant Irish population with its attendant level of social and economic grievances from which to ferment anti-British feeling.[51] This may help explain why English touring teams were never subjected to the provocative barracking which so antagonised Andrew Stoddart in Australia during the 1890s. Rather, New Zealand continued to agitate for various Imperial Federation schemes and for much closer social and political ties with Britain than the Australians ever deemed necessary or desirable. When, in 1931, the Imperial Parliament enacted the Statute of Westminster, removing the last vestiges of control from London and confirming the reality of New Zealand's shift from dominion to independent state, the measure was effectively ignored. Not until 1947, after twelve years of Labour government, was the Statute grudgingly adopted.[52]

The playing failure of New Zealand cricket teams only confirmed these ties to Britain. Despite promising beginnings and a surfeit of elite patronage, demographic, financial and climatic obstacles severely hampered the country's chances for success at international level. The performances of New Zealand cricket teams never justified alignment with notions of national self-assertion and statements of identity. There was nothing to match the exploits of Australian cricket teams from the late 1870s, New Zealand rugby teams from the mid-1890s or the Australasian contingents during the Anglo-Boer War and at Gallipoli, especially. Rather, New Zealand cricket lingered within a passive imperial ideology and a preoccupation which stressed form and convention ahead of success.

Without the large populations of Melbourne, Sydney and Adelaide, the provincial cricket associations and the New Zealand Cricket Council could not benefit from the revenue producing spectatorship that enabled the long-term development seen in Australia. Attempts to sustain a regular interprovincial competition or to provide sufficient guarantees for touring teams often foundered on a lack of funds. The problem became self-perpetuating in that an erratic first-class programme did nothing to sustain the public enthusiasm for cricket necessary to draw spectators to games. Even the Plunket Shield, presented in 1907 as a focal point for interprovincial cricket, failed to solve the problem. As matches were played on a challenge basis and on the home ground of the holder, the opportunities for all associations to profit were limited.

Financial difficulties can also be traced to provisions of the 1881 Public Reserves Act which prohibited any admission charge for fixtures played on publicly controlled grounds.[53] To cover costs, provincial associations and tour promoters were at the mercy of subscriptions and donations. With no obligation to do so, the public were seldom willing to contribute. Moreover, the 1885 amendment to the Act which allowed admission charges provided relief in name only. To circumvent the original Act Canterbury, Otago and Wellington plunged their resources into private ground ventures during 1882. These were to saddle them with considerable debts well into the twentieth century.[54]

Alfred Shaw, promoter of several English touring teams to New Zealand, identified particular disadvantages in the 1881 Act. He recalled that 1,000 Aucklanders refused to pay at the England XI match in 1882 as the ground was a public reserve. With no other ground available, 'We had no option but to play the match as arranged, and keep out those who thought we could afford to travel from England and play cricket without charge for their edification and amusement'.[55] Subsequent negotiations for an English visit in 1886–87 were not helped by the grasping attitude of the provincial cricket associations who saw the tourists as an ideal opportunity to supplement their meagre incomes and clear ground development debts.[56] Under these circumstances there were no full English tours of New Zealand from 1882 until 1903 and a vital sustenance for local cricket was removed.

To this restrictive chain of development must be added a more speculative explanation – that New Zealand cricket was hampered by an unfavourable climate. Cricket was too firmly established in English tradition ever to submit to the weather, but the elements may have determined choices made in new colonies and, perhaps, in Scotland and Ireland. The hotter climate of India and the West Indies was naturally conducive to cricket, but a more vigorous contact sport such as rugby gained almost no following – even among Europeans not bound by such considerations as Brahmin/Hindu objections to handling leather balls.[57] In Australia and South Africa, with a more temperate climate in the main settlement areas, both winter and summer sports flourished. In New Zealand, where the climate is rather more mild, winter sport held a distinct advantage over summer.

A statistical comparison with Australia suggests that a combination of temperature and rainfall contributing to damp, inferior pitches and ground quality had a dramatic impact on performance.[58] By 1914, 25.7 per cent of all completed team innings in Australian first-class matches produced totals in excess of 300 – 33.3 per cent for the period 1900–14. For New Zealand the overall figure is 7.2 per cent and 11.9 per cent for the period 1900–14.[59] By restricting opportunities for batsmen and placing bowlers at a deceptive advantage, New Zealand pitch conditions did not assist local players in developing the technique necessary to counter the superior skills of touring teams. Australian players, and Warwick Armstrong especially, frequently observed that New Zealand cricket would only improve when the quality of its pitches improved. Frank Laver, a tourist in 1905, suggested that better quality soil should be imported from Australia. After the next Australian tour in 1910, M. A. Noble added that there was little to be gained from playing on surfaces unfair to batsmen and offering no challenge to bowlers.[60]

Nor did such conditions prepare New Zealand players for the tours of Australia in 1899 and 1914. Daniel Reese, New Zealand captain from 1907 to 1914, considered that the failure of many batsmen was directly attributable to lack of experience on hard, fast wickets. Without being able to cultivate a proper match temperament, an inferiority complex developed among local players. Australian bowler and frequent tourist to New Zealand, Hugh Trumble, reinforced this with the observation that 'he would be inclined to back the New Zealanders, if they were batting at the nets'.[61]

While immersed in these struggles, cricket was superseded by rugby in participation and public consciousness. The winter code faced few of cricket's impediments. It was cheaper to establish and was not dependent on climate. The expensive ground developments which hamstrung the provincial cricket associations were also less of a factor in rugby. Although the first game under rugby rules was played in New Zealand as late as 1870, the game expanded rapidly to incorporate 438 interprovincial and international fixtures for the decade 1900–09. This compares with a total of 277 first-class cricket matches for the entire period 1864–1914.[62] From 1884 to 1914 representative New Zealand rugby teams, at home and on tour, won 118, lost seven and drew four of their fixtures. Against all opposition, touring teams in New Zealand won 42, lost 53 and drew six.[63] In stark contrast, New Zealand representative cricket teams won four, lost thirteen and drew one of their first-class matches during the same period. Against first-class opposition, touring cricket teams in New Zealand won 43, lost ten and drew fifteen. Of the losses, three were sustained by Tasmania, two by Fiji and two by the weak MCC side of 1907. Most of the draws were caused by bad weather. Of the 175 matches played by all touring teams, 114 were won, twelve lost and forty-nine drawn.[64]

The differing profiles of cricket and rugby are graphically illustrated by the 1905 All Black tour of Britain. By the end of a campaign in which they lost only one (still disputed) match against Wales, the All Black performances became the subject of immense colonial pride and political interest. Premier Richard Seddon seized on the tour to strengthen New Zealand's profile within the empire. Replying to a *Daily Mail* query as to reasons for the success of the team, he stated that 'The natural and healthy conditions of colonial life produce stalwart and athletic sons of whom New Zealand and the Empire are justly proud'. Seddon also suggested that results of the tour were received in New Zealand almost as eagerly as reports of the South African war had been.[65] While some sections of the press condemned the Premier's 'unabashed opportunism' in aligning himself with the tour, none could question his assessment of popular feeling. As the *Lyttelton Times* concluded at the end of the tour, 'It has remained for a band of young athletes to give the colony the widest advertisement it has ever had'.[66]

From this point on rugby was the national game, and the assertive imperial rhetoric which accompanied it was easily translated into emergent nationalism. At the same time, cricket remained in a passive and deferential relationship with Lord's. Indeed, the priorities of the New Zealand Cricket Council were unequivocally demonstrated in 1902 when it was confirmed that Lord Hawke's mostly amateur English team would tour during the coming season:

> The Chairman thought that nothing could be better for New Zealand cricket than the visit of a team such as that now proposed, and speaking for himself, he would rather see a team of English amateurs than a professional team or one from Australia.[67]

Significantly, this was the most profitable tour of New Zealand prior to 1914. Most, including the star studded Australian teams of 1881, 1896 and 1905, struggled to break even.[68] New Zealand spectators shared the same predisposition of players and officials towards the virtues of English amateurism.

In 1906–07 the MCC dispatched a weak team of little known amateurs on a financially disastrous tour of New Zealand. But this did not dim Cricket Council enthusiasm for contact with English teams. Every English tour of Australia was marked by strenuous efforts to persuade the tourists to play a few matches in New Zealand.[69] It is similarly revealing that the provincial cricket associations taxed their already strained finances with the extra expense of engaging professional coaches from England rather than Australia. There were three in Auckland during 1911, and another influx during the 1920s.[70]

After 1928, New Zealand's ongoing deference to English cricket came partly from a lack of support from Australia. Having determined that New Zealand was not of international standard, the Australian Board of Control fashioned an increasingly negative attitude. No Australian team visited New Zealand from 1928 to 1946, and there were only six visits in the forty years following New Zealand's admission to test cricket in 1929–30. Of the six New Zealand teams which visited Australia from 1925 to 1970, three were teams returning from England or South Africa which played three first-class games or less. Aside from one retrospectively recognised test match in 1946, the two countries did not meet regularly at international level until 1973–74.[71] Thus New Zealand was forced to look much more towards England for its international opportunities. Up to 1951, nineteen of New Zealand's twenty-two test matches were against England, and to date it has played twice as many test matches against that country as any other.[72]

The first New Zealand tour of England in 1927 and the first test playing tour in 1931 are instructive for their lingering tones of tutelage and deference. Summarising prospects for the first touring team in 1927, F. S. Ashley-Cooper declared that 'The Tour has been arranged, not with any idea of challenging our supremacy in the game, but from an educational point of view'.[73] When the team arrived in April, its captain, T. C. Lowry, Cambridge blue and former Somerset player, informed the British Sportsmen's Club that his men were 'Britishers anxious to appear on the cricket map, and accordingly came home not to beat the best sportsmen but to learn the rules as England taught them'.[74] At the end of the tour, the New Zealand High Commissioner, Sir James Parr, affirmed the underlying importance of the venture:

> The ties that held New Zealand and the home country together were ties of affection and loyalty which such visits helped to strengthen – such ties were stronger than written constitutions or bonds of steel. The team had played good cricket and had also been missioners of Empire.[75]

Four years later, although a test match was scheduled for the first time, the conception of the tour had not changed. Arthur Donnelly, President of the New Zealand Cricket Council, highlighted the dual objectives of the tour:

> They had come to England to improve the standard of the game in their own country and to promote, in some small degree, good feeling and understanding between the Mother Country and the most distant, but not least loyal, of the Dominions of the Empire.[76]

While praising the fine amateur spirit maintained by Lowry and his team, *Wisden* echoed Donnelly's sentiments: 'Representatives of one of our great Dominions beyond the seas, the New Zealanders looked upon the tour perhaps from a bigger point of view than the mere playing of cricket.'[77]

New Zealand's performance in almost winning the Lord's test of

1931 prompted the belated scheduling of two more test matches for the tour. But the next team in 1937 was still viewed as being on a steep learning curve, and that of 1949 was only accorded three days for each of its four test matches. When these were all drawn, it seemed that New Zealand had finally defied its own objections to the Statute of Westminster and achieved cricketing equality at least. But a disastrous waterlogged tour in 1958, including the only five-test series ever played between England and New Zealand, soon restored the balance. New Zealand did not win a test in England until 1983, and a series until the following summer.[78]

Beyond the specific focus of New Zealand tours, admiration for English cricket remained equally strong during the 1920s and 1930s. Ian Milner, son of the Rector of Waitaki Boys High School and an active socialist later implicated as a KGB agent, vividly recalled the fascination pupils felt for the distant game of England during his last year at school in 1929:

> Empire sentiment apart, England at cricket was the father of us all, Ashes in hand or no. A veteran like W. G. Grace was a dynastic figure . . . I had my Jack Hobbs of Surrey and England and Bert [sic] Sutcliffe, Yorkshire and England . . . After I'd straightened out the cream and green-covered mag, which had travelled twelve thousand miles into my hands, the first thing was to see how many Jack had made against Lancashire or Kent three months or more previously.[79]

In this Milner was not alone. Not only did the New Zealand sporting press give extensive coverage to the English County Championship and to test matches, but the major daily papers frequently editorialised on performances and developments within the English game.

New Zealand press and public reactions to the Bodyline controversy during 1932–33, for example, revealed a pro-English sentiment. The Christchurch *Press* accused the Australian media of sensationalism, recalled the damage inflicted on England by Jack Gregory and Ted McDonald in 1921, and praised the MCC for its strong condemnation of 'sweeping charges' made by the Australian Cricket Board. Others suggested that Bodyline was neither dangerous nor unplayable, and that the real fault lay in the techniques of Australian players.[80]

There is only one instance of New Zealanders challenging English cricketing values. The perceived aloofness of A. C. MacLaren's MCC team in 1922–23 moved several observers to question the appropriateness of class and social distinctions in English cricket. During a reception for the team in Christchurch, Daniel Reese, speaking on behalf of the New Zealand Cricket Council, suggested that although the MCC was admired as a great institution, 'its constitution was not democratic enough to suit the ideas of cricketers overseas'.[81] Taking this theme further, the Christchurch *Sun* insisted that the MCC should leave distinctions between amateurs and professionals at home, because New Zealanders would not treat the two groups differently. Moreover, in the lack of style, enterprise or spectator appeal shown by this predominantly amateur team, the *Sun* found an obvious explanation for England's heavy losses to Australia in 1920–21. 'English cricket needs to be "gingered up". It is wanting in imagination, courage and resource; virtues which are strongly characteristic of Australian play.'[82] But much of the controversy can be traced to the personal tactlessness of MacLaren and the detached opportunism with which he viewed a tour initiated to aid the recovery of New Zealand cricket after the First World War.

The response to MacLaren, however, is a reminder that any discussion of cricket and imperial ideology requires a degree of qualification. The views examined here are essentially those of an articulate and interested elite. Given the middle-class domination of New Zealand cricket outlined earlier, it is not at all clear how much relevance imperial themes held for blue-collar cricketers or the working class generally. A valuable lesson may be drawn from the British tour of the 1888–89 New Zealand native football team. While their matches against the elite rugby clubs of southern England attracted imperial rhetoric and a more acute awareness of the predominantly Maori composition of the team, such themes were almost entirely absent from coverage of the matches against working-class teams in Lancashire and Yorkshire. These markedly different personal and ideological responses suggest that caution is required in assessing the pervasiveness of imperial ideologies across class barriers.[83]

Cricket had only a minute impact on New Zealand's indigenous population. Although constituting more or less 10 per cent of the population, Maoris contributed no more than ten first-class cricketers prior to the 1990s. Of those who appeared before 1914, almost all can be traced to elite New Zealand schools and greater integration within the mainstream of European society. One, J. G. Taiaroa, was a solicitor and another, J. H. W. Uru, became a Member of Parliament.[84]

Most Maoris belonged to scattered rural communities. Only 11.2 per cent were urbanised by 1936 and 19 per cent by 1945. It was not until the late 1960s that they became a predominantly urban people.[85] Of course, the urban constraint did not apply to New Zealand rugby – in which sport Maori players have made a substantial international contribution since the early 1880s. It is only since 1990 that there have been any specific initiatives to develop Maori cricketers.[86]

Finally, it is important to appreciate that whatever the ideological homogeneity of the New Zealand cricketing elite, their approach to administration was marked by internecine bickering. The Wellington Cricket Association, in particular, was constantly at odds with the New Zealand Cricket Council over finance. As late as 1914, disgruntled Wellingtonians condemned the Council as a body with few achievements and little future.[87] Moreover, the selection of almost every New Zealand team from 1894 until the late 1920s provided a staging ground for displays of vitriolic interprovincial rivalry. Rather than choosing the best team, the New Zealand selectors were to some extent obliged to employ a system of provincial quotas in the interests of local appeasement.[88]

Such rifts mirror David Montefiore's characterisation of Australian cricket during the 1880s.[89] The idealisation of cricket as moral, imperial or national metaphor was circumscribed by the narrower realities of self-interest, personal ambition and regionalism. Successive generations of New Zealand cricketers and administrators may have been taught in the best public school tradition to pursue the game for its own sake, but they frequently behaved in a manner to suggest that the stakes were more immediate and tangible.

From the nature of its colonising pattern New Zealand, and Canterbury especially, developed a strong middle-class continuity which ensured a diligent replication of English cricketing form and philosophy. There is no mistaking that the playing of cricket in New Zealand during the nineteenth century was perceived as a vital component in preserving English characteristics and securing bonds of loyalty to the empire. Yet this imperial ideology did not develop in the assertive manner seen in Australia. The consistent failure of New Zealand teams at international level, set against the increasing domination of rugby, ensured that cricket maintained a narrow, deferential focus.

Only in the early 1970s did New Zealand begin to make a mark on the international cricketing stage. Both financially and in terms of playing experience, the New Zealand game benefited greatly from the overall expansion of test and one-day cricket. Most important in this context was the establishment of full international contacts with Australia in 1973. The national team increasingly contained players such as Glenn Turner, Geoff Howarth, John Wright and Richard Hadlee who had honed their technical and mental skills in English county cricket. Turner, especially, confronted the rather timid and traditional structure of New Zealand cricket with an unprecedented level of professionalism and confidence. His approach seldom won friends among amateur administrators,[90] but there were dividends in the form of consistently strong performances by New Zealand teams throughout the 1980s.

New Zealand finally secured its first victory over England at Wellington in 1978, more than a century after the first triumph by an Australian team. Some likened the achievement to VE Day, others to Hillary's conquest of Everest.[91] Whatever the true magnitude of the performance – and New Zealand fell rapidly to earth with heavy defeat in the next test at Christchurch – it could at least be said that cricketing parity had been achieved with the one opponent who still mattered above all others.

Notes

1 For a summary of results see E. W. Swanton, gen. ed., *Barclays World of Cricket*, London, 1986, pp. 100–2, 253–9, 309–16.
2 J. O. C. Phillips, *A Man's Country?*, Auckland, 1987, pp. 81–130; K. Sinclair, *A Destiny Apart: New Zealand's Search for National Identity*, Auckland, 1986, pp. 143–56.
3 See K. Sinclair, ed., *Tasman Relations: New Zealand and Australia, 1788–1988*, Auckland, 1987.
4 K. Sinclair, *A History of New Zealand*, Auckland, 4th rev. ed., 1991, pp. 57–61; W. D. McIntyre, ed., *The Journal of Henry Sewell: 1853–7*, vol. 1, Christchurch, 1980, pp. 31–2.
5 Sinclair, *History of New Zealand*, pp. 60–1.
6 E. G. Wakefield to Justice Chapman, 1 April 1850. Quoted in C. Lansbury, 'A Straight Bat and a Modest Mind', *Victorian Newsletter*, 49, Spring 1976, p. 13.
7 Figures derived from score reports of the *Lyttelton Times*, 1851–56, and M. Fraser, *New Zealand Parliamentary Record*, Wellington, 1913, passim.
8 *Lyttelton Times*, 2 April 1853, p. 10; 7 January 1854, p. 7; 29 April 1854, p. 7; 30 September 1854, p. 4.
9 See R. T. Brittenden, *100 Years of Cricket: The History of the Canterbury Cricket Association*, Christchurch, 1977.
10 All material relating to occupational composition of main centre cricket clubs is derived from my PhD thesis, 'Where the Game was Played by Decent Chaps: The Making of a New Zealand Cricket 1832–1914', University of Canterbury, 1996.
11 D. A. Wood, 'Athleticism: A Study with Particular Reference to Christ's College', research essay, University of Canterbury, 1985.
12 C. C. Corfe, obituary, *The Christ's College Register*, August 1935, pp. 93–5.
13 *Christ's College Sports Register*, February 1886, p. 33.
14 Wood, 'Athleticism', pp. 20–1, 27–8.
15 For example, *Lyttelton Times*, 10 December 1853, p. 10; 10 April 1888, p. 4; *The Press*, 18 December 1897, p. 7.
16 *The Press*, 17 August 1878, p. 3.
17 For example, *New Zealand Referee*, 3 September 1891, p. 27; 15 November 1894, p. 33; 15 September 1897, p. 36.
18 *New Zealand Colonist and Port Nicholson Advertiser*, 4 November 1842, p. 3; *Wellington Spectator*, 9 November 1842, p. 2.
19 Wellington Cricket Association, Annual Reports, 1880, 1890, 1900–14. See also my 'Cultural Baggage, Cricket and Class in Nineteenth Century New Zealand', *History Now*, 1, 1, May 1995.
20 Sinclair, *History of New Zealand*, pp. 49, 100.
21 *Auckland Cricketers Trip to the South . . . 1873–74*, Auckland, 1874, p. 4.

22 Auckland Cricket Association, *100 Not Out: A Centennial History of the Auckland Cricket Association*, Auckland, 1983, passim.
23 E. Olssen, *A History of Otago*, Dunedin, 1984, pp. 31–44.
24 G. Griffiths, 'Sale, Bradshaw, Wills, Manning and the "Little Enemy" ', notes on some early arrivals in Otago, no. 4, Dunedin, 1971.
25 *Ibid.*, pp. 22–4.
26 T. W. Reese, *New Zealand Cricket 1841–1914*, Christchurch, 1927, passim.
27 Otago Cricket Association, Annual Reports, 1880–1914.
28 K. A. Trembath, *Ad Augusta: A Centennial History of Auckland Grammar School 1869–1969*, Auckland, 1969, pp. 73, 87, 150, 172, 383–9; A. Sangster, *Pathway to Establishment: The History of Wanganui Collegiate School*, Wanganui, 1985, passim; H. A. Heron, *The Centennial History of Wellington College*, Wellington, 1967, pp. 29–56; T. D. Pearce and R. V. Fulton, *Otago High School Old Boys Register*, Dunedin, 1907, passim.
29 Sir J. Eliott, *Firth of Wellington*, Wellington, 1937, p. 178.
30 *School List of Christ's College*, Christchurch, 1935, passim; Trembath, *Ad Augusta*, pp. 383–9.
31 E. Olssen, 'Towards a New Society', in G. W. Rice, ed., *The Oxford History of New Zealand*, Auckland, 2nd ed., 1992, pp. 256, 272–3.
32 *New Zealand Statutes*, Shops and Shop Assistants Act, 1894, no. 32; Shops and Offices Amendment Act, 1905, no. 43.
33 Olssen, 'Towards a New Society', pp. 276–7.
34 Reese, *New Zealand Cricket*, passim.
35 *New Zealand Referee*, 26 June 1894, p. 26; 3 January 1895, p. 27; New Zealand Cricket Council, Annual Reports, 1895–1920.
36 *The Press*, 27 October 1863, p. 2.
37 *Ibid.*, 23 December 1863, p. 2.
38 Quoted *ibid.*, 12 November 1863, p. 3.
39 *Ibid.*, 17 December 1863, p. 2.
40 *New Zealand Herald*, 1 February 1877, p. 2.
41 *New Zealand Times*, 25 January 1882, p. 2.
42 *Lyttelton Times*, 19 September 1860, p. 4.
43 *New Zealand Herald*, 11 February 1905, p. 6.
44 *Otago Daily Times*, 2 February 1884, p. 2.
45 *Ibid.*, 21 January 1881, p. 3.
46 *The Press*, 31 January 1881, p. 3.
47 K. Sinclair, 'Why New Zealanders are not Australians: New Zealand and the Australian Federal Movement, 1881–1901', in Sinclair, *Tasman Relations*, pp. 90–103.
48 *Evening Post*, 27 December 1895, p. 2.
49 *New Zealand Herald*, 11 February 1905, p. 6.
50 *The Press*, 11 April 1928, p. 12.
51 Sinclair, *Destiny Apart*, p. 96. The Irish constituted *c.* 13 per cent of the New Zealand population, as opposed to *c.* 25 per cent in Australia.
52 *Ibid.*, pp. 96–103; R. Holt, *Sport and the British: A Modern History*, Oxford, 1990, pp. 231–3.
53 *New Zealand Statutes*, 1881, no. 15.
54 G. Tait, 'A History of the Otago Cricket Association in the Nineteenth Century', MA thesis, University of Otago, 1974, pp. 49, 61–2; T. W. Reese, *History of Lancaster Park*, Christchurch, *c.* 1935, pp. 1–10; D. O. Neely, *100 Summers: The History of Wellington Cricket*, Wellington, 1975, pp. 18–19, 25.
55 A. W. Pullin, *Alfred Shaw: Cricketer*, London, 1902, p. 74.
56 *Ibid.*, p. 96.
57 See J. A. Mangan, *The Games Ethic and Imperialism*, London, 1986, pp. 168–92.
58 G. Griffiths, 'History of Cricket in the South', unpublished manuscript, Dunedin, *c.* 1976.
59 Figures derived from B. Croudy, *A Guide to First-Class Matches Played in New*

Zealand 1863 to 1980, London, 1981; Reese, *New Zealand Cricket*; R. Webster, *First-Class Cricket in Australia: Vol. 1, 1850–51 to 1941–42*, Melbourne, 1991. A detailed summary is contained in my PhD thesis (see note 10).

60 F. Laver, *An Australian Cricketer on Tour*, London, 1905, p. 104; Reese, *New Zealand Cricket*, pp. 118–19; *Australasian*, 19 March 1910, p. 718, and 21 March 1914, p. 649.

61 D. Reese, *Was it all Cricket?*, London, 1948, pp. 390, 395; Reese, *New Zealand Cricket*, p. 116.

62 A. C. Swan, *History of New Zealand Rugby Football: Vol. 1, 1870–1945*, Auckland, facsimile ed., 1992, passim.

63 R. Chester and N. A. C. McMillan, *The Encyclopedia of New Zealand Rugby*, Auckland, 1980, pp. 379–82, 397–9; idem, *The Visitors: The History of International Rugby Teams in New Zealand*, Auckland, 1990, pp. 17–101.

64 F. Payne and I. Smith, eds, *1994 Shell Cricket Almanack of New Zealand*, Auckland, 1994, pp. 333, 335.

65 Quoted in T. N. W. Buchanan, 'Missionaries of Empire: 1905 All Black Tour', research essay, University of Canterbury, 1981, p. 22. See also J. Nauright, 'Sport, Manhood and Empire: British Responses to the New Zealand Rugby Tour of 1905', *International Journal of the History of Sport*, 8, 2 (1991); L. E. Richardson, 'Rugby, Race and Empire: The 1905 All Black Tour', *Historical News*, 47 (1983).

66 *Lyttelton Times*, 7 March 1906, p. 6.

67 New Zealand Cricket Council, Committee Minutes, 26 April 1902.

68 New Zealand Cricket Council, Annual Report, 1903.

69 Marylebone Cricket Club, Committee Minutes, 12 July 1909, 10 October 1927, 3 December 1928; Imperial Cricket Conference, Minutes, 25 July 1934, 15 June 1938.

70 Auckland Cricket Association, *100 Not Out*, pp. 115–19.

71 See my 'New Zealand' in *The Oxford Companion to Australian Cricket*, Melbourne, 1996, pp. 383–7.

72 Payne and Smith, *1994 Shell Cricket Almanack*, pp. 349–50.

73 *The Cricketer: Spring Annual 1927*, London, 1927, pp. 20–5.

74 *The Times*, 7 May 1927, p. 6.

75 *Ibid.*, 17 September 1927, p. 5.

76 *Ibid.*, 26 September 1931, p. 3.

77 *Wisden Cricketers' Almanack 1932*, London, 1932, pt. II, p. 2.

78 D. Neely, F. Payne and R. King, *Men in White: The History of New Zealand International Cricket*, Auckland, 1985, pp. 263–90, 583–600.

79 I. Milner, *Intersecting Lines: The Memoirs of Ian Milner*, Wellington, 1993, pp. 49–50.

80 For example, *The Press*, 20 January 1933, p. 8; 23 January 1933, p. 7; 25 January 1933, p. 8; 2 February 1933, p. 8.

81 Quoted in D. Kynaston, *Archie's Last Stand: MCC in New Zealand 1922–23*, London, 1984, p. 63.

82 Quoted *ibid.*, pp. 92–5, 135–6.

83 See my MA thesis, ' "The Originals": The 1888–89 New Zealand Native Football Team in Britain, Australia and New Zealand', University of Canterbury, 1992, pp. 48–67, 101–37.

84 G. Scholefield, *Dictionary of New Zealand Biography*, Wellington, 1940, vol. 2, pp. 357, 413.

85 M. King, 'Between Two Worlds', in Rice, *Oxford History of New Zealand*, p. 289.

86 T. Hyde, 'White Men Can't Jump: The Growing Polynesian Influence in New Zealand Sport', *Metro*, September 1993, pp. 62–9.

87 Wellington Cricket Association, Annual Report, 1910; *New Zealand Free Lance*, 24 January 1914, p. 19.

88 For example, *Otago Witness*, 15 February 1894, p. 32; 12 January 1899, p. 36; 29 October 1913, p. 53; *New Zealand Herald*, 21 January 1899, p. 6.

89 D. Montefiore, *Cricket in the Doldrums: The Struggle Between Private and Public Control in Australian Cricket in the 1880s*, Sydney, 1992.
90 V. Wright, 'High Noon for New Zealand Cricket', *NZ Listener*, 12 February 1977, pp. 20–3.
91 Neely *et al.*, *Men in White*, p. 503.

CHAPTER SIX

The Subcontinent

Richard Cashman

The paradox of Indian cricket is captured by Ashis Nandy:

> Cricket is an Indian game accidentally discovered by the English. Like chilli, which was discovered in South America and came to India only in medieval times to become an inescapable part of Indian cuisine, cricket, too, is now foreign to India only according to the historians and Indologists. To most Indians the game now looks more Indian than English. They find it only natural that cricket arouses more passions in India than in England.[1]

The strength of cricket on the subcontinent is paradoxical for many reasons. While cricket was played in India from 1721 and the Calcutta Cricket Club, founded in 1792, is probably the second oldest cricket club in the world, the indigenous population was not encouraged to play cricket for more than a century. For a long period Indians showed little interest in this colonial game and the first club for Indians, the Orient, was not established in Bombay until 1848. Cricket remained an exclusive game, the privileged monopoly of the colonisers until 1877 when the first contest between a British and an Indian (Parsi) side was played. For more than a century, sport (including cricket) was not an important colonial priority – it was an occasional form of recreation for the colonisers – nor did it become a part of the British civilising mission.

Despite this, cricket later became immensely popular on the subcontinent, particularly in post-colonial times when it became the defining sport of the subcontinent. An indication of this is that when Indians or Pakistanis settle in other societies such as Britain, an important activity is the formation of a cricket club. Such a club with a predominantly Asian membership is a significant way of maintaining culture in an alient environment.[2] The game has continued to expand its base and popularity in recent decades and it is ironic that there are now far stronger prospects for cricket on the subcontinent than in England where many believe that cricket is in a state of decline. The focus of world cricket has shifted from the home of the game, England, to its former colonies, particularly those on the subcontinent. While the first three World Cups were played in England, two of the next three were located on the subcontinent and the other in Australia and New Zealand.

Ashis Nandy signposts an important reason for the popularity of a colonial game on the subcontinent. The game has been reinvented so that it 'now looks more Indian [or Pakistani, or Sri Lankan] than English' to the post-colonial populations of the subcontinent. He goes on to suggest that cricket, like sport in general, can endorse and disseminate what are often contradictory messages. Nandy suggests that cricket was used equally as a critique of both native lifestyles and the colonisers (and their society):

> traditional English cricket (which is in many ways a reflection of earlier social hierarchies but is also unwittingly a criticism of the values associated with modern industrialism), modern cricket (increasingly an endorsement of the hegemonic, urban-industrial managerial culture and a criticism of the pre-industrial values now associated with defeated ways of life), imported cricket (the cricket which was exported to non-western societies as a criticism of native life-styles from the point of view of the industrialising West but which, as reconstructed by natives, brought out the latent function of the game in the West and became a criticism of the common cultural principles of capitalism, colonialism and modernity) and new cricket (the cricket by which its close identification with the industrial-managerial ethos is becoming increasingly an endorsement of the ruling culture of the world and a criticism of the victims of history).[3]

Sport, including cricket, represents a sponge which can absorb a variety of ideologies and this theme has been well documented in the film *Trobriand Cricket*.[4] The inhabitants of the Trobriand Islands totally transformed cricket to suit their own priorities and agendas, the game punctuated by tribal rituals and dances and the convention that the home side must always win the match. Cricket became a game which incorporated tribal agendas.

Several questions can be posed regarding subcontinental cricket. Why did the most English of English games inspire the indigenous population of the subcontinent? Why has the popularity of cricket on the subcontinent increased in the post-colonial era? When and how was cricket appropriated by a colonial population? Has the colonial game of cricket replaced some forms of indigenous culture? Mihir Bose has summed up the paradox that is Indian cricket:

Cricket, that very English game, is now one of the most prized of Indian institutions. It is the strangest, certainly the most unexpected, legacy created by Imperial rule. Nothing could be more English than cricket, yet nothing could be more Indian in the way the sub-continent has taken to the game and fashioned out something unique and very different to the English game.[5]

There are also gender issues yet to be explored. While cricket for women has been far less developed in India than in other cricket-playing countries and almost non-existent in Pakistan and Sri Lanka, women's cricket has attracted some astonishingly large crowds. Sub-continental cricket is different in its treatment of gender issues as it is in most other aspects of culture: in cities like Lahore, it is reported that there are women-only stands so that Muslim women can watch the game.

Sport, of course, was not a colonial priority when Britain established its Indian empire in the eighteenth century or while power was con-solidated in the nineteenth century. Organised sport on the subcontinent, so far as it existed, was a separate and exclusive activity confined to the colonisers. Cricket played by the British in India from 1721 was an occasional event played between traders, sailors, soldiers and ad-ministrators. Playing cricket, and sport in general, served a number of functions. Tony Mason has pointed out that the regiments played sport to maintain morale and relieve boredom.[6] Playing sport was a symbol of normalcy, maintaining British society in an alien environment. Sport played in the segregated confines of a club, a cantonment or some European-only facility also served a symbolic role as cultural state-ment of the privileged and exclusive character of British colonial cul-ture which separated the rulers from indigenous society. It was not thought desirable to teach Indians how to play cricket or any other British sport.

From 1835 the British articulated a policy of Anglicisation whereby an English-educated Indian elite was to be trained to become English in tastes, customs and manners to assist the colonial bureaucracy, and to act as a model for other Indians. Training Indians to play British sports was not a direct part of this policy, although the move to create 'brown sahibs' did lead to a longer-term but largely indirect promotion of sport. English-language colleges introduced elite Indians to many as-pects of English culture including sport. Princes like Ranjitsinhji at-tended elite colleges such as Rajkumar College where the enthusiasm of individual schoolmasters for cricket was transmitted to their Indian charges. The greater involvement of Indians in the bureaucracy and the army, too, helped introduce elite Indians to British sport. Indians drawn into the army also became drawn into the formal and

informal sporting customs of regimental life. Sport in the army simultaneously provided one way of 'breaking down barriers' while maintaining hierarchies and making them more palatable.

Casual football games provided a link between British and other
Indian ranks as one private in the Royal Scots recounted:

> In the evening we used to go along to have a chat with the Gurkha boys.
> We would invariably find them playing football and they would immedi-
> ately split up and demand that we join them. From then on it was
> everyone for himself, with about forty Gurkhas on each side, each having
> two or three British ranks playing with them and with the ball being
> passed to the British ranks by every Gurkha on their side.[7]

During the second half of the nineteenth century, sport gradually
became part of the British civilising process though there were some
initial reservations about the capacity of Asians (and any others who
were non-British) to understand and play English games, cricket in
particular. While there was no formal policy to use games to support
the Raj, many individual British officials – teachers in colleges, businessmen, bureaucrats in the railways and other government agencies –
were enthusiastic missionaries for sport and this enthusiasm was
conveyed to their Indian pupils, clients and subordinates.

When Indians took up British sports in the late nineteenth century
they were exposed to particular codes, forms of behaviour, styles of
dress, and techniques along with the ideologies associated with those
games. By the late nineteenth century cricket had been imbued with
many middle-class notions such as amateurism along with imperialism and British ethnocentrism. Indians who took up cricket were
exposed to such colonial ideologies. By embracing cricket some
Indians added credence to colonial cricket ideologies and helped
extend the power of those notions.

Organised sport had not been an important priority in Indian society
and imported sports such as cricket, soccer, hockey and, later, squash
had limited competition from any pre-existing sports. Peasants played
primitive stick and ball games, such as *gali-dandu*, which was played
with a wooden baton and wooden ball and was a simple game of hit and
catch. *Kabaddi*, a team pursuit game, had more elaborate rules. With
twelve players on each side in a small rectangular area (13 by 10
metres), *kabaddi* required no equipment whatever and a court could be
marked out on any open piece of ground. The game was not played in
organised form until 1923 and national rules were not adopted until
1944 with the Amateur Kabaddi Federation of India formed in 1950.
Wrestling, which has deep roots on the subcontinent, was one of the
few sports to become more organised in the twentieth century, though

there were many variant forms of wrestling from one region to another. The pre-British rulers, the Mughals, staged numerous tournaments and the winner of each was awarded a wooden club. As in any other pre-industrial society there were a variety of local and village sports mostly associated with festivals and often involving gambling and drinking. These included fights between animals, dart throwing, foot running, dancing, pigeon and kite flying. Most of these events were spontaneous or involved a low level of organisation. They were allied to other forms of recreation and culture such as dance.

The Indian princes who continued to rule about one-third of the subcontinent during the British period did have strong sporting traditions. Hunting, a favourite sport, was seen as an ideal preparation for war. Fights involving animals were popular at many courts; they involved elephants, deer, rams, water buffalo, dogs or rhinoceros. Other sports supported by the princes included archery, pig-sticking, fencing, wrestling, athletics and horse racing. Indoor games included chess and cards.[8] Aristocratic sport during the Mughal era was organised exclusively for the benefit of the court. The values promoted by princely sport were largely at odds with nineteenth-century British sporting ideologies: Indian princes enjoyed sport as a form of conspicuous consumption and the pursuit of pleasure.

Despite the existence of some sporting institutions in India, as in any other Asian societies, the major cultural traditions and the great festivals which attracted crowds and interest were religious or involved dance and drama rather than sport. A prominent sports administrator, Ashwini Kumar, even went so far as to claim in the mid-1980s that the notion of sport was alien to traditional Indian culture:

> Sport in our country is *khel-khud* (just a bit of fun), it goes against the grain of our country, against our tradition to play sports the way they do in the West. If a child in our country returns from the playground he is not asked by his parents how he fared, but slapped for missing his studies and wasting his time in *khel-khud*. Sport is against our Indian ethos, our entire cultural tradition.[9]

While it is difficult to compare the strength of sporting culture from one society to another, it is clear that the promotion of sport (apart from cricket) is still not an important priority for governments of the subcontinent. In the mid-1980s Ashwini Das bemoaned India's lack of sporting facilities:

> Out of some 600,000 schools we have ... some 1.8% have playgrounds. And I am not talking of the vast playgrounds in the West, but just a little piece of open land behind the school where the children can run, maybe. In a country of 800 million people there are only 11 gymnasiums. The

sports budget of the country is 80 million rupees (£5.5 million). We are just not organised for sports. The central government does not run it, education anyway is a state government subject so it falls between two stools.[10]

Interest in most forms of organised sport in India is below that in other societies. Certainly the Indian Government has done less to promote elite and mass sport – apart from cricket – than some other Asian countries such as China and Japan. Apart from a period of dominance in world hockey from the 1920s to the 1960s (which owed much to princely patronage and private sector support) and the achievement of Pakistanis in squash, the four countries of the subcontinent have achieved little in the Olympic Games and even the Asian Games. Any success in the Commonwealth Games has been largely confined to a few sports such as wrestling. All of which makes the national obsession with a colonial game largely played only in Commonwealth countries more fascinating and puzzling.

Although cricket was never directly promoted as part of the Raj, it was undoubtedly part of the colonial message. The appropriation of cricket by an elite minority community, the Parsis of Bombay – who had migrated to India from Persia many centuries before – was part of a long relationship of collaboration with the British. As a comprador group involved in trade and business, the Parsis developed close links with the British in the interests of enhancing both status and wealth. To the British they were 'ideal middle-men' who could act as cultural brokers advancing the interests of the Raj and interpreting its purposes to other Indian groups. The Parsis were enthusiastic Anglicisers, freely adopting British language, dress, furniture, literature and music, and taking on its customs and culture including cricket.

The Parsis were among the first Indian groups to form cricket clubs (from 1848) and to develop skill at the game, playing on the open area of Bombay known as the Maidan. They developed sufficient skill in cricket to earn the right to play against a European team in 1877 and an annual competition between the Parsis and the Europeans was initiated in Bombay from 1892. Such was the Parsi reverence for English culture and cricket that two Parsi teams toured England in 1886 and 1888. Playing against the British in India and defeating British teams there gave the Parsis a claim to superior status, as it advanced their claim to be an indigenous community at the pinnacle of Indian society. It also enhanced their opportunities for favours and promotions within the Raj and Parsis received many favours and preferments ranging from business opportunities to knighthoods.

The Parsis provided a model for other elite Indian groups to follow, leading to the development of the Bombay communal cricket tournament. The Hindus entered a team in the competition in 1907, the Muslims in 1911 and 'The Rest' (Indian Christians, Anglo-Indians) were added in 1937. With the formal participation of Indian groups in cricket competition – including competition among British groups – cricket became associated with imperial ideology and from the late nineteenth century onwards it became part of the ideological underpinning of the Raj.

Lord Harris, a powerful figure in the late Victorian and Edwardian cricket world, was president of the Marylebone Cricket Club (MCC) from 1896 having just concluded a term as Governor of Bombay from 1890 to 1895. Harris, a conservative politician critical of nationalist politics, linked cricket and sports-playing with imperial and Social Darwinian notions. Harris contended that British players were more suited to cricket-playing because by nature they were 'phlegmatic' whereas 'Oriental players' were excitable, apt to play rash shots and lacked concentration and stoicism. Unlike British players who could soldier on in the most oppressive conditions, Harris noted that Indian players were regularly calling for glasses of water. His views reflected British ethnocentrism, based on Social Darwinism, which suggested that non-British people (even Europeans) were ill-equipped by their 'racial' culture to appreciate and play 'manly' sports such as cricket. The terms 'French cut' or 'Chinese cut' implied that the best non-British peoples could achieve was an undistinguished mishit. In his private correspondence Harris referred to most 'natives' of India as 'effete', 'supine' and 'lazy', less manly and less vigorous than the colonisers. The exception to this rule were the vigorous 'martial races' such as the Sikhs, Gurkhas and Pathans whom Harris and other imperial thinkers considered the exception to the general rule of Indian passivity.

Like many conservative Englishmen of that era, Harris viewed India in communal terms. For him it was a country of many races, tribes and communities divided by religion, caste and tribe. This comfortable and convenient view helped underpin the Raj: the British governed and maintained the peace between the varied and often antagonistic communities. They alone could mete out justice in a fair and objective manner. By introducing an annual contest between the British and particular Indian communities, Harris helped popularise a Bombay cricket structure which reflected colonial agendas.

Ranjitsinhji (1872–1933), who became prince of Nawanagar, was India's most famous cricketer and an important symbol of imperial cricket. Enducated in India and England, his elevation to the English side in 1897 did not please all in the cricketing establishment – Lord Harris opposed his selection – but 'Ranji' later served as a powerful imperial symbol demonstrating 'to the British public that Indians were capable of absorbing the qualities their imperial overseers thought appropriate'.[11] 'Ranji' himself became an imperial spokesman and during the First World War he 'worked on recruiting campaigns and raised patriotic funds in both India and England'. Late in his life, Ranji described cricket as 'one of the greatest contributions which the British people have made to the cause of humanity'. He added that 'it is certainly among the most powerful of the links which keep our Empire together'.[12] Ranji and his nephew Duleepsinhji (1905–59), who also played for England, came to regard themselves more as English than Indian cricketers, and Ranji himself made a famous remark to that effect. In spite of an apparent disinterest in the development of Indian cricket Ranji was, as Mihir Bose has noted, an important and admired symbol of Indian cricket.

Whereas Harris had wondered whether Indian players could master cricket, Ranji's success playing for England and his innovative batting style – he helped to popularise the leg glance – generated a new range of imperial cricket myths which reversed the face of the earlier colonial ones. In English cricket writing there was much emphasis on Ranji's Oriental 'magic' and improvisation, reflected in the famous phrase that 'Ranji never played a Christian stroke in his life'. Neville Cardus helped flesh out the myth of the magic of Indian cricket when the described the batting of Ranji: 'When he batted a strange light was seen for the first time on English fields, a light of the East' which 'was lovely magic and not prepared for by anything that happened in cricket before Ranji came to us'.[13] It was the beginning of a colonial construction of subcontinental players that continued well into the twentieth century. Asian players were depicted as possessing a suppleness of wrist and superiority of vision enabling them to become attractive stroke players. The magic of Oriental players was later applied to the subcontinent's succession of spin bowlers who bowled with guile and mystery. While 'Oriental magic' was viewed as a positive attribute, it could easily slide into oriental trickery, cheating and chicanery. Pakistanis in the 1980s and 1990s, for instance, have often been constructed as bad sports and cheats. Australian journalist Mike Coward argued that the Pakistanis have been victims of 'racial, cultural and religious prejudice on and off the ground for many years'.[14]

By the 1930s there were many cricketing princes, players and patrons, who lavished great sums of money and energy to secure the top prizes in cricket, control of the game and captaincy of the side. Cricket politics were played out with great relish as it was part of the wider game. Cricket prominence provided the princes with more clout in the Chamber of Princes and enhanced their status with the British. It is ironic that cricket was progressively elevated to become the national game after 1947 because before Independence many of its primary backers, the Parsis and the princes, were not prominent in the nationalist movement. Rather, many were better known as supporters of and collaborators with the Raj.

There was no red-letter day in Indian cricket comparable to that in soccer when barefooted Indians, Mohun Bagan, defeated a booted European regiment at Calcutta in 1911. The defeat of the East Yorkshire regiment in the Indian Football Association (IFA) final in Calcutta – in the premier tournament of the country – on 29 June 1911 by the Indian Club, Mohun Bagan, was acclaimed both as a celebrated day for Indian soccer and as an event with wider political implications. The match was a David and Goliath affair with the barefooted Indians down by a goal at half-time against their booted opponents. When the Indian team rallied to score two goals and win the match:

> the crowd swarmed onto the pitch, [and] one Indian went up to the Captain of the Mohun Bagan team and pointing to the direction of Fort William said 'Brother you have lowered England's soccer colours. When are you going to lower those other colours?'[15]

While this interchange may be apocryphal, it does convey the euphoria created by this victory and the popular belief that it added to the Indian national movement.

Mihir Bose has argued that soccer should have become the national game of India because 'it is cheaper, it certainly permeated more layers of Indian society – even down to semi-rural areas – than cricket and, as in other parts of the world, could have been a metaphor for nationalism'.[16] Cricket was a game for middle-class Englishmen taken up by the Indian elites and middle classes. Bose argues that had the British been ejected from India in a more 'violent, revolutionary way', soccer rather than cricket 'would have become the major game'.[17] The argument is a persuasive one: Indians developed a love–hate relationship with their colonial masters. Many resented the presence of the British in India, but the hate was not extended to British culture. Irish nationalists, by contrast, developed a more thoroughgoing hatred of all things British including games, and promoted Gaelic games as an alternative to playing cricket or, to a lesser extent, rugby.[18]

There was no cultural critique of cricket whatsoever during the period of the nationalist movement. The only criticism was of the communal form of competition played in Bombay and copied in cities such as Karachi. In Bombay, contests between the Europeans and Parsis evolved into an annual Pentangular competition. India's nationalist leader, Mahatma Gandhi, criticised this competition in the 1940s because it encouraged a more communal conception of India whereas Gandhi and the nationalists were promoting a more plural and secular India. Others were critical because they believed that communal cricket enhanced communal tensions, though whether it did or not (or acted as a safety-valve) remains a matter for conjecture.

There was no direct conflict between the British-introduced games of cricket and the nationalist movement. Many nationalists themselves, educated in English-language schools and in England itself in some cases, had developed a love of the game. Jawaharlal Nehru, India's first prime minister, was educated at Harrow where he was exposed to cricket and became a keen supporter after India's independence. Similarly, there was some overlap between cricket and nationalism. While not a 'strident, jingoistic nationalist', acting captain Vijay Merchant told the Marylebone Cricket Club during the 1946 tour of England 'that it must not believe that an exchange of cricketers would bring the two countries together. Only independence could do that'.[19] The support of Indian princes – such as Ranji, Duleep, the Nawab of Pataudi Sr and Jr – also enhanced the Indian acceptance of cricket. While Ranji and Duleep played only for England, the Nawab of Pataudi Sr played for England between 1932 and 1934 before captaining the Indian side on the 1946 tour of England. His dual representation added to the cultural continuity between English and Indian cricket.

The development of a distinctive Indian culture of cricket was another important reason for the popularity of the game after 1947. Indeed, such a cricket culture was so well developed before 1947 that cricket on the subcontinent no longer appeared to be a British game. An Indian cricket culture included distinctive ways of playing and watching the game. Because cricket in India in the 1930s was a fashionable game, cricket tours of India included lavish entertainment and hospitality. India by then had developed its own forms of competition, such as the Ranji Trophy and late monsoon contests played on wet and lively wickets. A central element of Indian cricket was the glamour associated with the game and those who played it. This has remained a factor on the subcontinent where contemporary test players are idolised in similar fashion to film stars.

Cricket fired the imagination of many Indian princes in much the same way that it had appealed to aristocrats in eighteenth-century England. It offered a convenient outlet for intrigue, pomp, selfish ambition and conspicuous consumption. The princes enhanced the colourful and distinctive culture of Indian cricket. In *Plain Tales from the Raj*, Englishman H. T. Wickham, a member of the Indian Political Service from 1904 to 1922, recalled what happened when the Maharaja of Kashmir came to bat:

At three o'clock in the afternoon the Maharaja himself would come down to the ground, the band would play the Kashmir anthem, salaams were made and he then went off to a special tent where he sat for a time, smoking his long water pipe. At four thirty or thereabouts he decided he would bat. It didn't matter which side was batting, his own team or ours. He was padded by two attendants and gloved by two more, somebody carried his bat and he walked to the wicket looking very dignified, very small and with an enormous turban on his head. In one of the matches I happened to be bowling and my first ball hit his stumps, but the wicket keeper, quick as lightning, shouted 'No Ball' and the match went on. The only way that the Maharaja could get out was by lbw. And after fifteen or twenty minutes batting he said he felt tired and he was duly given out lbw. What the scorers did about his innings, which was never less than half a century, goodness only knows.[20]

In many respects, Indian cricket before 1947 drew more on eighteenth-century cricket notions which emphasised patronage, specialisation and social hierarchies – than it did on nineteenth-century notions which stressed cricket as a pure and moral process of character-building. Because of their lavish promotion of the game, princes captained their own sides and sometimes even captained their country.

Many princes batted in carefree and extravagant style. The Yuvraj of Patiala, for example, came in to bat in a match with India perilously placed at 4/66 in the second unofficial test against the touring Australian side in 1935–36. Captaining India, the Yuvraj played a highly entertaining innings of 40 runs in 30 minutes – with five sixes and one four – but was criticised by the press for playing an inappropriate innings for a four-day match which India lost by a wide margin.

Princes rarely bowled and were often reluctant to exert themselves fielding. The Maharaja of Vizianagaram, who captained India on the 1936 tour of England, was reluctant to bend in the field and some of his fellow players referred to him as the 'Arsenal footballer' who used his boot on the field. There were many other parallels between Indian cricket in the 1930s and the eighteenth-century game. Princely ambition created divisions detrimental to the performance of the national team and which were particularly manifest on the 1936 tour to England. Many Indian sides were led by princes who restricted their activity to batting while the bowling was undertaken by 'commoners', many of whom were employed by the princes. Indian cricket also suffered because the rivalry between one prince and another often loomed larger than co-operation in the interest of national success.

Indian crowds were colourful, excitable and occasionally volatile, and also drew on eighteenth-century cricket-watching traditions. Matches were often watched by crowds in gaily decorated shamianas (tents). When princes organised matches, including international tours in the 1930s, match times were freely adjustable according to the whim of the maharaja to allow for a shooting party in the early morning or after lunch. Princely patronage enabled lavish facilities to be attached to cricket grounds. When Brabourne Stadium at Bombay was opened in 1937, the Cricket Club of India Stand combined the facilities of a club, a hotel and a pavilion.

Indian cricket has long been played in a festival or carnival-like atmosphere, with continuing noise a distinguishing feature, and some foreign players have found batting there disconcerting. Vijay Merchant recalled a conversation with Keith Carmody of the Australian Services team of 1945. After he had stepped back from the wicket several times waiting for the crowd to settle down, Carmody asked: 'How can I concentrate on the bowling?' Merchant replied: 'If you show that you are taking notice of the crowd they will carry on. Best to disregard the noise if you can.' West Indian players' concentration was disturbed during the second test of the 1948 series when the crowd noise was augmented by frequent explosion of fireworks and bomb-crackers and the blowing of bugles.[21] Another disconcerting practice was the use of mirrors to reflect the sun into the batsman's eyes. In Ranji Trophy matches it was quite common for spectators to invade the ground to congratulate a centurion or a player who has hit a six to garland them, or give them sweets and even money.

Well before Independence, Indian crowds had developed a reputation as passionate supporters of cricket. Australian player Neil Harvey later wrote that Indians constitute 'probably the world's most fanatical followers' of cricket 'who easily pay the highest prices'. In later decades Tony Greig stated that he enjoyed playing in India more than any other country because 'nowhere does a Test match create such fervour; and nowhere else in the world is a cricketer made to feel so important'. The extroverted Greig enjoyed 'clowning to amuse the packed crowd' because he realised that 'they delight in the antics of the top players'.[22] Greig was popular because he appreciated the festival character of Indian cricket.

The segregation of Indian cricket crowds was another feature established well before Independence. Whereas English and Australian grounds were mainly divided between members and outer patrons, Indian cricket grounds of the 1930s separated Europeans from Indians, club members from outer members, commoners from elite, men from women. There were also distinct areas for particular communities, based on their club membership. When the touring English team played at the Bombay Gymkhana Ground in 1933–34 there were five separate enclosures for the Willingdon Club, the Islam, Parsi, Hindu and Catholic Gymkhanas, another twenty-two sections for individual cricket clubs, along with separate sections for colleges and schools and another section for twenty-one cricket clubs and commerical firms. The public stand occupied only about one-quarter of the space. There were far fewer communal and sectional compartments in the Indian crowd after 1947, though the contrast between the comfortable accommodation for the elite in places such as Brabourne Stadium – where the captains of industry rubbed shoulders with high-ranking government officers and film stars – and the crowded concrete terraces of the East Stand was remarkable, suggesting a continuing semi-feudal structure of Indian cricket.

Over the century before Independence, India developed its own rich and distinctive culture of cricket which was a product of the environment (cricket was played in hot and often humid weather, on low-slow wickets and, occasionally, on grassless outfields), social configuration and the cultural structure of the subcontinent. Indian cricket developed different rhythms and styles of play. Cricket is played mostly during the winter months (December–February), necessitating early starts at 10 a.m. due to fading light in the early evening. To fit in with international timetables, some international matches have been squeezed into the oppressive pre- or post-monsoon heat and humidity of March–May and September–November.

From the 1930s onwards India became known for its batsmen, who plundered runs remorselessly on some of the easy-paced batting wickets of the subcontinent which were favourable to spin but decidedly unhelpful to fast bowlers. There were very few fast bowlers of note produced from the 1930s to the 1970s, though medium-pacers and fast bowlers found more favourable wickets in Pakistan.

When the British left India in 1947, cricket was not yet the national game. Hockey and soccer were equally, or more, popular in certain parts of the country and amongst peasants and working-class Indians. Cricket's strength was firmly located in urban India, particularly in Bombay, and its support was greatest amongst the middle class.

Yet the ingredients for the post-colonial prosperity of the game were present in 1947. Cricket was the fashionable and glamorous game which had developed its own stars. The British had lent a hand by introducing test match series between England and India from 1932 onwards, and prior to 1947 three Indian teams had toured England – in 1932, 1936 and 1946 – to play against full-strength

English sides. An English team also toured India in 1933–34 led by England's infamous Bodyline captain, D. R. Jardine, who had been born in Bombay where his family was prominent in legal circles and who later developed an interest in Indian philosophy and mysticism. It was ironic that England was prepared to recognise India as a separate cricket nation some fifteen years before India achieved Independence.

A second advantage for cricket was that it had support in high places after 1947: in government, business and media along with that from the former princes. Government support was particularly noticeable in Pakistan during the period of military rule when generals who ran government agencies, such as the water board, employed prominent cricketers and organised cricket teams. The association of government with cricket was undoubtedly an attempt by the generals to secure a more 'popular face'.[23] Government has frequently involved itself in cricket politics. When the form of the national team has been considered unsatisfactory the Government of Pakistan has, on more than one occasion, dismissed the Board of Control, replacing it with a new one. Sri Lanka has the unusual custom that team selections must go to the Ministry of Sport for approval.[24]

Businessmen, particularly in Bombay, became the new patrons of cricket, taking over where the princes had left off. Firms such as Tata, Nirlon and Mafatlal employed cricketers, providing them with generous salaries and leave to pursue a cricket career. These businessmen took over from the princes because cricket was established as an attractive form of popular culture by 1947. Wealthy entrepreneurs enjoyed the glamour and status associated with cricket by this time. The support of government and media interests was even more important, because not only did cricket receive extensive media coverage on the government-controlled radio and, later, television, but from the 1960s onwards major cricket matches were broadcast in Hindi and all the major regional languages as well as in English.

Broadcasting in Hindi and other significant languages was, perhaps, the most important element of de-Anglicisation of cricket after 1947 and, undoubtedly, was an important factor in its spread beyond the middle classes into rural India and to regions where cricket had been weak. Hindi commentators developed a curious hybrid language to describe cricket which combined a number of English cricket words (cricket terms) within the context of a Hindi sentence.

Cricket received far more favourable media exposure than any other sport, leading to occasional complaints in the media. *Link* raised the issue in 1970:

Why this partiality for Test cricket, the running commentary of which is on the national hook-up. It is difficult to understand. Or is it? Occasionally, the finals of a premier football or tennis or badminton final get time on the AIR [All India Radio], but it is mostly not on the national hook-up. Thus a very large number of sports lovers do not get the benefit.[25]

Another advantage enjoyed by cricket in 1947 was that its strength was based in Bombay, which city plays an important role in disseminating popular culture throughout India. Bombay has long been influential in two separate but overlapping ways. As India's most cosmopolitan city with the strongest links to the West, Bombay has acted as a cultural filter where Western and international culture is interpreted, adapted and repackaged for Indian consumption. Bombay is also the film heartland of India and has generated its own cultural images and symbols throughout the subcontinent. In Bombay cricket and film culture run parallel, with cricketers and film stars both adorning the huge billboards around the city.

With the support from high places, cricket became more genuinely popular in the 1960s and 1970s and was *the* national game by the 1980s and 1990s when it had widened its social and geographic base. Whereas there had been many test players from privileged backgrounds in the 1930s, along with some from less affluent backgrounds, the great majority of test players in the 1960s came from middle-income families and from a wider number of regions throughout the country.[26]

Male cricketers on the subcontinent are accorded film star status and are idolised to a greater extent than cricketers in any other society. Imran Khan in Pakistan and Sachin Tendulkar in India, in particular, have achieved iconic status in their societies providing them with social status, wealth and potential political power. Imran has often been referred to as a 'proud Pathan', or as the 'lion' or 'warrior' of Pakistan, thereby associating him with the martial traditions of the subcontinent and restating in a modern theme one of the imperial cricket myths.

In part as a result of this reverence, there is a greater gender gap between male cricketers and female cricketers on the subcontinent than in many other cricket-playing countries. Women's cricket was much slower to develop in India with the first international tour taking place in 1975, some four decades after England toured Australia and England and Australia played the first Test series. No women's team represented Pakistan or Sri Lanka in a major international competition until Pakistan played its first World Cup in 1997.

There are several reasons for the relative backwardness of women's cricket on the subcontinent. Women have been discouraged from participating in sport in Islamic countries. It has also been thought inappropriate for women to appear in mixed company in crowded public enclosures (where women are thought to be subject to moral danger) and in some places, such as Lucknow and Patna, there have been separate enclosures for women. In more cosmopolitan cities such as Bombay, elite women are part of the crowd in the members' pavilion though are not present in the popular stands. Appropriate costume has been another problem facing women playing cricket, though this was solved by women appearing in trousers rather than wearing culottes (a divided skirt) which is the practice in England, Australia and New Zealand.

When Indian women started playing test cricket in the 1970s, some astonishingly large crowds were recorded: 70,000 turned up in one day at Patna and a crowd of 35,000 was recorded at Calcutta in the late 1970s. The size of the crowds astonished touring Australian players watched at home by tiny crowds at best. It is ironic that most people in the large crowds which came to watch Indian women play cricket were men by a ratio of five to one. There have been various explanations for the size of these crowds. When the Indian women took the field in one test 'they shared a joke that the predominantly male audience had come in the belief that they would play in shorts or skirts and would be disappointed to find them clothed in trousers'.[27] The novelty of women playing cricket was another factor in such initial crowd support of women playing cricket. Sizeable crowds were also reported in Australia when women first started playing cricket, but dwindled once the novelty wore off. It is also likely that the popularity of the male game is so great that Indians will watch any form of cricket.

There has been very little exploration of gender issues in subcontinental sport, so there are more questions than answers. Why is subcontinental cricket so dominated by male culture? What values are admired in ideal cricket males such as Imran and Tendulkar? In what ways do women participate in cricket culture? What barriers are there to future participation?

Although imperial cricket and its ideological underpinnings are long dead, issues which date from the colonial era still figure in the debates and politics of world cricket. Post-colonial adjustments remain lively issues in the cricket world because many newer cricket nations believe that colonial mentalities (and the relics of the colonial era) are still a factor in the political balance of power in world cricket. This has occurred at several levels.

Although the British left India in 1947, and by the 1970s there were four independent powers on the subcontinent and by the 1980s three test-playing nations, the power of world cricket was still dominated by institutions set up in Britain, the MCC and the International Cricket Council (ICC). While the ICC changed its name from the Imperial Cricket Council (formed by England, Australia and South Africa in 1909) to the International Cricket Council to reflect the wider membership of other countries, much world cricket power still resided in the first world. It was not until 1993 that the ICC ceased to be administered by the MCC – though it continued to meet at Lord's – and appointed its first chief executive, Australian David Richards. Englishmen have chaired the ICC for most of its history, though West Indian Sir Clyde Walcott was Chairman from 1994 to 1997 when he was replaced, in controversial circumstances, by Indian businessman Jagmohan Dalmiya.

During the 1980s and 1990s there have been tensions and differences between those whose power is based in the first world of cricket – the largely 'white' empire which first played test cricket – and an emerging power bloc led by officials based on the subcontinent. This has emerged in part because some of the 'brown' and 'black' cricket powers have regarded themselves as victims of decisions made by the 'white' cricket countries. Pakistanis and, to a lesser extent, West Indians and Sri Lankans have seen themselves as victims. Mike Coward has argued that West Indian pace bowlers were convinced that the ruling by cricket's 'conservative First World establishment' on short-pitched deliveries was designed to deprive them of power and influence. Pakistanis have long believed that Western perceptions of an Asian Muslim cricketing power have given rise to myths, based on prejudices, that Pakistanis practise cheating and gamesmanship far more than other countries.[28] There has also been a move to make the political structures of cricket reflect the burgeoning strength of the game on the subcontinent which contrasts with the relative decline of the game in England.

During 1995 there were tensions between PILCOM, the subcontinental organisers of the sixth World Cup, and the ICC over the running of the event and whether there should be a boycott of the matches staged in Sri Lanka. During the same year the vote for the new Chairman of the ICC resulted in bloc voting with the older cricket nations supporting Australian Malcolm Gray, while the subcontinent and many of the newer cricket nations backed an Indian candidate, Jagmohan Dalmiya. Because none of the three candidates won the required two-thirds majority the vote was postponed for twelve months after which time Dalmiya was selected.

The reverberations of the 'imperial era' are far from dead in these post-colonial times. The decolonisation of cricket is a complex process because the cricket politics and structure in Asian countries are much different from those of England and Australia. Imran Khan, with his social and political connections, was far more powerful than an Allan Border or a Mike Atherton. Imran always had a much freer hand in recruiting untried talent to the national side. The Government of Pakistan has long played an active role in cricket politics, dismissing the Pakistan Board of Control for Cricket on a number of occasions. Similarly there are close links between cricket and politics in Sri Lanka. The Ranatunga clan, for instance, is powerful both in cricket and politics. A brother of former captain Arjuna, Prassanna is acting chief minister of the country's western province and another, Dhammika, is chief executive of the Sri Lankan Board of Control. Sri Lankan team selections have to be approved by the government, in the person of the Minister of Sport.[29]

The past of the subcontinental cricket culture, then, dominates its present and will certainly determine its future.

Notes

1 Ashis Nandy, *The Tao of Cricket: On Games of Destiny and the Destiny of Games*, New Delhi, 1989, p. 1.
2 Jack Williams, 'South Asians and Cricket in Bolton', *The Sports Historian*, 14, May 1994, pp. 56–65.
3 Nandy, *The Tao of Cricket*, p. ix.
4 Released in 1976 by the Papua New Guinea Office of Information.
5 Mihir Bose, *A History of Indian Cricket*, London, 1990, p. 16.
6 Tony Mason, 'Football on the Maidan: Cultural Imperialism in Calcutta', in J. A. Mangan, ed. *The Cultural Bond: Sport, Empire, Society*, London, 1992, pp. 142–53.
7 E. S. Humphries in Charles Allen, ed., *Plain Tales from the Raj*, London, 1978, quoted in Mason, 'Football on the Maidan', p. 2.
8 M. N. Pearson, 'Recreation in Mughal India', *British Journal of Sports History*, 1, 3, December 1984, pp. 335–50.
9 Mihir Bose, *A Maidan View: The Magic of Indian Cricket*, London, 1986, p. 19.
10 Quoted *ibid.*, p. 19.
11 Ric Sissons and Brian Stoddart, *Cricket and Empire: The 1932–33 Bodyline Tour of Australia*, Sydney, 1984, p. 32.
12 Quoted in Richard Cashman, *Patrons, Players and the Crowd: The Phenomenon of Indian Cricket*, New Delhi, 1980, p. 35.
13 Quoted *ibid.*, p. 35.
14 27–28 November 1993.
15 Bose, *A Maidan View*, p. 35.
16 Bose, *History of Indian Cricket*, pp. 16–17.
17 *Ibid.*, p. 17.
18 R. Cashman, 'Cricket and Colonialism: Colonial Hegemony and Indigenous Subversion?', in J. A. Mangan, ed., *Pleasure, Profit, Proselytism: British Culture and Sport at Home and Abroad 1700–1914*, London, 1988, pp. 258–72.
19 Bose, *History of Indian Cricket*, p. 112.
20 Allen, *Plain Tales from the Raj*, p. 238.
21 Cashman, *Patrons*, p. 119.

22 Quoted in Jack Pollard, ed., *Six and Out: The Legend of Australian and New Zealand Cricket*, North Sydney, 1975, p. 348; A. Greig, *Test Match Cricket*, London, 1977, p. 91.
23 Richard Cashman, 'The Paradox that is Pakistani Cricket: Some Initial Reflections', *The Sports Historian*, 14, May 1994, pp. 21–37.
24 Malcolm Knox, 'Clan Cricket', *Sydney Morning Herald*, 24 August 1996.
25 Quoted in Cashman, *Patrons*, p. 148.
26 *Ibid.*, pp. 95–6.
27 *Ibid.*, pp. 138–9. See also Rachael Heyhoe Flint and Netta Rhienberg, *Fair Play: The Story of Women's Cricket*, London, 1976, pp. 111–13.
28 Cashman, 'The Paradox that is Pakistani Cricket'.
29 Knox, 'Clan Cricket'.

CHAPTER SEVEN

Other cultures

Brian Stoddart

Where the British flag went, so too went cricket, to the extent that 'Games' might well have been a legitimate addition to the maxim that imperialism was about 'God, Gold and Glory'. Unlike football (soccer, as it is known in some parts of the world to distinguish in from more localised versions of the kicking game), cricket did not become a globalised game, but its geographical spread matched that of British expansionists who were part of the direct and indirect British empire. As the essays in this book show, the impact in areas of formal British expansion was substantial as missionaries, bureaucrats, traders and educators took British mores with them around the world. In some ways, however, many of the more interesting stories about cricket and culture occurred outside those areas of British control.

In the United States, for example, cricket survived what was the great cultural schism of 1776 and lasted almost until the mid-nineteenth century as an important, if localised, symbol of a British link in some quarters.[1] It was to be into the second half of the nineteenth century, and after the Civil War, before baseball took on its great supremacy and became what for some analysts is the cultural representation of America. Cricket survived all that, and with a largely imperial connection. From the later nineteenth century, in many large centres like New York the game was carried on by migrants from areas of British dominance. Significant among them were West Indians who worked on ships which plied between the Caribbean and the east coast centres in north and south America.[2] That significance lasted well into the twentieth century. Later waves of migration enhanced the effect and extended, particularly, into Canada where physical conditions and cosmopolitan patterns of settlement helped retard cricket as a significant national pastime. Tours into the north American centres from both England and Australia during the nineteenth and early twentieth centuries helped keep interest in cricket there alive, but it remained a niche sport. Later twentieth-century demonstrations of the one-day game in places like the Toronto Skydome saw a persistence of interest, but cricket now stands more as a testament to the power of cultural memory than it does as a sport of significance.

In Malaysia (as it is now known), cricket came in with the British administrators, traders and teachers, and some senior members of the service (like Sir Frank Swettenham) were thought to favour officers who had cricketing skills. But cricket's continuity and current existence is owed to another group entirely.[3] As in other parts of the empire, India provided large numbers of labourers for Malaysia. Many of these were Tamils from Ceylon (now Sri Lanka) where the game held great sway. Among other occupations, the railways were pre-eminent in the spread of the game throughout the Malay Peninsular as Tamil workers took cricket into centres like Taiping and Ipoh. Even now, many of the competition sides in Malaysia hire professional players from Sri Lanka, so maintaining the connection.

Just to the south in Singapore, the Singapore Cricket Club was formed in 1852 and by the 1880s was an institution of great social significance and one of the major centres of white exclusiveness. That was maintained for a very long time. The club held a significant piece of real estate, which added to the exclusiveness, and was one of the few to hold out against multiracial membership until well into the twentieth century. In 1960 non-Europeans were admitted to the rugby union section as invitees, and that was the beginning of change which culminated in 1963 with the declaration of open membership.[4] Even now, membership of the club is considered a mark of social distinction.

The Hong Kong story was similar, with the exclusive white club holding on the island a piece of land eventually sold to make way for the new bank building which now dominates the downtown area. The Hong Kong Cricket Club (HKCC) was founded in 1851 and was thought to represent the 'unassailable tradition of the British way of life and fair play in the Far East, with the players being selected very carefully because respectability was to be kept up'.[5] Interestingly, there were said to be Chinese ground bowlers in both Hong Kong and Shanghai (where the game was also a British preoccupation), but that community was never encouraged by the British to take up the game seriously – what that really meant, of course, was that the Chinese were not encouraged to see cricket other than as a variation upon domestic service. That was noted with great seriousness in 1997 as one of the reasons cricket might struggle to survive the territory's reincorporation into the People's Republic of China.

Elsewhere in the empire, similar patterns of exclusion and dominance prevailed. Rule 4 (a) of the Nyasaland Cricket Club, for example, ruled that 'only persons of European and Asian descent shall be eligible to become members of the Club'.[6] What that points to, of course, is local specificity. Where white numbers were substantial enough, the clubs could be rigidly exclusive. Where numbers were sparse, a cultural taxonomy was introduced. In this case the Asians were largely drawn from India where there was a playing credential. In other places, like the Chinese in Hong Kong and the Malays in Malaya, groups were positively dissuaded from becoming players. It was a trade-off between getting sufficient numbers to allow play to continue and maintaining some sort of social hierarchy.

Brief though they are in the telling here, these stories confirm several of the key characteristics of cricket's social format in the more significant playing areas. First, cricket was taken into these locales with as much a social as a physical purpose and intent. Second, the game was socially constructed in all its locations by the selective nature of its playing membership. Third, it was seen as a continuing link with the 'old country' and, more specifically, the way of life and culture to be found there. Fourth, the introduction of local populations to the playing ranks was carefully controlled. The differences displayed in these places of smaller significance were of degree rather than of substance.

In other countries, however, the substance changed much more dramatically, making the game a struggle between local tradition and the imported British dominant culture. In most places, that is, cricket came from Britain and remained to remind of things British. India springs to mind as a good example as do New Zealand and Barbados in that while there were variations, they were largely minimal. Local populations were not so accommodating in some places, notably the Pacific.

In a marvellous account of the game in Fiji, Philip Snow (colonial servant brother of the novelist C. P. Snow) revealed how an orthodox introduction of the game became modified by local practice and needs.[7] The first club was formed in 1874 by European colonial civil servants prompted by senior officers like Sir Edward Wallington, as he later became. At that time he was private Secretary to Governor Sir Edward des Voeux, himself a cricket enthusiast. An old boy of Sherborne and Oxford, Wallington was a classical 'cricket as a civilising agency' enthusiast and encouraged local populations to join in. A later Colonial Secretary, A. W. Mahaffy, insisted that all his staff stop work at four in the afternoon and go to the practice nets.

Indigenous Fijians took to the game with gusto and incorporated it into other traditions. From one region came reports of clubs which were more like medieval guilds, sporting scarlet uniforms replete with badges and being in tune with local political movements. One 'club' even elected its own Governor, Chief Secretary, Chief Judge and all the rest of the offices. According to Snow, some cricket clubs were even part of sorcery groups. And the paramount power of the chiefs was taken over into the cricket practices with their power thought to preclude defeat, to warrant their batting first and to justify their own personal proclaimers in the crowds. Many chiefs turned up for play in their ceremonial dress of rank and took the games seriously. In one inter-community game the host chief claimed the right to bat first given his higher status, was dismissed second ball, and so took out the stumps and banned the playing of cricket.

While the earlier organisation of Fijian cricket had been largely inter-racial, separation appeared early in the twentieth century to produce some familiar patterns. In Suva there grew up separate competitions for Europeans and Fijians in what was labelled an 'unwritten policy of segregation'. On the eve of the Second World War the Suva Cricket Club's competition games were staged on the best wickets in the middle of the city, with the United Cricket Association's matches for Indian and Fijian sides being held on inferior wickets around the edges of the town. The Fiji Cricket Association took control in 1941, but by then the spirit of separation had created a great competitive edge. The Dewar Shield (donated by the whisky family) became the same symbol of success as had similar trophies elsewhere in environments of dis-crimination. In 1932 Nandi won the trophy and held it for several years, with the dominance being regarded in Suva as commoners' impertinence. During the early 1940s the most successful team came from the Fijian Police and displayed marvellous attacking cricket. Then in 1948 an Indian side won the Dewar for the first time, marking another symbolic triumph over adversity.

There was in Fiji, then, what might be described as a mixed cricket culture within which local tradition found a place, only to be later taken over by an institutionalised segregation which served to rein-force the local social and political hierarchy which sprang from the organisation of the colonial state. Since independence, Fijian cricket had occasionally been seen on the world stage with, at one stage, its players wearing a white version of the *lavalava* which returned memo-ries of earlier Fijian practices. Needless to say, the political revolutions of the 1980s and the consequent social shifts have had their effects upon the Fijian game.

Away to the north-west, cricket in the Trobriand Islands took an even more radically different form, as depicted brilliantly in the ethno-graphic film produced in Australia by an American anthropologist assisted by a Trobriand student.[8] The game was introduced to the islands by European missionaries in the 1920s and 1930s as part of an overall 'civilising' mission which included the usual changes in dress tradition and social practice. Very quickly, however, the Trobrianders refashioned the game to be more in line with local needs and fashions. For one thing, restrictions on the numbers of players per team were done away with, the only thing that mattered being an even number of players per side (this was characteristic throughout the Pacific). Legitimate bowling actions were replaced by spear-throwing ones which in turn, because of their accuracy, led to a reduction in the size of the stumps. The ball was carved from local material and the bats resembled more the old eighteenth-century versions seen wielded by the Hambledonians. The fall of each wicket was greeted by dance celebration, and teams practised elaborate demonstration rituals which included face and body painting derived from older war party styles. Games were inevitably accompanied by feasting, and became part of inter-village political activities. And far from the sobering tones sought by the missionaries, the chants and songs frequently took on ribald forms.

This was excellent demonstration of the power to resist the cultural norms which underlay the purely English form of the game and, inevitably, raises questions about why some of the more dominant cricket cultures did not follow similar lines. Those questions are only deepened when the case of Western Samoa is considered. The modern visitor to those islands arrives by plane and is driven to Apia, the capital, along several miles of road lined with the trees and shrubs for which the south Pacific region is renowned. Standing out, however, are the strips of concrete in the middle of almost every village's common area, surrounded by the residences and village buildings. They are cricket pitches in the style to be found throughout Australia and New Zealand, but the games played upon them are quite unlike those found in the two neighbouring countries. The pitches also represent well over a hundred years of distinctive playing tradition.

Unlike in most places, it is possible to date precisely the take-off of the game in Samoa. William Brown Churchward became the British Consul in Apia in 1882 where he remained until 1885. The son of some minor landowners in England, he was educated in private schools and in France. He joined the army and saw service in New Zealand during the land wars of the 1860s. After a spell of diamond-hunting in South Africa and sheep farming in Tasmania, he wound up in Apia at a sensitive time politically. Not only were the British, Germans and Americans in competition for control of Samoa, the local clans were also in dispute over natural sovereignty. As a result, warships arrived regularly in Apia and the crew of one of them, the *Miranda*, sparked life into cricket in 1881. The Apia Cricket Club was formed, with play occurring on land provided by the recognised king, and the first game saw a European side from the town take on the ship's crew. A ground was sought, messages were sent to Sydney for more cricket gear, and membership subscriptions canvassed.[9] But it was not until two years later that the game boomed.

The root cause of the take-off is significant. Cricket was already played in Tonga, and a team from there arrived in Apia and promptly challenged the locals. They went to Churchward to seek his support and that of the sailors to instruct them in cricket 'Fa'a Peritania' (English style) rather than 'Fa'a Tonga'. The game became a craze as it had done in Tonga where there was a law restricting play to one day a week. As Churchward himself noted, however, the English game soon held little attraction for the local players.[10]

Very quickly, all that was left of the English game was a ball being delivered to a bat with all the rest, as Churchward put it, 'purely of their own manufacture'. The game provided opportunity for feasting and parading (as it would later in the Trobriands), and involved all members of the village including women and children. On match days the umpires (judges) led their teams to the match site, penny whistles and drums playing, banners in the breeze. Much money had been spent on uniforms which the players wore as they marched military-style. Each player carried a bat as a soldier would a rifle and, upon a leader's command, would perform 'an entire special manual exercise'. Those leaders would often be dressed in naval uniform, complete with cocked hats, carry swords and would 'inspect' their ranks. After that group would come the followers, also dressed up but carrying the all-important food.

The games themselves were equally dramatic with no restriction on the number of players, demonstrations followed dismissals or spectacular batting, and significant amounts of gambling. Churchward reported seeing games involving up to 200 players per side, with 30–40 per side being commonplace. The playing equipment, too, became localised with bats reverting more to the style of three-sided clubs. (The Museum of Anthropology at the University of British Columbia, whose collection is based on that donated by a major Pacific artefact 'lifter', Frank Burnett,[11] has a cricket bat labelled as a war club.)

All this activity had developed by 1885, demonstrating the rapidity with which adaptation could occur. Moreover, cricket had become part of the complex political fabric. Churchward noted that the Apia teams, as part of their demonstrations, would stop outside his consular office, receive the order to 'Salute' at which they would 'present' their bats as in rifle drill while the accompanying band played. Needless to say, the Germans became very suspicious about these displays of apparently pro-British behaviour. They were bothered even more by some direct action. In mid-1885 there were disputes between the acknowledged king and a rebel one. The king was keen to avoid the displeasure of the foreign powers, but his supporters put 200 'cricketers' into canoes and sailed off to stage a match which turned into a fight. The king himself stopped that action after having second thoughts. On another occasion, some villagers thought they were about to be annexed by the British and staged a big game of indefinite length so that they would be unavailable for official business should the British arrive. Little wonder, then, that the Germans forbade the playing of cricket by the king at his official seat of government. The official reason for the banning was a very European one which revealed the clash of cultures – cricket of this kind took far too long to play, and distracted the local population from useful and productive work. Cricket's concept of time, then, fell in perfectly with the social patterns and needs of the Samoans.

One excellent case from 1885 confirms the point about customisation and localisation. During a particularly tense period politically, a group of Samoans decided to appeal to Queen Victoria to promulgate a British intervention. During the time taken by the mail ship to reach England, a massive cricket match was to be played and, so, prevent any other major alternative from being carried out by the British or the other powers during that period.[12]

The English style of game was all but obliterated under this onslaught, and in some ways demonstrated the fragility of imperial rule in any of these settings. Significantly, it shows how the analysis of popular culture can provide a touchstone to deep-seated cultural mechanisms. While Churchward and others noted the importance of cricket at this time it is ironic that Te Rangi Hiroa, the great Maori anthropologist, gives it no mention at all in his work on Samoa,[13] despite his emphasis on the social value of Samoan community games in the promotion of social interaction via feasting and celebration. That was shown in the continued flowering of the game throughout the 1880s. One 1888 mission report described a game of 200 aside, typical of the vigorous excitement generated by these affairs. Elders were on hand with staves to intervene if proceedings got out of hand, and the level of seriousness was a major concern for both church and state.[14]

By the 1890s visitors were returning from remote villages to report that everything was 'dead' (quiet, that is) except for cricket.[15] In particular, the game was seen to threaten the Sunday observances which had been inspired amongst the Samoan people by the missionaries. Cricket matches began to replace church services in some villages and that was seen to set a trend.[16] The heights of all this may be gauged from the report of one particular match.[17]

It was played between the villages of Matautu and Salealua which turned into a four-day affair after an earlier series of games had produced inconclusive results. Matautu won the game which according to custom (by all reports) allowed them to take the opponents' flag and replace it with their own. The vanquished objected to this and a fight broke out in which one player's head was smashed with a bat and the losing chief was hit by a stone. Things died down but then, also according to custom, the losers claimed the right to burn the opponents' village. Notice was given, the Matautu people shifted out their belongings and went off singing to the boats. In came the sackers and destroyed fifteen houses.

There were regular reports of such matches, significantly some of them involving women. From the beginning women were a major part in all this and they became skilled players. The *taupo*, the village or district princess, frequently led teams in their matches, and in one 1893 case was the playing captain for Laulii against the Sogi district captained by two women (Mrs Trood, wife of the British deputy-consul who was a long-term resident, and Mrs Scanlon who was the wife of the local policeman).[18] In another match a few months later, a team of men from HMS *Katoomba*, who all batted left-handed, lost to a team of 'native women'.[19] There were several matches during this period which had different communities playing against each other: what were routinely reported as 'half-caste' teams played against Europeans, visiting ships' crews, women and others. As in many other cricket locations these might have been the only times at which these communities did interact, given some local practices of social exclusion. What is more interesting, however, is that these matches were invariably played in local style rather than English style. And when the English style was played the local style experts won frequently.

Against the background of increasing missionary anxiety about the hold gained by cricket, there came a report that the Revd Goward and his Tuese College students were clearing a cricket ground for their use.[20] Local inventiveness continued, though, on this front. In one episode, hundreds of people gathered to witness and play cricket at a ground near Apia. Reports abounded of days of shouting, chanting and noise, work was said to be neglected with men and women alike 'demoralised' (which suggests that drinking was involved). It turned out that the losers had to pay 1s per head towards the building of a church for indigenous Samoans in and about the town. The missionaries belatedly discovered the practice and tried to stamp it out.[21]

The extent of the churches' concern appeared in various ways. One of the most interesting was a detailed report of goings-on which appeared in New York in the *Catholic World*. It described a day of cricket in Samoa which began with drums and trumpets in the morning. A big procession involving all villagers then proceeded to the site of another village. Some players were painted, and wore what were described as 'grotesque' clothes. Dropped catches meant that the unfortunate players were taunted with being 'old women' (a frequent derogatory remark around the cricket world, of course), while good hits were greeted by wild applause. In some cases games lasted up to a week and during that time the visitors were housed, fed and entertained by their hosts, which again emphasises the deeper purposes which underlay the surface activity.[22]

John Charlot has pointed this out nicely.[23] As early as 1890, he shows, cricket had been incorporated into stories about activities of the gods, and were contexted in the political struggle involving the European powers and the local chiefs. The playing of cricket became noted as an activity of the gods, and this in itself was a device for the telling of human needs and actions. Perhaps the key observation is the confirmation that cricket matches were used as fronts for war councils. The overall message is that a good many European-introduced cultural practices became subordinated to local needs and customs. Which is why, precisely, the European powers paid so much attention to them.

One report in 1905 noted that many white residents were criticising the government (in German hands by then) for not acting against the latest flare-up in the cricket craze which spread as quickly as any other virus, according to the writer.[24] The critics argued that the games led Samoans away from work (in its Western context) and into debts and fights. What they were really concerned about, arguably, was that the games indicated a deeper level of discontent and unrest. A detailed description of one match demonstrates this point further.[25]

An important point is that the story was told by an American observer not so distracted, perhaps, by the game form as an English aficionado might have been. It begins with the decision as to which side bats first. The two captains were served *kava*, the local ceremonial drink, tossed the cups to the *taupo*, spat into an outstretched palm of a hand, and the first one to have a fly land on the palm got to bat first along with his sixty-seven team-mates for this encounter. This was a match to decide an island championship and, so, involved much ceremony. The visitors were feasted by the hosts with evenings taken up in drinking and *siva-sivas*. These were dance and song parties at which the sexes mingled and which offended the European sense of decency. They were much frowned upon by the Europeans who tried periodically to stamp them out. An earlier report noted one such 'impudent revival . . . in all its native simplicity and indecency' in which the women dancers ended up naked, or nearly so, and indulging in actions which the European observers thought lewd, indecent and suggestive.[26] In this case, then, cricket was used to promote the survival of a number of indigenous cultural practices.

The fielding side scattered to the sounds of drums, conch shells and horns. Dismissals were greeted by the fielding side with great pageantry. Running and shouting and chanting, the whole of the fielding side formed into a war dance line-up and then, 'with rhythmic clappings of hands and stampings of feet', advanced tauntingly upon the ranks of the waiting batsmen. This was all very reminiscent of traditional battle customs, especially because of the traditional dress and markings evident.

One incident, as recounted by Lewis Freeman, revealed the integration of culture and cricket. Among the observers in the midfield hut was a dwarf who was the mascot of one of the chiefs. He was hit hard by a ball smashed away by a batsman, and this was seen as an unprecedented omen by the players and observers, who were said to have regarded such people with awe.

At a more technical level, the 'field' had no boundaries, and if the ball ended up in the sea then the runners could complete as many runs as possible. Buildings and trees were a legitimate part of the field, and so was any dog that might make off with the ball. While there were 'overs', the stumps consisted of a single wicket. The batsmen did not run; rather, there were specialist speedsters who did that in an effort to increase the total score. That practice was said to have begun when an injured chief, who had to play for ceremonial purposes, was allowed to bat with a runner as in the English code.

Anything was fair in this game. The home side's *taupo*, her attendants and dignitaries were all seated in a hut right in the middle of the field, and the hut was surrounded by fielders waiting to make catches of the deliveries which bounced off the roof. The *taupo's* chief attendant ventured out to distract the visiting chief's son, a leading player while he was in the field. After a while her playful behaviour, of the kind at the centre of the debate between Margaret Mead and Derek Freeman, got the better of him. He missed a catch, the batsmen made several runs, and he was chased off into the bush by his irate teammates, and there he was made to stay until he promised to give up chasing women until the completion of the game. His honour was restored a couple of days later when he scored 82, including 15 all run when one of his drives dislodged a beehive and so upset the fieldsmen. On day five the home side had been dismissed for 1,386 runs. By day nine the visitors needed almost 400 to win with only twelve batsmen left. They fell just 4 runs short, losing on a disputed catch. All of this was clearly invested with much social meaning, and incorporated a great deal of customary practice revolving around ritual, politics, belief systems and gender relations. This was cricket, certainly, but cricket of a very specific kind and tailored for the social context.

In 1900 the Germans assumed authority over Samoa and they, in particular, were worried by the cricket movement and began legislating against it. This was achieved by having Samoan custom law agencies take the decisions themselves. In 1902, for example, stick- and spear-throwing and cricket alike were prohibited except where they lasted for under two hours and involved fewer than twenty people.[27] As we have seen, such an edict cut at the heart of cricket, Samoan-style. Even so, two years later Wilhelm Solf, the German administrator, noted that cricket playing for money or goods was becoming a nuisance in Savaii where it kept people away from work for days, even months.[28] This suggests that cricket had become a principal means of Samoan resistance to the imposition of Western concepts of work and time. British authorities sought a compromise by restricting play to one special day, and by encouraging a return to the English-style game.[29] That revealed a minimal appreciation of what the customised game had come to mean to the Samoans. Solf took a proposal to the indigenous law forum to impose such restrictions, but was persuaded to withdraw it on the grounds that the craze was thought to be dying out anyway.[30]

That seemed to be the case for a short while, but further reports of playing filtered in from various parts of the islands. In 1906 the German authorities were again alarmed by the incidence of matches, so banned all contests between villages, restricted intra-village matches to the afternoons only and set down fines and/or imprisonment for violation of the edicts.[31] Two years later the point had still not been taken by the villagers as, in one case, sixteen villagers were fined for transgressions. That must have raised some resentment because, shortly after, they were pardoned by the German authorities.[32] A month later a really big match, with thousands of taros and pigs at stake, was played by two villages.[33] The Germans resorted to even tougher restrictions a few months later in the view that leniency had not worked: challenges between towns were banned, matches could occur only inside villages on Wednesday and Saturday afternoons, there was to be no playing for money or trade goods, the fines were increased steeply, and transgressing individuals could be jailed for between one day and three months.[34] But as the outbreak of the First World War loomed and the German control of Samoa waned, cricket persisted, despite attempts to curb it which even included the Germans ploughing up pitches. The game had quickly become too much a part of the social fabric.

When New Zealand took control of Western Samoa after the conclusion of the war, sport became part of their 'civilising mission' just as the British had done. Rugby union naturally (given New Zealand's addiction to that game) received a big boost and that marked the start of the rise of that sport to international prominence. Cricket continued but, as on earlier occasions, with a bent towards the revival of the English form. In 1926 one village celebrated the opening of a new pitch with a big feast and great rejoicing, the villagers pledging to master the English way. A village XV beat the European visitors by an innings. The only real problem came after the match when the villagers did not distribute left-over food to the visitors because they did not contribute, but the Europeans were waiting for a sign of what the villagers wanted to receive.[35] The social rituals still drew a big distinction between English and Samoan cricket.

Given earlier links between cricket and politics, it was inevitable that similar connections be seen between the game and the Samoan independence movement which developed during the 1920s. In one spectacular case, about 1,000 women in blue uniforms paraded through Apia as they headed off to stage a cricket match. By this point the New Zealand authorities were clamping down on anything that smacked of political demonstration, but were put in a dilemma by something connected with sport which they were trying to promote as a social building exercise. Nevertheless, several of the women were arrested and charged with sedition, because the authorities took exception to their dress. While Rosabel Nelson, a prominent pro-independence leader, claimed that they were cricket dresses, she admitted that the white hem which all the women sported symbolised the Mau movement which was spearheading the political cause. The women were convicted and discharged.[36] Just a few months later, at least one Mau supporter was arrested when fights broke out during one big inter-village match and a policeman was hit over the head with a bat.

As the independence movement gained strength and the process of decolonisation moved towards a conclusion (beginning in 1948 and finalised in 1962), cricket clearly remained an integral part of Samoan village life as an introduced form moulded into a local one. A New Zealander who headed the teachers college just after the Second World

War recalled the centrality of cricket in the lives of his students.[37] One of his Samoan staff members, as part of a course on local custom, organised a big cricket match and picnic at a local village, and the students were to play the villagers. Practice was taken very seriously and then the day arrived. Six busloads of splendidly dressed college people made their way to the village to make a grand entrance, bearing large amounts of food as gifts, and being greeted formally by the village council. Speeches, gift exchanges and other formalities were then completed and the game commenced, 26 a side. The villagers were very good players and the college kids novices, with the inevitable result, and the villagers extracted a high price – the new uniforms worn by the College team for the occasion. It was a variation on the burning of houses.

Again, Irwin described all the characteristics of Samoan cricket noted since the later nineteenth century: horns, whistles, acrobatics in the field, singing, dancing and fast action. There was a story during his time there of a batsman, upset at being dismissed, who killed the umpire with one blow of his bat/club. The curious social balance was also there. A village which won a giant sum like £1,000 might need all that just to feed the visitors during a long and important match.

Another traveller at about the same period made similar observations.[38] He noticed two small boys covering hundreds of leaves with latex from a banyan tree. After it dried, the latex was peeled off and wound around another latex core to form a hard rubber cricket ball of the type still to be found in Samoa. Gibbings then watched a match and commented on the mass participation, the continuous bowling, the specialised runners, the instant formation of new rules, the singing and dancing and chanting. For the two weeks he stayed in one village, there were three games of cricket going on morning and afternoon. If the rain came, up went the umbrellas and the game continued.

At another village, Gibbings was present for the opening of a new pitch which was marked by a 30-team competition (this time with just twelve players a side). Over 2,000 people gathered, and they had dispersed to them 16,000 taro roots, 1,500 loaves of bread, 22 cattle, 90 large pigs and uncountable small pigs and chickens. The first day was given over to marching, speeches, hymns, prayer and pageantry, all in front of huts decked out like 'the pavilions of medieval knights'. There were even the ritual sacrifices of bulls. The pitch was decorated with flowers and ribbons, the teams marched on in uniform and behind their banners, the ribbons were cut, shots fired, and the singing lasted until midnight. Next day the cricket began.

This activity was unappreciated by a succession of colonial powers, all of whom viewed it from a Western standpoint and pronounced it socially unproductive. Read in the Samoan context, it was highly productive and culturally significant. And it persists to this day. Early in 1988 I visited Western Samoa, and driving about one afternoon chanced upon a game in a village. The villagers were dressed traditionally, the pitch was a road running through the village. In one hut an elder, the umpire, had command of a bag full of money, the stake for the game. The stumps were as described in the literature, and so was the ball. The bats were beautiful, carved from trees in the traditional club shape, bound at the top to make a grip. In addition, though, they were intricately painted to the owners' specifications and in traditional markings. The play was full of fun and activity, the ball ending in the sea on several occasions or being lost behind huts while the runners were urged on and the fielders got more frantic trying to locate the ball.

This game had its origins in the same one I had learned in New Zealand from coaches and manuals produced in England, which underlines the real force and point of the game as it has existed and continues to exist in the other cultures. Cricket everywhere is a product of its environment, whether in subtle or in spectacular form. It is contoured by the social and cultural needs and inclinations of its players and supporters, and to read cricket is to read life.

Notes

1 See George B. Kirsch, *The Creation of American Team Sports: Baseball and Cricket, 1838–72*, Champaign–Urbana, 1989.
2 The celebrated case was that of William Shepherd of Barbados, one of the pioneers of working class cricket there.
3 Interview material, Professor R. Ratnalingan (Rhodes Scholar, former Malaysian captain), Penang, 1996–97.
4 Ilsa Sharp, *The Singapore Cricket Club, 1852–1985*, Singapore, 1985.
5 *Hong Kong Cricket Club: Centenary, 1851–1951*, Hong Kong, 1951.
6 *The Nyasaland Cricket Club*, Blantyre, NCC, MCMLI.
7 Philip A. Snow, *Cricket in the Fiji Islands*, Christchurch, 1949.
8 *Trobriand Cricket*, a film by Jerry Leach.
9 *Samoa Times*, 4 June 1881, 11 June 1881, 30 July 1881.
10 W. B. Churchward, *My Consulate in Samoa*, London, 1887, pp. 142–9 refer to the following points.
11 See the Burnett Collection files, UBC Archives, and for the flavour of the activity, read the Francis Dickie preface to Burnett's *Summer Islands of Eden*, London, 1923.
12 Churchward, *Consulate in Samoa*, pp. 146–7. The story is repeated in H. E. Holland, *Samoa: A Story that Teems with Tragedy*, Wellington, n.d. [1918?].
13 Te Rangi Hiroa, *Samoan Material Culture*, Honolulu, 1930.
14 Derek Freeman, *Margaret Mead and Samoa: The Making and Unmaking of an Anthropological Myth*, Cambridge, Mass., 1983, p. 146.
15 *Samoan Weekly Herald*, 4 February 1893.
16 *Ibid.*, 25 March 1893.
17 *Ibid.*, 18 March 1893.
18 *Ibid.*, 20 May 1893.
19 *Ibid.*, 19 August 1893.

20 *Ibid.*, 1 August 1896.
21 *Ibid.*, 25 September 1897.
22 *Ibid.*
23 John Charlot, 'The War Between the Gods of Upolu and Savaii: A Samoan Story from 1890', *Journal of Pacific History*, 23, 1, April 1988, pp. 80–5.
24 *Samoanische Zeitung*, 15 April 1905, in Pacific Manuscript Branch (hereafter PMB) 479, National Library of Australia.
25 Lewis R. Freeman, 'An Account of an Historic Samoan Cricket Match', *Pacific Monthly*, 20, 6, December 1908, pp. 569–80. A later version of the same story which appeared in *Mid-Pacific Magazine*, 23, April 1922, pp. 347–51, is much more detailed and, importantly, contains a number of informative photographs.
26 *Samoa Weekly Herald*, 26 November 1892.
27 Mataafa to Schnee, 13 August 1902, PMB 479 – Western Samoa: English Summaries of Papers Relating to the German Administration, 1900–1914. The bulk of these papers are held in the New Zealand National Archives in Wellington, with the references here seen in microfilm as held by the University of Queensland.
28 W. Solf, memo, 7 May 1904, PMB 479.
29 C. Taylor, memo, 16 June 1904, PMB 479.
30 C. Taylor, memo, 16 August 1904, PMB 479.
31 L. Schulz, memo, 11 February 1906, PMB 479.
32 Fa'ifa'i to Schulz, 3 December 1908; Schulz to the People, 16 January 1909, PMB 479.
33 Village report, 4 February 1909, PMB 479.
34 Solf, report on new cricket ordinance, 17 September 1909, PMB 479.
35 *Samoa Times*, 26 March 1926.
36 *Samoa Herald*, 4 March and 17 March 1930.
37 George Irwin, *Samoa: A Teacher's Tale*, London, 1965, pp. 29–35.
38 Robert Gibbings, *Over the Reefs*, London, 1948, ch. 11.

CHAPTER EIGHT

At the end of the day's play: reflections on cricket, culture and meaning

Brian Stoddart

The cultural landscape of cricket alone signifies the game's centrality in both imperial and post-colonial social construction. While there has been much discussion about who was included in playing the game, for example, it is as important to note those excluded – for a long time that involved such diverse groups as women in most areas, working-class blacks in the Caribbean, ethnic communities in Australia, Maori in New Zealand, non-whites in South Africa and sub-communities on the subcontinent. Those patterns have begun to shift, certainly, but as the essays here demonstrate, the origins and development of and the reasons for the patterns were socially significant. In all locations, even those who hate cricket as a game must deal with its social contours and profile.[1]

Implicit in the term 'cultural landscape' is the idea that cricket everywhere goes along with art, literature, music, scholarship, religion, industry, business, commerce and politics to produce a distinctive representation of a country or nation state, say, to the world at large.[2] If anything, these representations are now more important than ever given that the concept of globalisation contains the possibility of homogenised experience.[3] Something of this stalks Samuel Huntington's much discussed thesis about world politics taking on civilisational rather than national lines.[4] Had he paid more attention to world sport dimensions he might have revised his theory because, as most students of sport world argue, activities *sportif* arouse far more patriotic/nationalistic fervour than probably any other human endeavour (much to the chagrin of those in high culture).[5]

A useful starting point for a discussion about trends within the game lies with the ICC (International Cricket Conference, successor to the Imperial Cricket Conference) Trophy '97 played in Kuala Lumpur, Malaysia, as the qualifying tournament for the 1998 World Cup. From the remnants of the empire came Bermuda, Gibralter and Scotland (although some Scots might not appreciate that political tag). From the former British imperial world came East-Central Africa, West Africa, Kenya, Singapore, Bangladesh, Ireland and the hosts, Malaysia – the tournament was also a forerunner for Malaysia's hosting of the 1998 Commonwealth Games where cricket is to be an included sport for the first time. (Significantly, as its contribution to the nation's Vision 2020, by which time Malaysia would be a 'developed' country, the Malaysian Cricket Association aims to have test status by that year.) From the old informal, economic empire came Argentina. From the (technically) non-imperial world came Italy, Denmark, Holland, the United States of America, the United Arab Emirates (UAE) and, spectacularly, Israel.

'Spectacularly' because as an Islamic state, and a leading member of the Organisation of the Islamic Conference, Malaysia has long had a policy of non-engagement with the Jewish state. On this occasion the Malaysian Government, led by Prime Minister Datuk Seri Dr Mahathir Mohamad, very quietly agreed to the Israeli team being admitted to the country as a way of showing the 'benign' face of Islam which allowed Malaysia to play a full and growing regional and international role. Unfortunately for the government, the more hard line Islamic Party, PAS, disapproved of the visit and staged demonstrations at grounds where the Israelis were to play. One of those demonstrations was very large and broken up by security forces using water cannon, so spectacular television footage of the events appeared around the world. At least one newspaper report hinted vaguely at a connection between the demonstrators and the sighting of a so-called Shi'ite prayer practice at the mosque from whence the demonstrators came (among other things, Malaysia has been keen to curb what it considers to be 'deviationist' practices of the Islamic faith).[6]

The significance was that the Malaysian Government promotes a dual line of social development, preference for *bumiputera* (sons of the soil) but tolerance and participation for other communities, especially the Chinese (largely Hokkien and Cantonese speaking) and Indians (largely Tamil and Punjabi speaking). Cricket has a stronghold amongst the Indians, many of whom spring from Sri Lankan Tamil-speaking origins, has a small foothold in the Chinese community and support from elements of the Malay elite. Given the Commonwealth Games inclusion it was inevitable that the Malaysian Government try to downplay controversy, because staging a successful games had become labelled as a major test of the country's progress. Given the complexity of the Malaysian position politically, it was no surprise that in the week following the tournament the government voted at the Non-Aligned Summit for a freeze on relations with Israel in protest at its actions on the West Bank which allegedly contravened the Middle East peace accord.

Bangladesh, meanwhile, won the ICC Cup final against Kenya with both teams going through to the World Cup proper, while Scotland won the consolation final to secure a place as well. The Bangladeshi victory aroused great emotions not only at home but in Malaysia itself, where the large-scale presence of both legal and illegal Bangladeshi workers has been a controversial matter. One newspaper cartoon on the day of the final depicted Kuala Lumpur as taken over by the Bangladeshi population in a sort of Bhaktinian triumph. All teams in the tournament, in effect, showed the residual effects of empire: the UAE team was replete with Pakistanis and Indians, the Kenyan side (as historically with its field hockey teams) was sometimes referred to as the Indian second eleven, the Canadian side contained several Caribbean players as did Bermuda, the Dutch and Danish sides contained players with English experience (and both countries have long had coaching assistance from imperial world players). Bangladesh itself was coached by the great Barbadian, West Indian and Hampshire opening batsman, Gordon Greenidge, again showing the power of cricket to reproduce itself, moving from colonial disposition to post-colonial definition.[7]

With that theme in mind, we can begin to analyse some features of cricket's cultural landscape. A most obvious feature concerns the playing arenas themselves. In cities around the world 'the cricket ground' is a shorthand reference to a site where, regularly, thousands of people gather to participate in civic ritual.[8] In Australia, for example, the cricket ground abbreviations MCG (Melbourne Cricket Ground), SCG (Sydney Cricket Ground), WACA (Western Australian Cricket Association), the Gabba, the Adelaide Oval as the test playing sites have all played considerable roles in their cities' histories as well as in the folklore and collective memories of their citizens.[9] While one among many ritual activities staged there along with football (various codes), royal visits, the Olympic Games (in the Melbourne case), athletics, rock concerts, papal tours and Billy Graham crusades, cricket still denotes the prime cultural purpose of the sites. In the subcontinent the giant Brabourne Stadium in Bombay and the evocative Eden Gardens in Calcutta provided exactly equivalent roles but, if anything, in a more powerful way even than in Australia because cricket was being transported across a cultural divide. In the Caribbean Kensington Oval in Barbados, Queens Park Oval in Trinidad, Bourda and Guyana and the magnificently backdropped Sabina Park in Jamaica have all staged defining moments in the histories of their communities.

Above all, of course, Lord's in London has remained the prime example of a cricket ground (solely) which has taken on a far more symbolic social role: 'the cathedral of cricket' as it was once dubbed by Sir Robert Menzies, the long-serving Prime Minister of Australia and firm believer in the binding cultural power of the game.[10] For over two hundred years Lord's has commanded pilgrimage aspirations for players, spectators and administrators alike, *the* source of authority as the India Office, the Colonial Office, St Paul's, the Old Bailey, Guy's, Parliament, the Royal Academy, Oxford and Cambridge were in their respective spheres. As Bernard Cohen has pointed out in a different context, the architecture of imperial authority had a profound effect on the colonial condition, and the architecture of cricket was no different – the elitist Long Room at Lord's spawned equivalents around the world so that 'the Members'' stand would become the focus of social, even class envy.

What was really created in these arenas was social space and separation. At the SCG, for example, the crowd on the now disappeared 'Hill' for years derided 'the wankers' in the Members' stand in a sometimes belligerent display of apparent class or, at least, group solidarity. That was highly significant in a society which perpetuated myths of egalitarianism. Such separation was replicated around the world, as Orlando Patterson pointed out for Jamaica – in his case, there were references to the disposition of European bullfight rings with wealthier patrons in the shaded areas and poorer ones in the full glare of the sun.[11] In the cricket case, of course, that is most apposite in that very hot climates prevail in many of the major playing countries. More recently, an additional element of social space has been the proliferation of corporate boxes in which the captains of industry and commerce dwell as evidence, first, of the increasing penetration of commercialism into cricket and, second, of the classed nature of the game.

In that sense the arena plays an immensely important role. Historically, the major cricket ground has provided a temporary suspension of social reality as its inhabitants apparently came together in celebration of the game, irrespective and unmindful of the normal condition of social ranking, economic disparity, religious belief, ethnic background or gender. It was, of course, only apparent because the very composition of the crowds belied the claims to equality – in Australia there were few women outside the Members' stand, almost certainly no aboriginal people and a mere sprinkling from the so-called ethnic communities. Similar typologies of crowds were to be and are still found throughout the cricket-playing world. But the apparent social harmony allowed sermonisers to recite the homilies found throughout these essays about cricket being the bond of empire, the social element for peoples of different backgrounds, and the continuing cultural thread in a changing world.

While this has concentrated on the elite stadium world, it must be remembered that the ground played a similar function at all social levels of the game. The English village ground, for example, was celebrated in the idealised literary works of Hugh de Selincourt, Edmund Blunden and, famously, A. G. MacDonnell.[12] The very sense of social equality might well be regarded as having begun at that village level, which helps explain why late twentieth-century allegations about corrupt practices in the running of the national village championship were taken so seriously. There is an obvious point to make here, too, about the cricket pitch being the figurative, and sometimes literal, centre of schools in England and throughout the empire.[13] In the West Indies, for many players in poor black clubs a visit to a more elite opponent provided a rare opportunity to meet the socially powerful in the same venue.[14] That those meetings were strictly controlled was immaterial, the meetings still occurred. Surjit Mukherjee makes the same case in recalling matches played in the High Court compound of pre-Independence Patna in India. There he got to mix, in a vague way, with the British rulers and their colonial helpmates.[15] In many places around the world, the cricket ground put together social worlds which otherwise would never have met.

In Perth (Western Australia) grade cricket in the 1970s, for example, university teams might travel to play in the very outer suburb of Midland to meet the powerful Midland-Guilford sides.[16] Most university players were drawn from upper status, wealthier riverside suburbs like Nedlands, Dalkeith, Claremont and were predominantly the private school educated offspring of professional and commercial families. Midland-Guilford, on the other hand, comprised mainly players from lower status, more artisan backgrounds educated in state schools. Interestingly, Midland-Guilford teams also carried players from ethnic community backgrounds because the area had long been a centre for southern European settlement. While there were exceptions to these social depictions, there was no mistaking the social perceptions that stalked the players of both teams, the 'haves' versus the 'have-nots'. No matter that the perceptions were probably illusory, they ruled the minds of those involved.

Variations upon that theme, stemming from the village green, are found throughout the world. The famous Wanderers ground in Johannesburg was and is part of an exclusive private club which played a central part in the strict social marking which dominated South African life officially until the early 1990s and which, in some ways, still marks it unofficially. The concrete pitches which characterise Samoan villages provided both a focal point for village life itself, and for staging interaction with other village communities. The smallest of village grounds throughout the Caribbean perform similar functions. Outposts like the marvellous Brockton Oval in Vancouver, Canada, provided a focal point for the continuity of at least one stream of British culture in a society which became increasingly hybridised with that of the adjacent American one. Ashburton Oval, the New Zealand ground where I played much of my early representative cricket, was a replica of many English grounds, surrounded by trees in a parkland setting with families and other spectators enjoying picnics amidst the smell of freshly mown grass and the very English sounds of 'Well played' and 'Bad luck'. Those comments often came from the imported English coaches. (It was to be very different when I shifted to Australia where my sense about the cultural specificity of cricket would become highly developed.) It was another variant on the vast garrison ground in Secunderabad in India where I could watch literally dozens of games proceeding at the same time, and at the nearby elite venues like that of Hyderabad Blues (home to the great 'Tiger' Pataudi and Abbas Ali Baig). At all levels, then, the theatres of cricket reveal the stories of the cultures that produce and support them, and so form perhaps the key component in the cultural landscape of the game.

But what is it that the crowds who have flocked to all these venues sought and, for the most part, found? That is a more difficult question to answer, not just for cricket but for most world sports, because the research to date has been limited. Nevertheless, some points are worth making. At one level there is simple entertainment. In most cricket locations in the late nineteenth century, for example, games provided some of the limited public entertainment possibilities in an era before radio, film and television. Cricket was cheap, in some cases free, and it spread over a long time which suited an urbanising environment beginning to gain increased leisure time. Cricket, like other sport, provided controlled competition along with thought-provoking strategy and tactics, so that spectators were never passive consumers. On the contrary, they developed sophisticated understandings of the game which produced its own intellectual momentum and specialised knowledge. That, in turn, produced social discourse – how would West Indies/ South Africa/New Zealand 'do' against England? (In more recent times, of course, the question has been more in the reverse.)

That process, in turn and as Bill Mandle pointed out years ago, then provided social benchmarking opportunities.[17] How the *team* was 'doing' became transformed into how the *community/country* was 'doing'. For most cricketing nations the first development stage

[155]

was completed by an official test victory over England, the 'Home' of cricket and social development alike. While Australia achieved that in 1877, it took New Zealand another century. Consequently, it is tempting to trace the development of relations between Britain and the two countries in quite different ways, Australia moving towards a republic while New Zealand still cultivates something of an English gentility (while carving out a Pacific and Asian trading network under the nose of the big neighbour). The West Indies triumphs of 1950 sparked unprecedented social response in communities heading towards political independence, while the famous 'Blackwash' photograph which encapsulated the 5-0 series win over England in 1986 was, in some ways, the ultimate post-colonial triumph. Pakistan's first test win just a few years after the gaining of a bloody sovereignty by way of the Partition was interpreted as a very promising sign for nationhood. Similarly, the Sri Lankan triumphs of the later 1990s against the background of a terrible war have also provided a vague social continuity.[18] Again, the accession of Bangladesh to World Cup status was greeted by the populace as a milestone in the social development of South Asia's poor cousin.[19]

It is not far from that to a point about spectator escapism, of course. The real significance of Lewis Eliot's visit to the county cricket ground at the beginning of the *Strangers and Brothers* sequence (referred to in chapter 1 by Keith Sandiford) is that it is an escape to an idealised world of the 'perfect' England. That is why change has been so hard to produce in the game everywhere, its social heartland looks confidently towards the past rather than the future. Kerry Packer's sin in 1977 was, for spectators and administrators alike, not so much that he changed a game but that he changed a social practice, a comfortable convention and a reassuring social bolt-hole. How else could it be explained that the world's best players performed before a handful of spectators on one side of the road in Perth while, on the other side, Australia's second or even third eleven played their counterpart nonentities before respectably sized crowds? They were not watching cricket so much as social convention. Exactly the same points can be made about the introduction of the one-day form, super sixes and four quarter matches – their acceptance comes through an education about social change. More specifically, cricket devotees need to be convinced that new forms fit their social world.

Attempts by cricket administrators to attract 'new' crowds frequently founder upon this point. Cricket, like all sport forms, survives and flourishes because those who follow it find meaning within its playing and representational 'text'.[20] If modern cricket faces danger, it is that audiences will no longer relate socially to what is being played out before them.[21] Just as new literary or music forms often meet hostile receptions initially (think here of James Joyce and *Ulysses*, Igor Stravinsky and *The Rite of Spring*) so, too, do new cricket ones.[22] What really happens, of course, is that the same crowds will often seek different sensations in different forms of the same activity, cricket in this case. The cadences of test cricket (involving subtleties over time, to reduce it to a possibly over-simplistic statement) are quite different from those of a one-dayer (which involve direct action over a shorter period), yet the one watcher may derive benefit and pleasure from both depending on the social circumstances in which they occur. For example, a day-night 50 overs match played through the working week provides one form of cultural sustenance, a five-day test match watched while on holidays another one entirely.

Similar matters of context and meaning are attached to players' participation in cricket. Over the past century or so of organised, competitive cricket in all its locations, the game has meant different things for different people. As Keith Sandiford argues, for the Victorian amateurs (as for their successors like the Revd David Sheppard) cricket was as much about moral code as physical activity and achievement. Cricket was a means to a social and cultural end. For others, however, it was an end in itself. For English professionals from the later nineteenth century onwards, the game provided a livelihood – when they finished playing they could turn to coaching or to umpiring (and that pattern, of course, continues to this day where names like John Hampshire, John Shepherd and Peter Willey spring to mind with umpiring and Ray Illingworth, Bob Woolmer, Bob Simpson and Geoff Marsh in coaching).[23] In Australia, New Zealand and South Africa professionalising the game took much longer. In earlier times potential professionals headed for England and the leagues or county cricket. Ted McDonald grasped the opportunity in the 1920s, Cec Pepper and Bill Alley a couple of decades later, Glenn Turner and Barry Richards a couple of decades still later. In their home countries, though, the game was still amateur or shamateur. With the maturation of commercialism has come the full professionalisation 'enjoyed' by the current test stars of those countries.

That pronounced difference between the English game and its counterpart in the White Dominions, as they were identified well into the twentieth century, is as significant for its cultural point as for its playing one. The cultural role of the game in England was different, which really means that its social ritual function was different. While the county was the defining level in England, it was more the club in those other countries. In some ways, the urbanising of the game occurred much earlier in the colonial sites while the English form attempted to hold on to its rural antecedents for much longer, and with decreasing success. In some ways it was a repeat of the Industrial Revolution – Great Britain inaugurated it, and later powers drew on that experience to leapfrog into a new generation. So with cricket – in Australia, the urban clubs produced the supply lines for the state sides, while in Britain the public schools and the industrial areas proved increasingly incapable of supplying players in the numbers they had once done.[24]

In the West Indies and the subcontinent it was different again. While the 'cricket as the only way out of the ghetto' story is sometimes overplayed, it has substance. The Everton Weekes story bears that out perfectly. Born poor, he grew up on the edge of Kensington Oval and came to the attention of an influential member of the white cricketing elite in Barbados. Because he was socially unacceptable to the main clubs, a way was found for Weekes to join the army which had a team in the competition. From there he moved quickly into the Barbados side, became a West Indies star, played the leagues in England and made a career. Once his playing days were over, his cricket fame helped him secure alternative careers, as did his prowess at bridge. Asked about it all many years later, Weekes commented that he had 'paid his dues'.[25] It might have all been so very different for him, as it was for the countless others who never made it. In India, the career of Kapil Dev is as instructive. While in his country and in Pakistan many of those who went on to professional careers came from sometimes privileged backgrounds, he did not. From a socially degraded position, his cricket still allowed him to go on to a much greater social and economic career than he might otherwise have dreamed of.[26]

It is worth noting that players and umpires are not alone in owing their economic status to cricket. Over the last hundred years in all the cricket sites, people have made careers as groundsmen and women (John Maley of World Series Cricket fame in the 1970s and the innumerable local legends at West Indian venues), administrators (like Bill Jeanes in Australia and Peter Short in the West Indies), promoters (like Spiers and Pond in the 1870s), writers and broadcasters and telecasters (Bruce Harris, Johnnie Moyes, E. W. Swanton, John Arlott, Alan McGillivray, Tony Cozier), scorers (Bill Frindall), statisticians (Ross Dundas), equipment makers (Duncan Fearnley) and repairers, masseurs and physiotherapists (Errol Alcott), managers, coaches (Bob Simpson), trainers (Denis Waight), baggage masters (Bill Ferguson), player agents, advertisers, grounds painters (of all the new on-field logos), scoreboard attendants, concession stall proprietors, gatekeepers, souvenir sellers, booklet publishers, booksellers (John McKenzie and Roger Page), auctioneers catering for the now professional collectors of memorabilia, photographers (Patrick Eagar). The 'profession' of cricket has grown remarkably since the mid-nineteenth-century beginnings of its organised form, and that growth shows little sign of slowing either geographically or in disciplinarity.

In many ways, this is a spread in search of respectability and self-esteem as much as it is in search of an economic future, and that quest unites many elite level players with their counterparts in humbler levels of the game. For generations of players and supporters, the game has given meaning to their lives with the working week being merely that slab of time which keeps apart the playing weekends.[27] For them, the year is still as seasonal as it was for those who formulated the game in pre-industrial societies: summer is the high point of the year, autumn the reflective season, winter the contemplative and spring the expectant. It is from among the diehards of that cultural spectrum that come the touring parties to accompany the players – in recent years the English 'Barmy Army' has been best known, but Australian parties to the West Indies and elsewhere have provided as much food for thought. Similarly, from among these masses come the distinctive crowds and characters of India, West Indies, Australia and the rest, the Yabbas and the King Dyals. In the exaggeration of form and behaviour (as in carnival), we are best able to recognise ourselves and what we would like to be and do. In the sports crowd and watching the sports form we come close to revealing the inner self.[28]

That might range from the sense of self-satisfaction gained as a player in a lowly grade team, from the status accorded local cricket heroes, from the memories of once having 'been someone' in a past sporting life, from the friends-for-life made in cricket, from the sense of power some gain from a captaincy or a presidency to replace a vacuum elsewhere in their existence, from a sense of family continuity through membership of the same club for generations. There is, too, in this very male world a rare chance for interaction between father and son in playing together, and less rarely by going to watch matches together – it is from such bonding that many males derive their personal 'meaning of life' which often defy the march of the women's movement and the change in men's roles generally. These social resonances, too, help explain that other phenomenon – the difficulty faced by players and other participants at all levels when the time comes to retire. If a player has no other social string (as Bradman, Greg Chappell, Ted Dexter and Clyde Walcott did in business; C. T. Studd, Brian Booth and G. C. Grant in religion; John Inverarity, Paul Sheahan in education; Stanley Jackson, Wes Hall and Roy Fredericks in politics), then life after cricket can be short and/or tragic (as it was for Andrew Stoddart,

Fleetwood-Smith and Jim Burke). As with any other civic activity, cricket can be socially enabling or inhibiting, and the dark or the negative side of cricket shows up at all levels: gambling, immorality, cheating and petty-mindedness are found throughout the game, simply because it is socially constructed by people.

Which, in turn, raises the question about how the game is socially mediated: that is, how is its 'story' communicated from person to person, country to country, generation to generation? It is an important question because it concerns the social values of cricket, their construction and dissemination and alteration. Much of it begins with family and education where the lessons of cricket are lessons in life, and for many people the social platform is set there. From then on, much has to do with the people we play with or are administered by, and by the commentators on the game. This last group is both the most important throughout most participants' lives, and the most complex.

Cricket has an overwhelmingly large literature.[29] While much of it remains hagiographic, sycophantic and self-serving, there is also a body of work which carries compelling stories of people's lives, socially reflective messages and ideals by which many more people might live.[30] But there is a sense in which the writers about cricket (and about a good many other sports) have elevated the laudable and downplayed (or, worse, gilded) the less acceptable. There is an episode in the contemporary television sitcom series 'Men Behaving Badly' in which one of the 'heroes' cheats on his girlfriend – the mind immediately springs to the cricket (for which read 'sports') tour. On his tour of England, Fleetwood-Smith was said to have slept with dozens of women. While the press then was a lot more inhibited (no 'Bonking Botham' tabloid headlines), the tour books never hinted at any of this, nor at the drinking which has been legendary on some tours (as has the smoking of funny cigarettes on some). In some ways, that might be preferable to the deifying of Walters, Marsh and Boon for their liquid amber exploits.[31]

When Roland Fishman wrote a sad, and technically bad, little book about an Australian tour to the West Indies, he was pilloried by the cricketing fraternity not for being illiterate in the game, but for exposing (in quite a veiled manner) the lives of some of the players – the braggadocio womanising, the drinking, the lack of interest in local peoples and cultures, the narrowness of outlook and the belligerent arrogance.[32] In an age when politicians, priests, writers, movie stars, television presenters and business people have their private lives paraded before the public, it is curious to see just how shielded cricketers themselves can be. Leaving aside legal considerations such as libel and journalistic ones such as not risking a source, it might be that such protection harks back to the idealised world of cricket and its iconic status within the social realm. Cricket, as it were, was the last bastion of normality – hence the quick denials of match fixing, gambling, ball-tampering and bribery in recent years. Should those matters be proved, then cricket would take a terrible blow to its image as the moral educational arm of the imperial and post-colonial world.

What we 'know' of cricket, then, is a 'mediated' form. But there is an important point to be made here. This is not the mediated form dismissed so pejoratively by some intellectual analysts (whose argument is largely about commercialisation).[33] It is more a form which accommodates rather than challenges the idealised version of cricket in the view that the game does have a social role (although many purveyors of the view would have an inchoate understanding of it, at best).[34] Thus in print, radio and television there is a still undeveloped 'investigative' approach to cricket. Until very recently, the afficionado had to be part of the cricket network itself to uncover the 'real' story about player selection, captaincy, scandal and the like. Now the mainstream mediating agencies are being supplanted by the Internet and its innumerable discussion groups which quite openly spread gossip and news absent from the more obvious news streams.[35] This trend may prove to be a big challenge for the survival of the idealised cricket world.

Modification to that ideology is inevitable, given the shifts in playing power which have occurred in recent years. Until well into the 1970s England, Australia and South Africa were the 'big' cricket powers. While other nations had their Warholian fifteen minutes of fame, those three enjoyed success and cultural dominance. But with the rise of the Clive Lloyd-led West Indian teams of the late 1970s, that dominance was challenged. This was then matched by Pakistan, India and, more recently, Sri Lanka on the playing fields. England sank into the abyss and, with its 1997 Ashes loss, went five series against Australia without a series win, reminiscent of its thrashing at the hands of the West Indies throughout the 1980s. South Africa was excluded from the cricket world for a long time, was reintroduced over-quickly after the restoration of democracy in the form of President Mandela and, after brief initial success, had to begin rebuilding. Australia, too, suffered a period of decline before its mid-1990s partial restoration.

This can be seen as the cricket version of the colonial and post-colonial literature story, the re-creation of a world order.[36] It is about the refashioning of style, attitude and order. The troubled election of Jagmohan Dalmiya as President of the ICC (mentioned here by Richard Cashman) makes the point perfectly – its interpretation in India was about the former imperial elite and its acolytes being unwilling to acknowledge the shift in the world's axis (in some ways, ironically, it was an argument that India had now reached the benchmarks of acceptable development set by Lord Harris a century earlier). Earlier versions of this political orthodoxy had been the palpable reluctance of England, Australia and New Zealand to act against South Africa and its institutionalised racism. West Indies, India and Pakistan worked very hard to make an impact on that attitude. The allocation of World Cup sites was a more muted but, nonetheless, sharply felt matter. Just as the only Commonwealth Games to be held outside Great Britain, Canada, New Zealand and Australia before 1998 was Kingston in Jamaica in 1966 so, too, the World Cup was hard to prise away from the 'developed' nations. The one staged in India and Pakistan was marked by administrative controversy, the Australian refusal to play in Sri Lanka (because of the ongoing civil war) and argument about television rights. West Indies is still searching for the right to stage the 2003 event, despite its greatness as a player power. For those on the receiving end, of course, arguments about infrastructure and preparedness are statements about post-coloniality and, so, felt sharply. Yet the very palpability of those political issues made them infinitely easier to deal with than some of the more intangible ones.

The prime case in point concerns West Indies tactics and strategy in becoming the top playing nation during the 1980s, blessed with an array of outstandingly skilled and strong fast bowlers. Clive Lloyd dispensed with spin almost entirely so that opposing batsmen throughout the order were subjected to unrelieved pace. Added to that, those fast bowlers exploited to the utmost their skills with the short-pitched delivery. By then the use of the batting helmet was almost *de rigeur*, but even that did little to placate those on the receiving end. There was much ill-informed talk of the return of Bodyline, unfair advantage, and even some regressionist mutterings about 'the unfair advantage of natural black athletes'.[37] A series of rule changes, ranging from a limitation on the number of permissible short-pitched deliveries to the minimum number of overs required to be bowled in an hour or a day, was widely interpreted in the Caribbean as an attempt by Prospero to restrict Caliban from maximising a new found advantage. It was, if you like, the equivalent of requiring Edward Kamau Braithwaite and other Caribbean writers to express themselves in 'real' English rather than nation language. The further dimension, as in other cases, was that the 'white dominions' were almost invariably seen to be on the side of the former imperial power, with the 'newly independent non-white nations' arrayed opposite. In that way, there was still a clash of cultural wills over what was the specific form of the cricket ideology. The clear point is that the underpinning beliefs in the role of cricket were by now quite different in the myriad of consuming sites.

The struggle for control over a form of cultural practice – cricket in this case – is really a struggle to determine how at least one part of the human world should 'look': that is, to determine whose view of the world should prevail. On the one side are those who created or, at least, formulated the practice, on the other those who have modified it in order to give it more meaning for them and, in some cases, for a 'newer' world order. If that is accepted, then what does cricket 'look' like now and how might it project its future? That question really asks, what are the points of continuity in the game alongside those of disjunction in a cultural sense? The very fact that the game survives into the new millennium indicates its core of continuity, a game which inspires passion in millions of followers in very different societies and cultures around the world. As researchers, though, we are a very long way from understanding fully the wellsprings of that passion in all its forms. Similarly, we recognise many of the superficial signs indicating change without really comprehending the 'deep structure' (as Clifford Geertz might label it[38]) which drives that change.

As cricket continues to professionalise, then, to alter its geographical centres of playing and governmental power, to embrace new communities, to add to that massive extant literature, to occupy large amounts of radio and television time, as more players join Sachin Tendulkar and Shane Warne as extremely well-paid media (as opposed to sports) stars, as women continue to search for equal recognition, and as spectators world-wide continue to devote much of their attention to an activity which is largely unproductive socially, we interpreters need to ask more searching questions and to engage more fully with the post-colonial project as a whole. Because while the return of Hong Kong to the People's Republic of China suggests that the sun *has* finally set on the British empire in the political sense, the persistence and even the flourishing of cricket shows that 'the imperial game' might well be one of the empire's major lasting influences.[39]

Notes

1 This point was made to me by a (rare) non-lover of cricket in Barbados. It is interesting to note in this connection, too, the comments by Mulayam Singh Yadav (Indian Defence Minister and conservative politician) that cricket was a 'servitude' game imposed on India by British imperialists and, so, should be rejected in favour of 'Indian' games among which he included field hockey, itself a dubious claim: 'Minister's Attack On All Things English', *New Straits Times*, 30 August 1997. Of course, this was a much less intellectual variation of the point made about the West Indies nearly thirty years earlier by sociologist Orlando Patterson, 'The Ritual of Cricket', *Jamaica Journal*, 3, 1969, and reprinted in Hilary Beckles and Brian

Stoddart, eds, *Liberation Cricket: West Indies Cricket Culture*, Manchester, 1995.

2   I discussed this approach in my keynote address to the Sporting Traditions X Conference, Perth 1997: 'Sport in Asia: The Future in the Past'.

3   Some outlines for the globalisation of sport debate may be seen in the special edition of the *Journal of Sport and Social Issues*, 20, 2, August 1996.

4   See Samuel Huntington, *The Clash of Civilizations and the Remaking of World Order*, New York, 1996.

5   An interesting commercial version of this point is to be seen in Jean-Paul de la Fuente, 'Forget the Consumer at Your Peril', *Sport Business*, 11, June 1997, p. 12.

6   The story of these events may be followed in *New Straits Times*, 1997: 31 March, 5 April, 6 April, 12 April.

7   For the Greenidge career, see the encapsulation in Rob Steen, *Desmond Haynes: Lion of Barbados*, London, 1993, pp. 109–17, which recounts how Greenidge was born in Barbados, taken to England at fourteen, played county cricket at a young age but then opted to play for West Indies and frequently felt as though he belonged to neither culture.

8   Some ideas on this line of analysis may be gained from the essays in Karl Raitz, ed., *The Theater of Sport*, Baltimore, 1995. John Bale also provides many important insights here; see his *Landscapes of Modern Sport (Sport, Politics and Culture)*, Leicester, 1996.

9   For Melbourne, see Keith Dunstan, *The Paddock that Grew: The Story of the Melbourne Cricket Ground*, Melbourne, 1962, and for Sydney, Philip Derriman, *The Grand Old Ground: A History of the Sydney Cricket Ground*, Sydney, 1981.

10 See the 'Cricket' folders in the Menzies Papers, National Library of Australia, for frequent references along these lines.

11 Patterson, 'The Ritual of Cricket'. For the bullfights: Ernest Hemingway, *Death in the Afternoon*, New York, 1940, and Kenneth Tynan, *Bull Fever*, New York, 1958.

12 For some ideas, Brian Stoddart, 'Cricket, Literature and Culture: Windows on the World', *Notes and Furphies*, 30, April 1993. This was the published version of my presentation to the annual Barry Andrews Memorial Lecture series which commemorates the work of a pioneer in the analysis of cricket literature.

13 The standard work on the role of sport in the public school is J. A. Mangan, *Athleticism in the Victorian and Edwardian School: The Emergence and Consolidation of an Educational Ideology*, Oxford, 1981. For a specific case study, Keith A. P. Sandiford and Brian Stoddart, 'Cricket and the Elite Schools in Barbados: A Case Study in Colonial Continuity', *International Journal for the History of Sport*, 4, 3, December 1987, reprinted in Beckles and Stoddart, *Liberation Cricket*.

14 Brian Stoddart, 'Cricket, Social Formation and Cultural Continuity in Barbados: A Preliminary Ethnohistory', *Journal of Sport History*, 14, 3, Winter 1987, reprinted in Beckles and Stoddart, *Liberation Cricket*.

15 Surjit Mukherjee, *The Autobiography of an Unknown Indian Cricketer*, New Delhi, 1996.

16 This point is drawn from ethnographic experience.

17 W. F. Mandle, 'Cricket and Australian Nationalism in the Nineteenth Century', *Journal of the Royal Australian Historical Society*, 59, 4, December 1973.

18 For the incongruity of this, see Emma Levine, *Into the Passionate Soul of Subcontinental Cricket*, New Delhi, 1996.

19 For the response to the victory, see 'Man Stabbed To Death As Fans Celebrate Entry Into World Cup', *New Straits Times*, 10 April 1997.

20 Some will see post-modernism embedded within this point, others merely social anthropology built on the concepts of ritual. For an excellent work which raises many considerations along these lines, see Mike Marqusee, *Anyone but England: Cricket and the National Malaise*, London, 1994.

21 Richard Guilianotti makes some interesting points along these lines in relation to modern English football – see his 'Football Media in the UK: A Cultural Studies Perspective' to be found in *Lecturas Educacion Fisica Y Deportes: Revista Digital* which may be found at http://www.sirc.ca/revista/lect_03w.htm.

22 David Rowe draws some excellent parallels between modern popular music and sport in his *Popular Cultures: Rock Music, Sport and the Politics of Pleasure*, London, 1995.

23 The standard reference to the English professionals is Ric Sissons, *The Players: A Social History of the Professional Cricketer*, Sydney, 1988.

24 Of course, this is a highly generalised point – country areas in Australia have produced many test players, and in England the traditional suppliers still produce the odd player. Even so, the point is that traditional development lines alter over time and have to be accounted for.

25 Interview material, Barbados, April 1985.

26 It is important not to overplay this general point, of course. As many analysts have pointed out in the case of African-Americans, the idea of the 'ghetto escape via sports' is flawed in that vast numbers of, say, basketballers do not reach the professional ranks. Nonetheless, players like Weekes and Kapil Dev do persuade others to try and follow.

27 For a wonderful view of Australian country cricket and its role, see Charlee Marshall, *I Couldn't Bowl for Laughin'*, Thangool, 1988. The quintessential soccer (football) work on this aspect is Nick Hornby, *Fever Pitch*, London, 1993, which recounts the life of an Arsenal fan. For some theorising, Alec McHoul, 'On Doing We's: Where Sport Leaks into Everyday Life', *Journal of Sport and Social Issues*, 21, 3, August 1997.

28 While it is many years since I lived in, then left, New Zealand, I can still 'barrack' for no other rugby union team than the All Blacks. There is an interesting work to be done on the affiliations of sports historians and sociologists – I support West Indies in cricket (for reasons apparent in my work), the Dodgers in baseball (because of Jackie Robinson and Roger Kahn), West Coast Eagles in Australian football (because I was in at their beginning in a peripheral way, and because I spent long enough on the littoral to feel the separation), Miami Dolphins in American football (because of Don Shula and Dan Marino), Greg Norman (because he is a wonderful player disliked by so many American sportswriters) and Bob Charles (because he inspired me to keep playing left-handed), Babe Didrickson (because she showed what women could do), Merlene Ottey (black women are doubly marginalised) – that is enough of a list to dismiss any vestigial trappings of dispassionate social science.

29 See E. W. Padwick, *Bibliography of Cricket*, London, 1985.

30 Here we might think, naturally and inevitably, of C. L. R. James, but also of Conrad Hunte, Vijay Hazare, Ray Robinson, Dick Brittenden, Alan Ross, Fred Root, Michael Manley (even if his history is flawed), Bruce Francis (on South Africa, because he was provocative).

31 The death of Australian football star Darren Millane was a terrible case in point about how the lessons could be interpreted so wrongly – nicknamed 'Pants' (as in conqueror of women) in an AIDS-conscious world, Millane died by driving his car under a truck while drunk. His death was characterised as a 'tragedy', not in the sense that it was a cautionary tale but that he had 'been an adornment to the game'.

32 Roland Fishman, *Calypso Cricket: The Indies Story of the 1991 Windies Tour*, Melbourne, 1991. For a much better book in the same vein, Francis Edmonds, *Another Bloody Tour: England in the West Indies 1986*, London, 1986.

33 For example, Ian Harriss, 'Packer, Cricket and Postmodernism', in David Rowe and Geoffrey Lawrence, eds, *Sport and Leisure: Trends in Australian Popular Culture*, Sydney, 1990.

34 Of course, none of this can be separated from commercialism in an analytical sense, but the thrust of the point here will be clear enough.

35 See my general argument about sport and the rise of the Net in 'Convergence: Sport Upon The Information Superhighway', *Journal of Sport and Social Issues*, 21, 1, February 1997.

36 For an introduction to some of the points here, see Bill Ashcroft, Gareth Griffiths and Helen Tiffin, *The Empire Writes Back: Theory and Practice in Post-Colonial Literature (New Accents)*, London, 1990.

37 For a latter-day American demonstration of the potential heat in this argument, see some of the discussion on the sociology of sport website (sportsoc@ vm.temple.edu will provide registration and access to the site) about John Hoberman's *Darwin's Athletes: How Sport Has Damaged Black America and Preserved the Myth of Race*, New York, 1997.

38 Clifford Geertz, 'Deep Play: Notes on the Balinese Cockfight', *Daedalus*, 101, Winter 1972. The passage of time has not dimmed the importance of this article as an indicator of how superficial form can mask complex inner workings, and it should be re-read from time to time by all historians and sociologists of sport.

39 For some comments on the interaction between sport and the Hong Kong handover, see 'Beer, Sweat and Tears', *Far Eastern Economic Review*, 10 April 1997.

INDEX

Note: 'n.' after a page reference indicates the number of a note on that page.

amateurs and professionals, 1, 4,
   24–5, 157
appeal of cricket, 156
Ashes, 51–2
and Australia, relationship
   between, 34–7, 39–40, 44, 42–9,
   51–2, 64
economic issues, 23–4, 25
education, 14–19, 21–2
Edwardian era, 25
entry charges, 43
form and style, 7, 157–8
Georgian era, 9, 10, 24
institution, cricket as, 28, 29
literature, 26–7
and New Zealand, relationship
   between, 93–4, 95–7, 100–2,
   103–4, 105, 106–10, 111–12
paternalism, 23, 26
playing conditions and pitches, 85,
   153, 154
playing power, 161
race and ethnicity, 6
racism, 90
religion, 14, 19–22, 28–9
rise of cricket, reasons for, 27–9
social class, 12–14, 22–3, 24, 25–6
social evolution of cricket, 7, 10
social importance of cricket, 9–12,
   21–2
and South Africa, relationship
   between, 56–66, 69–72
spectators, 10–11
and subcontinent, relationship
   between, 116–19, 121–5, 128–9,
   131–2
test victories over, significance of
   first, 156
and West Indies, relationship
   between, 6, 80, 81, 83, 84–5, 90
women's cricket, 5
Ensor, R. C. K., 29
entertainment value of cricket, 155
entry charges
   Australia, 43
   England, 43
   New Zealand, 105
   South Africa, 69
Esher Cricket Club, 12
ethnicity, see race and ethnicity
Eton, 15, 16

Evangelicism, 20
Evatt, Dr H. V., 47–8
Ewing, Patrick, 89

Far East, 6
   see also named countries
Farnborough, 15
Fearnley, Duncan, 158
Ferguson, Bill, 158
Feries, J. J., 60
Ferris, Jack, 45, 46
Fichardt, Charles Gustav, 58
Fiji, 106, 137–8
Fiji Cricket Association, 138
Fingleton, Jack, 49
Firth, Joseph, 98
Fishman, Roland, 160
Fleetwood-Smith, L. O'B, 160
Flood, Edward, 37
Foley, C. P., 17, 18
football, 124, 128, 135
Ford, P. G. J., 17, 18
form and style, 6–7
   England, 7, 157–8
   India, 7, 127
   New Zealand, 111–12
   Pakistan, 7, 128
   West Indies, 7, 86–7
Fortune, Charles, 69
Francis, Bruce, 165n.30
Francis, George, 90
Fraser, Bishop, 19
Fredericks, Roy, 87, 159
Freeman, A. J. ('Dol'), 67, 69
Freeman, Derek, 144
Freeman, Lewis, 144
Friendly Societies, 21
Frindall, Bill, 158
Frith, David, 48, 50
Fry, Charles Burgess, 22, 26, 60

gali-dandu, 119
gambling, 42
Gandhi, Mahatma, 124–5
Garner, Joel, 6
Geertz, Clifford, 163
gender issues, see women's cricket;
   women's roles
geography, 6–7
   New Zealand, 99
George IV, 11

Steel, D. Q., 16
Steel, H. B., 16
Stephen, Francis, 37
Stephen, Leslie, 20
Stephenson, H. H., 16
Stevens, E. C. J., 102
Stewart, Major R., 61
Still, W. C., 35
Stoddart, Andrew, 48, 104, 159
Stoddart, Brian, 39, 42, 48–9
Streatfield, E. C., 17, 18
Studd, C. T., 159
style, *see* form and style
Surrey County Cricket Club, 12
Sussex County Cricket Club, 12, 84
Suva Cricket Club, 138
Swanton, E. W., 158
Swettenham, Sir Frank, 136
Sydney Cricket Ground (SCG), 42, 153

Taiaroa, J. G., 110
Tamils, 136
Tanganyika, 69
tapeball, 87
Tasmania, 106
Tendulkar, Sachin, 130, 131, 163
Thesiger, Frederic John Napier, 17
Theunissen, Nicolaas Hendrik, 58
Thomas, Faith, 38
Thomas, Freeman, 14
Thomson, Arthur, 25
Thring, Edward, 14, 15, 22
ticket prices, *see* entry charges
Tomlinson, D. S., 64
Tonga, 140
Transvaal Cricket Union, 69
Triangular tournament, 64
Trickett, Ned, 36
Trinidad, 80, 81, 82, 89, 152
Trobriand Cricket, 117, 138–9
Trobriand Islands, 117, 138–9
Trood, Mrs, 142
Trott, Albert, 45, 60
Trumble, Hugh, 106
Trumper, Victor, 46
Tuese College, 142
Turner, Glenn, 111–12, 157

Uganda, 4, 69
United Arab Emirates (UAE), 151, 152

United States of America, 135, 151
and Australia, relationship between, 40, 41, 51
and Canada, relationship between, 2–3
and West Indies, relationship between, 89
universities, 16–18
Uppingham, 14, 15, 16
Uru, J. H. W., 110

van Zyl, Commandant, 59
Vaughan, C. J., 14
Victoria, Queen, 11, 12, 141
Vizianagaram, Maharaja of, 126
Vogel, Julius, 100
Vorster, John, 59, 71, 72–3

Waddy brothers (E. L., E. F., P. C.), 42
Waight, Denis, 158
Wakefield, Edward Gibbon, 94, 95, 97
Walcott, Sir Clyde, 132, 159
Walford, H., 14
Walker, I. D., 15
Wallington, Sir Edward, 137
Walrond, Colonel, 13
Walters, Doug, 160
Wanderers, 5, 82, 83, 154–5
Ward, Revd A. R., 20
Warne, Shane, 163
Warner, Lady, 67
Warner, Sir Pelham ('Plum'), 6, 17, 49, 64
South Africa, 61, 62, 63
West Indies, 80
Warton, Major R. Gardner, 60
Watson, Cheeky, 73
Waugh, Revd Thomas, 20
weather, *see* climate
Weekes, Everton, 90, 158
Wellington, NZ, 97, 101, 111
Wellington College, NZ, 98
Wellington school, England, 16
Wells, C. M., 15
West Africa, 151
Western Province Cricket Club, 56
Western Samoa, 139–48, 155
West Indies, 1, 4
broadcasting, 89